Irish Media

Irish Media: A Critical History maps the landscape of media in Ireland from the foundation of the modern state in 1922 to the present. Covering all principal media forms, print and electronic, in the Republic and in Northern Ireland, John Horgan shows how Irish history and politics have shaped the media of Ireland and, in turn, have been shaped by them.

Beginning in a country ravaged by civil war, the book traces the complexities of wartime censorship and details the history of media technology, from the development of radio to the inauguration of television in the 1950s and 1960s. It covers the birth, the development and – sometimes – the death of major Irish media during this period, examining the reasons for failure and success, and government attempts to regulate and respond to change. Finally, it addresses questions of media globalisation, ownership and control, and looks at issues of key significance for the future.

John Horgan demonstrates why, in a country whose political divisions and economic development have given it a place on the world stage out of all proportion to its size, the media have been and remain key players in Irish history.

John Horgan is Professor of Journalism at Dublin City University, which has pioneered the development of undergraduate and postgraduate journalism education in Ireland. His own work has broken new ground in the study of Irish media history, and he is also the author of a number of acclaimed political biographies, notably of Sean Lemass (1997) and Noel Browne (2000).

Irish Media
A Critical History Since 1922

John Horgan

London and New York

First published 2001
by Routledge
11 New Fetter Lane, London EC4P 4EE

Simultaneously published in the USA and Canada
by Routledge
29 West 35th Street, New York, NY 10001

Routledge is an imprint of the Taylor & Francis Group

© 2001 John Horgan

Typeset in Goudy by Taylor & Francis Books Ltd
Printed and bound in Great Britain by
The University Press, Cambridge

British Library Cataloguing in Publication Data
A catalogue record for this book is available from the British Library

Library of Congress Cataloging in Publication Data
Horgan, John, 1940–
Irish media: a critical history since 1922 / John Horgan.
Includes bibliographical references and index.
1. Mass media–Ireland–History–20th century. I. Title.
P92.I76 H67 2000
302.23'09417'0904–dc21   00–045938

ISBN 0–415–21640–0
ISBN 0–415–21641–9

For Mary Jones

Contents

Abbreviations

Archival sources

NAI
: National Archives of Ireland. References in the text take the form of the abbreviation, followed by the Department of State from which the archive document has come, followed by the document or file reference number.

NLI
: National Library of Ireland. References in the text take the form of the abbreviation followed by the call number of the book or item in question.

USNA
: United States National Archives. References in the text take the form of the abbreviation followed by the reference number of the document concerned.

Parliamentary debates

DD
: Dail debates. References in the text take the form of the abbreviation, followed by the date of the relevant extract.

Principal newspapers consulted

BT
: *Belfast Telegraph*
II
: *Irish Independent*
IN
: *Irish News*
IP
: *Irish Press*
IT
: *Irish Times*
NL
: *(Belfast) Newsletter*
SBP
: *Sunday Business Post*
ST
: *Sunday Tribune*

Introduction

The 1916 Rising in Dublin, when Britain and her allies were in the throes of the First World War, was speedily and ruthlessly – too ruthlessly, as it turned out – suppressed. Within six years, there was a new government in Dublin, and the Irish Free State, still technically under the Crown but with a freedom to manoeuvre it was not slow to exploit, began the complex task of nation-building even as it turned its guns on its own countrymen in a brief but vicious civil war.

To many observers in Britain and elsewhere, the 1916 Rising came as a complete shock. Irish political concerns, it appeared, had been largely pacified by the end of the nineteenth century, and the island, while not as docile as Wales or Scotland, seemed integrated, for the most part, into a United Kingdom whose politics, mores and media were those of the Edwardian era.

More perceptive observers than many of those in Dublin Castle or the Dominions office in Whitehall, however, would have been able to spot bubbles of change bursting on the surface of what was otherwise a quiet, even stagnant political scene. Nowhere was this more evident than in the media. Since the late 1890s, in Belfast as well as in Dublin itself, a rash of small periodicals had been appearing. Some were political, some literary, some a mixture of both. What they had in common was the conviction that good government was no substitute for self-government. Some of them were edited by men who believed that argument should be accompanied by organisation. Some of them, supported by political subventions, were a vital part of the secret work of rebellion.

The world they inhabited was utterly foreign to that in which the mainstream media held sway. The *Irish Independent*, founded in 1905, was the voice of the increasingly wealthy, articulate and mildly nationalist Catholic middle class, taking over from the ailing *Freeman's Journal*. The *Irish Times*, founded in 1859, was the voice of Southern Unionism: equally articulate – patrician, even – monied, Protestant, and tinged with a liberalism which found few echoes among the Unionists' co-religionists in Belfast and the surrounding counties. In that region, still united with the rest of the island, the bitterness of at least two and a half centuries had divided the population into two self-sealing blocs, each with its own media. Northern nationalists read the *Irish News*, their unionist fellow-citizens the *Belfast Newsletter*. The *Belfast Telegraph* alone straddled the sectarian divide, to a large extent because the market was too small to support two evening, as well as two morning newspapers.

This book examines the history of the print and broadcast media in both parts of the island in the eight decades from the Anglo-Irish Treaty to the present day. Its analysis is not merely chronological, but is grounded in the belief that the relationship between the media and the communities they serve is a complex and subtle one, symbiotic and mutually revelatory. The media inform social and political change, as well as reflecting it, and the economics of the media industry are peculiarly vulnerable to changes in the wider economic field, where fluctuating advertising trends, the emergence of new media forms, and changing patterns of consumption, all pose continually new challenges.

There are few neat divisions into which these eight decades can be put, and any division runs the risk of being to some extent arbitrary, but some of the major fault-lines can readily be discerned. The new State in 1922 inherited what was essentially the old order, in legislative as well as in cultural terms. The period of readjustment (Chapter 1, 1922–31) took the best part of a decade, for much of which the media landscape was essentially as lopsided as its political counterpart, where up to 40% of the electorate remained unrepresented in the national parliament. When militant Irish Republicanism came in from the cold with the creation of the Fianna Fail party in 1926, the stage was set for a further realignment of national media: this duly occurred with the establishment of the *Irish Press* by the leader of Fianna Fail, Eamon de Valera, in 1931. Radio, seen at least in part as one of the necessary trappings of nationhood, was tame, tightly controlled and didactic.

The decade and a half between the establishment of the *Irish Press* in 1931 and 1947 (Chapter 2) saw the increasing involvement by the state in areas of media policy. The 1937 Constitution was notable for its attempt to address key questions of freedom of expression. The Second World War, in particular, ushered in a most stringent form of media censorship, and the legislative weapons that were forged at this time not only constrained the mainstream media but were used to considerable effect against minority political publications on both left and right. Fascinated by media, Irish politicians saw, in short-wave radio, a way of reaching out to the Irish diaspora and simultaneously airing political grievances about Northern Ireland on the world stage.

The decade between 1947 and 1957 (Chapter 3) was marked by political volatility, economic hardship and by governmental *dirigisme* of a high order. The establishment of the Irish News Agency marked a significant development in the government's media policy, albeit one which was to die a long and lingering death. The beginnings of a policy of media management become apparent. The Cold War produced a renewed interest, by foreign as well as domestic intelligence services, in the political affiliations of Irish journalists. Towards the end of the decade, the reins were relaxed in radio, and a new political openness towards the rest of the world, and Europe in particular, was mirrored in the openness to the UK-based television services, now widely available within the borders of the Irish state.

Chapter 4 (1957–73) sees a major concentration on one medium – television – as the debates which surrounded its establishment and its early years of existence reflect with great clarity the substantial cultural and other changes which were taking place in Irish society. This combination of a new medium and rapid social change produced, in turn, an additional set of tensions between government and broadcasters. Following a series of skirmishes, major hostilities erupted with the outbreak of violence in Northern Ireland in 1969. The resulting ban on the broadcasting of certain material, which was to remain in existence until 1994, marked a new era in media control.

The year 1973 marks a watershed in the development of the print media (Chapter 5), with ownership changes both at the Irish Independent group (where Dr A.J. O'Reilly assumed effective control), and at the *Irish Times*. Two major groups – the Independent and the Press – attempted diversification, with varying results – more successfully in the case of the former. Overall, after the serious economic problems of the mid-1970s caused by the oil price rises of that era, growing Irish national prosperity sharpened national and international competition. New titles were established, and UK papers – tabloids in particular – took a renewed interest in Irish sales. In broadcasting, the growth of pirate radio produced a new set of problems for governments and for the State's own radio services; the politics of broadcasting policy moved for a time to the top of the public agenda, and by 1985 had become a cause of considerable political dissension.

Broadcasting again features prominently in Chapter 6 (1985–95), more especially in the light of the unsuccessful attempt, in the Republic, to come to terms with the reality of pirate radio and the political controversies surrounding the attempts at political regulation. Not least because of these factors, media again begin to move up the political agenda, and the most overtly political medium of all – the Irish Press group of newspapers – goes into terminal decline. In Northern Ireland, there was a continuation – and intensification – of the tensions within broadcasting, as the electronic media generally became the focus of attention by local politicians, their governors and national regulators, as well as by the security forces, to a greater extent than ever before.

Further developments and trends, between 1995 and 2000, have led to a situation of extraordinary pluriformity (Chapter 7), qualified to some extent by the growing role of one media giant, Independent Newspapers, which has taken major expansionary initiatives, not least across the border into Northern Ireland. Globalisation has begun to affect all Irish media, and rationalisation and agglomeration is becoming a major factor in the media internally. New titles and broadcasting outlets are being created frequently, and at the same time there is a growing public interest in questions of media ethics, led by concerns about 'tabloidisation' under the influence of UK competition. Nor is competition exercised only in terms of sales: UK media interests are showing an increasing interest in purchasing Irish titles, both national and provincial; and the Independent group is showing, with its purchase of the *Independent* (London) that this commerce can be a two-way street. In broadcasting, the development of digital TV, as well as the presence of new competitors, is forcing the national broadcasting station to adopt new policies, and possibly seek commercial partners, as it looks for the massive levels of investment that will be needed in the future.

All these developments raise many questions, some of which, ironically, mirror the self-same issues which faced the media eighty years ago at the time of the foundation of the State. What role do the media play in the modern state? Will access to the media continue to be a function of social or economic power? What are their responsibilities, as well as their rights? What are the most appropriate mechanisms for regulation? To what extent will the future of the media be determined by technology, and to what extent by commercial or political considerations? How dramatically will the new media alter the shape of the playing field and the duration of the match? These and other questions involve projections for the future which will have to be answered in the light of the experiences of the past and the challenges of the present.

1   The new order, 1922–31

The establishment of the Irish Free State in January 1922 may have marked the beginning of the dissolution of the British Empire, but this was as yet far from apparent, and, in Dublin, such global considerations were far from people's minds. In every sphere of public and private life, the business of adjustment began apace. The media were not exempt; indeed, they were as unprepared as any sector in society for the sea-change that was in progress, and in some cases had rapidly to adopt, chameleon-like, a range of new editorial positions as they grappled with emerging political and social realities.

The media landscape in 1922 had been disturbed, but not fundamentally altered, by the trauma of the War of Independence, which effectively began in 1919. The advanced nationalist press had to a considerable extent disappeared under the censorship legislation – notably the Defence of the Realm Act – after the 1916 Rising, and, although a number of subterranean or *samizdat*-type publications, notably the *Irish Bulletin*, had become extremely efficient propaganda outlets for the growing Irish Republican military and political forces, mainstream media were still by and large conservative: they supported Home Rule rather than Republicanism, or Unionism rather than Home Rule. During the most intense period of the War of Independence, they cooperated for the most part willingly with the office of the censor, so much so that, when he finally relinquished office at the time of the Treaty, he was moved to write to the editors expressing his appreciation at the degree of understanding they had shown for his task (NAI: Chief Secretary's Office: Press Censorship Records, 1916–19).

Prior to the Treaty, the existence of the United Kingdom of Great Britain and Ireland was reflected in the nature of the media available in the smaller island, and in the balance between British and Irish titles. At this remove in time, no circulation figures can be quoted authoritatively, but circumstantial evidence suggests that the major British newspaper titles had substantial circulations in Dublin, Belfast and elsewhere on the island. There was a large Protestant population, amounting to some 10% of the total population of the island, and 5% of the total population of the Republic, whose present boundaries were defined authoritatively almost immediately as Northern Unionists took advantage of the opt-out clause in the Treaty to create the entity known since then as Northern Ireland.

The *Irish Times*, whose circulation at this time was static, or falling, at around 20,000 copies a day, was predominantly the paper of the Protestant commercial and professional classes: Protestant land-owners and the titled gentry would have read, instead or additionally, the *Times*, the *Daily Telegraph* or the *Daily Mail*: lower middle- and working-class Irish Protestants would have read the more popular British titles. Few of them would have read any of the Independent group of titles – the *Irish Independent*, *Sunday Independent* or *Evening Herald*: this group of papers appealed primarily to the growing Irish Catholic middle classes and to the farming community. Since 1905, when they had been re-launched, they had become the first indigenous newspapers whose circulation was effectively national.

They did not have the field entirely to themselves: the *Freeman's Journal*, which had a chequered history going back to its foundation in 1763, and whose by now vestigial anti-clericalism attracted the lingering admiration of James Joyce, had suffered enormously from supporting Parnell after his divorce and was experiencing a terminal slide in circulation. Protestants even had an evening paper to reflect their special interests: the *Dublin Evening Mail*, founded in 1823 (it was to drop the word 'Dublin' from its title in 1928).

Outside the major urban centres, a whole range of weekly provincial papers survived and even prospered. The oldest of them, the *Limerick Chronicle*, had been founded in 1766. It was a journalistic landscape which had evolved dramatically in the second half of the nineteenth century, as the old network of small, Protestant-owned papers, situated for the most part in garrison towns, was supplemented, challenged and in some cases obliterated by the growth of nationalist papers whose success was based partly on rising educational and income levels among the Catholic population, and partly on developing forms of political self-expression from the Land War in the 1880s onwards. Only in Northern Ireland was the traditional bifurcation maintained, with both nationalist and Unionist local papers continuing to flourish, some of them appearing twice or even three times a week.

There were, inevitably, newspapers which did not fit neatly into this geographical or social set of categories. Waterford boasted two evening papers, the *Evening Star* (founded 1917) which lasted until 1940, when it became a weekly, and the *Waterford Evening News* (founded 1848), which was to last until 1957 when it was amalgamated with its weekly stable-mate the *Waterford News* (later amalgamating with its rival to form the *Waterford News and Star*). In Cork, the principal papers were the *Cork Examiner*, and its sister paper the *Evening Echo*, under the control of the Crosbie family since shortly after its foundation in 1841. After the collapse in 1924 of its Unionist rival, the *Cork Constitution* (founded 1822), these were the only examples of daily newspapers outside Dublin and Belfast. The group also published the *Cork Weekly Examiner* until 1981. Ireland had no indigenous broadcasting: the BBC, however, was widely available and listened to; its schedules were published as a matter of course in all the daily newspapers, and its programmes were the subject of weekly commentaries by radio critics.

As the new government took power, an accelerated period of readjustment ensued. Of all the national daily papers, the *Freeman's Journal* was the most enthusiastic supporter of the administration. The *Irish Independent*, long a supporter of Home Rule, found the transition to *de facto* independence relatively easy to make. Even the *Irish Times*, which in 1916 had called for further executions of the leaders of the Rising, and for 'sedition [to be] rooted out for once and for all', discovered unexpected reserves of enthusiasm when it editorialised:

> No Irishman can watch without pride and hope the beginnings of our native Parliament … the temper of this assembly of young and untrained men, its practical quality, its skill in intricate debate are one of the happiest omens for the country's future.
>
> (22 September 1922)

The welcome probably would have been more grudging but for the fact that Eamon de Valera, the sole surviving commandant of the Rising, had, together with many who had fought in the War of Independence, rejected the Treaty and walked out of the Dail after they were on the losing side in the vote to ratify it. A government led by W.T. Cosgrave and manned by the pro-Treaty majority was a different proposition from one which might have included de Valera himself and firebrands like Liam Mellows and Cathal Brugha. Not only were these men determined on a total break with Britain, some of them, like Mellows, were infected by an even worse disease: socialism. Their exclusion not only from government but – by their own action – from the Dail itself, not only put a premium on supporting Cosgrave, but made it a more congenial task.

The learning curve, for journalists and politicians alike, was to be a steep one. On 14 April 1922 the dissident Republicans occupied the Four Courts, the centre of the judicial system and the repository for the public records of Ireland going back to the fourteenth century. After a few months of stalemate, the Civil War broke out in earnest, and was to last almost until the end of 1923.

The conflict was not only military. There was a plethora of newspapers published by or on behalf of both sides. The government published *An Saorstat* ('The Free State') from February to November 1922. It was only notionally a newspaper, in that its columns were mostly filled by commentaries on current events, and by appeals to specific groups for political support (e.g. 'Women and the Treaty', 18 March). These commentaries alternated with attempts at satire aimed at de Valera and his followers; an article titled 'Revised Definitions – A Dictionary for the Times' noted, under 'de Valera' 'See "Dictator"' (11 April). The infrequent advertisements in its pages, when they were not for political meetings to be addressed by pro-Treaty leaders, were for expensive consumer items such as motor-cars and fur coats, indicating strong support for the embattled government from the upper social classes. Government supporters P.S.

O'Hegarty and Sean Milroy published similar papers entitled *The Separatist* and *The United Irishman* respectively in 1922 and 1923. Ministers even briefly considered, before rejecting, a scheme by a military officer to start a new pro-government paper in the west of Ireland, an area in which pro-government sympathies were noticeable by their absence. The government also accepted the suggestion of its press adviser, Sean Lester (a former news editor of the *Freeman's Journal*) to ban public advertising from provincial weekly newspapers sympathetic to the Republican cause (Horgan 1984a: 55).

The Republicans had their own papers, including *The Fenian*, a semi-underground paper which appeared for the first time in July 1922 and intermittently after that until October. It contained war bulletins on the activities and occasional successes of the anti-Treaty forces, and used on its masthead the date-line 'The 7th year of the Republic', in place of a more conventional chronology. Its articles were, for obvious reasons, all unsigned, and habitually referred to the 'Slave State' rather than the Free State. *Eire* and *Poblacht na hEireann*, which was suppressed in December 1922, were similar publications. Labour published its own sectional paper, *The Voice of Labour*, for the first time also in 1922 (it lasted until 1927). In this welter of short-lived political journalism, the foundation of *Dublin Opinion* in 1924 stood out: a magazine specialising in light humour, it had a remarkable existence until 1970.

Government and republicans alike realised early on that the newspapers were as important as any territory being fought over, and both sides evolved media management techniques that varied from the persuasive to the intimidatory. The newspapers, for their part, while generally supportive of the government, felt it necessary from time to time to defend their independence, to an extent which ministers sometimes found little short of treasonable.

The government set up censorship mechanisms in a hurry. One of the chief issues was the way in which the anti-Treaty forces would be described. As far as the government was concerned, any description which tended to give the impression that the struggle was between two equally legitimate forces was anathema: so the publication of the military ranks used by the anti-Treaty forces was banned, as was the use of the words 'forces', 'troops' or 'army' to describe their combatants. Worst of all was the term 'Republican'. The members of the Cosgrave government, although they had been forced to accept a political solution which fell short of the hoped-for Republic, still regarded themselves as ideological Republicans, and did not take kindly to their opponents' appropriation of the word.

Even as the hostilities intensified, there were differences of opinion within the government. Michael Collins, who was chiefly involved with prosecuting the war, wrote to one of his colleagues on 26 July:

> The censorship was too strict for my liking. It is unquestionably a fact that the average reader of the newspaper discounts to an undue extent censored news, and in any case we have the situation so well in hand now from the public and military point of view that the newspapers themselves may be

trusted to do what is right if only they are spoken to occasionally. If there are rare instances of departure from the spirit in which we allow freedom of the press, then I think we should take such cases up separately.

(NAI: Taoiseach: S 1394)

On 20 October, some two months after Collins's death, another government military leader, General Richard Mulcahy, called all the newspaper editors in to urge them to convey the impression that the fighting was over by suppressing or minimising the reports of activities by the 'Irregulars', as the government preferred their opponents to be described.

This was a response to the fact that the government's censorship policy was not operating in a vacuum. The Republican forces were engaged in widespread intimidation of newspaper proprietors and editors in areas of the country (principally the south, south-west and west) over which they exercised a large measure of control. The *Kerry People* in Tralee and the *Nationalist* in Clonmel, Co. Tipperary, were two of the most prominent casualties: in Cork, where the entire city was for a time under the control of Republican forces, the *Cork Examiner* and its evening paper were forced at gunpoint to carry the full text of Republican press announcements.

Nor were their activities confined to provincial newspapers. Captured papers from the period in the Military Archives (MA: A, 10657; US, 10) suggest strongly that Republicans had directly intervened with the managements of both the *Irish Times* and the *Irish Independent* in an attempt to secure more balanced coverage, and that these interventions had to some extent been successful. It was not so critical for the *Irish Times*, whose core circulation was in Dublin; but the *Irish Independent*, which had a large proportion of its sales in non-metropolitan areas, was susceptible to a boycott which apparently lasted for two weeks. Although the paper vigorously denied that it had come to any understanding with the government's opponents, the government censors believed that it was:

insidiously, rather than openly, doing its best for the Irregulars ... by the mere working of a passage to imply that this is not a revolt against a constituted government ... but a fight between two factions.

(NAI: Taoiseach: S 1394)

The *Freeman's Journal* did not disguise its loyalty to the government, and suffered in consequence. When it published in March 1922 accurate, but uncomplimentary, information about the inner workings of the Republican movement, which had been deliberately leaked to it by the authorities, armed Republicans entered its city centre premises in Dublin and destroyed the machinery with sledge-hammers. Newsagents in counties Sligo and Mayo were terrorised into refusing to stock the paper, and the Irregulars then adopted a more labour-effective method, by intercepting the mail train at Limerick junction and burning all copies of the *Journal* destined for counties Limerick, Cork,

Tipperary, Waterford and Clare. The headquarters of the IRA, as the Republican forces described themselves, issued instructions to their local units to expel hostile journalists from their areas (NAI: Justice: H5/55).

As hostilities tailed off, leaving only a few pockets of resistance, the government turned its attention to other threats, notably from foreign correspondents based in Ireland. When the army complained about the tone of articles appearing in the London *Daily Mail* in February 1923, the government seized all copies as they were being unloaded from the mail-boat in Dun Laoghaire, and suppressed it for four days. The London *Morning Post* fared even worse: its correspondent in Dublin, T.A. Bretherton, had already suffered the indignity of being horse-whipped on the steps of the Kildare Street Club by the nationalist Conor O'Brien (O'Brien 1998: 38) for comparing the Catholic Irish to monkeys. He now enraged the authorities to such an extent by a series of articles in March and April 1923 in which he maintained, *inter alia*, that:

> The Irish Free State has no assets, is spendthrift, is already heavily in debt, and has in its midst a large and, it is to be feared, growing section of the people who deny the existing government's claim to represent the nation or sign its notes of hand.
>
> (Horgan 1984b: 52)

The government's Director of Publicity, Sean Lester, recommended that Bretherton be either imprisoned or deported. Wiser counsels prevailed, however, and the government confined itself to making diplomatic representations about the miscreant. Military censorship itself withered and died after the *Irish Times* successfully defied, in July 1924, a government instruction not to print the military ranks ascribed to Republicans in its paid death notices.

A more permanent casualty of the hostilities was the *Freeman's Journal*. Although it had resumed publication after the destruction of its presses by the republicans, the growth of the *Irish Independent* had left it completely without a market niche. It moved briefly to sensationalism in an attempt to boost sales, but this backfired when the police, stirred into action by a strident campaign it was waging against the city's numerous brothels, raided one of them only to discover a senior journalist from the paper enjoying its facilities (Oram 1983: 155). Despite its fading fortunes, however, it represented an attractive option for the Republicans, partly because it had an existing readership (however small), but more so because of its tradition of independence in the late nineteenth century. Now that the Civil War was over, de Valera and his allies were actively canvassing the possibility of taking over or starting a daily newspaper to counter the overwhelmingly anti-Republican ethos of all the other dailies. They set their sights on the *Freeman's Journal*.

They nearly succeeded – indeed Lester believed that they had all but managed to amass the purchase price – when the Murphy family, proprietors of the *Irish Independent*, stepped into the breach as the *Journal* ceased publication in December 1924 and bought paper and premises for £24,000. Conspiracy theorists might hold that this was done at the instigation of the government; but the more likely explanation is that it was a purely commercial move designed to stifle the possibility of any opposition in the market-place. William Lombard Murphy, the chairman of the company, was reported in his own newspaper a year later as confidently expressing the opinion that the most fundamental characteristic of newspapers was that they were:

> great Irish industries, which had been built up by years of hard work, and by enormous expenditures of time, energy and money; and which, when they were successful, paid into the coffers of the State a large sum in income tax, and, whether successful or not, gave a very large amount of employment.
>
> (*II*: 18 December 1925)

These 'great Irish industries' were operating in a climate in which freedom of expression, despite the termination of military censorship, was shortly to come under attack from other quarters. Article 9 of the Constitution of the Irish Free State laid down, in a somewhat negative context, that 'the right of free expression of opinion as well as the right to assemble peaceably and without arms, and to form associations and unions is guaranteed for purposes not opposed to public morality.' In 1926, elements in the defeated Republican forces – still without a newspaper of their own – formed a new political party under de Valera, called it Fianna Fail, and began their tortuous journey towards full participation in democratic politics. In 1927, de Valera made one of a number of visits to the United States which combined fund-raising for his new organisation with a detailed study of newspaper ownership models and management practices.

His impatience on the subject of starting a newspaper was particularly evident when one of his political opponents, Ernest Blythe, made a speech in 1929 suggesting that Ireland was happy to remain in the British Commonwealth. De Valera told one of his correspondents:

> If we had a daily paper at this moment I believe that Blythe's statement could be used to waken up the nation, but the daily press that we have slurs it over and pretends that nothing vital has been said. The English press of course are broadcasting it wherever they can. This is natural enough, for it is Britain's final victory over what remained of the Collins mentality and policy.
>
> (Longford and O'Neill 1970: 270)

This development effectively marked a decisive split in the anti-Treaty forces: many of Fianna Fail's former comrades maintained that this was a betrayal of principle and remained on the margins, a potent source of political and social tension. Their military organisation, the so-called Irish Republican Army, was proscribed, IRA publications were outlawed by the Public Safety Act of 1927, Section 9 of which made it a crime to publish anything 'aiding or abetting or calculated to aid and abet an unlawful organisation'.

More censorship was in the air, but this time of the social or moral rather than the military or political variety. Already in 1923 the new government had passed, with barely a ripple of dissent, legislation to censor films. This was a powerful expression of the work of a number of important interest groups, notably the Vigilance Association, which had been set up by a group of Catholic priests and laymen in 1911 to safeguard Irish public morality particularly against the incoming tide of foreign newspapers, magazines and motion pictures, but which had registered little success under British rule. The chief spirit of this organisation was a Jesuit priest, Fr Richard Devane, who had been known to confiscate British publications from unwilling newsagents in his native Limerick and, with his helpers, set fire to them publicly. He was ably assisted by the Irish Christian Brothers, a religious order dedicated to the education of Catholic boys, for whom they established the periodical *Our Boys* in 1924, partly to offset the spread of British publications for young people. Devane alleged that 'many of the boys' papers are, in effect, recruiting agencies for the British boy scouts which, in turn, are a recruiting agency for the British Army and Navy' (Coogan 1993b: 11).

Both these organisations now turned their attention in 1925 to the new Minister for Justice, Kevin O'Higgins, firmly believing that a native Irish administration would pay more attention to their entreaties than a distant government in Westminster (Horgan 1995: 62). The minister was supportive, but unwilling to move without evidence of widespread public support. His hesitation was overcome by a meeting with a deputation of Catholic bishops in January 1926, after which he immediately appointed a 'Committee on Evil Literature' to examine the whole question and to furnish him with a report (NAI: Justice 7/1–3). The committee's report, which was delivered by the end of 1926 and published in early 1927, was the foundation for the 1929 Censorship of Publications Act, which was to remain in force without major modification until 1967. One of the Act's principal progenitors, the Revd R.S. Devane S.J., although not a member of the committee, influenced it strongly both by giving voluminous evidence of wrong-doing by imported journals and by writing copiously on the subject. In one of his effusions, he noted:

> In this question we must remember we are not dealing with the liberty of the Irish press but with the licence of an extern press. Hence I suggest that the proposed legislation be not directed against the home press, but to the outside press. To my mind Irish journalism and the Irish press are as near perfection in this matter as any press can be. (At least 99% of the Irish press. I am not unaware that a few Dublin productions are giving, at times, some cause for anxiety. The Irish provincial press is such as the most exacting could demand in the matter under consideration.)
>
> (Devane 1927b: 16)

Where newspapers and periodicals were concerned, the main effect of the new legislation was felt – and was intended to be felt – by imported rather than domestic publications. Insofar as this operated to restrict competition from outsiders, Irish newspapers tended to welcome the establishment of the committee, or at least to suggest that public morality needed attention. The *Irish Times* noted, with a sideswipe at the new government, that:

> Today ... the Free State is not only a less industrious, but a more immoral country than it was fifteen years ago. Parents are losing the capacity to control their children. Extravagance in dress is almost universal, and is most reckless among the very people who can afford it least. Fifteen years ago few women of the middle classes touched strong liquors, even in their own homes. Today many of them take wine and whiskey in public places.
>
> (9 February 1926)

This comment was penned before the announcement of the establishment of the committee. When the news broke, it rowed back a little, suggesting that the problem was perhaps not all that great. It detected:

> the smug voice of cant ... in the demand for a moral censorship of the press [which would] merely feed the national vice of self-complacency ... The things which defile Ireland today come not from without, but from within.
>
> (19 February 1926)

The *Irish Independent*, its mass circulation more at risk commercially from British competition than that of the *Irish Times*, was vociferous in its support:

> There are stringent regulations to deal with the sale of anything that may prove poisonous to the body; but there is no attempt made by the law to prevent the indiscriminate circulation of imported papers that poison the soul ... The fact that the vilest newspapers are flaunted in the face of the public every Sunday, while no prosecutions ensue, is evidence enough that the present law is powerless, unless, indeed, one assumes there is no desire to enforce it.
>
> (19 February 1926)

The *Irish Independent* warmly welcomed the report itself, and described its proposals as 'no more an attempt to interfere with the liberty of the press or of the subject than does the legal code against criminal libel or against bigamy' (1 February 1927). The *Irish Times*, on the other hand, went some distance in its attempt to reconcile its liberal Protestant ethic and demonstrably middle-class concerns. Public opinion and 'old fashioned manliness' were more effective censors than legislation, it suggested. Moreover, the proposed Board's power could easily be 'perverted to the use of the faddist with an unhealthy mind'. It added:

We have seen in Ireland attacks upon improper literature entrusted to young people who ought not to know that there is such a thing, and often the crusade has done more to taint innocence than the thing against which it was directed. A healthy child can be loosed among the classics without danger; but the little prig who is taught to peep for matter to denounce in every print can hardly fail to be infected.

(1 February 1927)

When the Dail debated the report, the moral majority was evident on all sides. The Minister for Justice, Mr FitzGerald Kenny (O'Higgins had been murdered by the IRA in the interim) told parliament:

We will not allow, as far as it lies with us to prevent it, the free discussion of this question [contraception] which entails on one side of it advocacy. We have made up our minds that it is wrong. That conclusion is for us unalterable.

(DD: 18 October 1928)

The Censorship of Publications Board which was set up as a result of the committee's report had a major effect on the development of Irish literature over the next three decades. The main effect of the legislation so far as the newspapers were concerned, however, was to make the importation of any material containing information about contraception a criminal offence. For many years thereafter, this legislation was operated on a class-specific basis: it was used, for example, to proscribe British newspapers like the *Sunday Chronicle* and *Reynolds News*, which carried small advertisements for family planning requisites. Another paper to fall under the ban was the *Daily Worker*, whose political sentiments were unwelcome but not illegal: its small advertisements for birth control materials were a convenient excuse for banning both message and messenger. On the other hand, publications like the *New Statesman* and *The Spectator*, which carried identical advertisements, never attracted official attention in the same way, presumably because their middle-class and better-educated readers were assumed to be impervious to such temptations. Impervious or not, these did not want for other distractions: their house journal the *Irish Tatler and Sketch*, whose social agenda had been impoverished by the departure of the Viceroy in 1922 but which was still otherwise largely unaltered, recorded in 1927 that no fewer than 20,000 of them attended a military tattoo at the rugby grounds in Lansdowne Road, after which a civic ball was attended by such luminaries as Oliver St John Gogarty and Lord Longford in fancy dress (de Vere White 1967: 22).

Broadcasting: a badge of independence

The establishment of the BBC in 1922 was undoubtedly a factor which provoked interest, and an early attempt at emulation, in the infant Free State. In much the same way as in the 1960s the national airline became a badge of independence and self-sufficiency for a number of former colonies, the creation of a national broadcasting service was to assume a high priority, even as the country struggled to extricate itself from the huge cost of the Civil War, which ended only in May 1923.

As it happened, the Treaty which had established the Free State, and which had led directly to that civil war, also had a bearing on the establishment of a radio service. This was because the British negotiators, conscious as ever of Ireland's place in the scheme of imperial defence, had included a clause (not published at the time) restricting the right of the new government to establish radio stations with a capacity for broadcasting outside the national territory. Any such stations had to have prior British agreement: this was to become relevant later, when the power of broadcasting apparatus was increasing rapidly, and when a number of commercial organisations sought to use Ireland as a base for their activities.

Even at this time, many of the early moves into radio were being made by entrepreneurs rather than by governments. These entrepreneurs, in turn, were primarily interested in technology rather than in content: inventors, manufacturers and distributors of wireless receiving apparatus, they conceived of broadcasting as a way of selling their wares, and of broadcasting content primarily as a means to this end. The BBC itself was formed initially by a consortium of commercial organisations which had been operating independent experimental stations, and which were pushed together by the Post Office. One of these organisations, the Marconi Wireless Telegraph Company, was simultaneously directing its attention to the neighbouring island. Marconi had carried out many of his early experiments in wireless telegraphy from suitable vantage points in Co. Cork, and, in May 1922, when Ireland was in the early stages of its civil war, he applied to the Irish government for permission to set up a station. A similar, almost simultaneous application, was received from the *Daily Express*. The *Daily Express* application was not proceeded with, and Marconi's was turned down 'owing to the present disturbed conditions in Ireland' (Gorham 1967: 5). Undeterred, Marconi went ahead with experimental transmissions over a range of some 7 miles from Dun Laoghaire, in the southern part of Co. Dublin, to the Dublin Horse Show in August 1923: the government disapproved, and his apparatus was dismantled and sent back to Britain.

As the 'disturbed conditions' ameliorated, rivalry and emulation went hand in hand: the Irish Postmaster-General (his title, like much else, borrowed from the UK administration) proposed in November 1923 that broadcasting be established as a commercial concern under the effective control of native private enterprise, but doubts about this in the Dail (i.e. parliament) prompted, instead, the establishment of a Dail Committee in the following month. The committee, whose work was bedevilled by a scandal involving alleged links between one of its members and a private organisation involved in lobbying for the right to set up a radio service, presented its interim report in January 1924 and its final report in March of the same year. In one Dail debate on the issue, Walsh warned that the Dail risked surrendering Irish broadcasting to 'British music hall dope and British propaganda'; one of his Southern Unionist critics replied tartly that 'if we are to have wireless broadcasting established on an exclusively Irish-Ireland basis, the result will be *Danny Boy* four times a week, with variations by way of camouflage' (McLoone 1991: 3).

The peculiar form which the debate on Irish broadcasting took at this time can be explained at least in part by the peculiar nature of the Irish parliament. Those of its members opposed to the Treaty had withdrawn from the assembly just before the beginning of the Civil War. They had not re-entered the arena of constitutional politics, and indeed were not to do until the Sinn Fein organisation split, leading to the creation of Fianna Fail in 1927 and that party's subsequent *rapprochement* with the Dail. In the interim, and in the absence of any political opposition which could unseat the government, individual members had considerably more control over the executive than later became the case. In this case, they were able to prevail, not only over the doubts of the Postmaster-General, but over the delaying tactics employed by the Department of Finance (Farrell 1991: 13).

This was the context in which the Postmaster-General found his proposals rejected, and the administration found itself saddled with a broadcasting model, and a broadcasting philosophy, which was in many respects not of its own choosing. The Postmaster-General was J.J. Walsh, who, before 1916, had been a telegraph operator. He believed he had devised a model which would allow the government to control broadcasting content without having to pay for the staff and technology used to prepare and transmit it, because it would be operated on a concession basis and financed by a licence fee; but it rapidly became apparent that the erstwhile revolutionaries in the Dail would not be content with anything that fell short of full political control, and were little short of evangelical in their view of the potential for the new service.

Walsh had told the committee of his own belief that 'any Irish station is better than no Irish station at all' (Gorham 1967: 12), but his enthusiasm markedly abated when he encountered the views of the committee. This was because the committee not only recommended strongly that the new station be set up as a state monopoly (with cost implications which Walsh clearly foresaw, and which he felt unable to justify in the light of the financial stringencies being visited on his department in the aftermath of the civil war) but had a vision of the future content of broadcasting with which he found himself out of sympathy.

The committee's final report was almost hyper-Reithian in its view of the future. It considered broadcasting:

> to be of incalculable value: it views the use of wireless telephone for entertainment, however desirable, as of vastly less importance than its use as ministering alike to cultural and commercial progress ... a lecture, which otherwise would require to be repeated at different centres involving no little inconvenience and multiplied cost can be heard simultaneously in a thousand schoolrooms and in the home of all who desire to learn ... In this

way the pupils may learn the elementary principles of hygiene, of gardening, of fruit-growing, bee-keeping, poultry-raising and the like direct from men of recognised authority in the subjects. Similarly, expositions of the reasons for and the application of new laws, lessons on the institutions of government and civics generally might be disseminated in an attractive fashion ... As compared with its power for promoting such valuable ends the Committee regards the employment of Broadcasting for entertainment purposes as quite subsidiary and worthy of consideration, here, rather as a possible source of revenue than as an essential element in the problem.

(DD: 28 March 1924)

The asperity with which Walsh greeted this manifesto was undoubtedly related in part to the fact that, on the very day on which the debate took place, the government had had to secure parliamentary approval for a reduction of a shilling in the old age pension. He warned against accepting the degree of financial responsibility involved and added, even more darkly, that the only other country in the world which was tempted to choose the path of total state control was Russia. He went on:

The people want amusement through broadcasting; they want nothing else, and they will have nothing else. If you make amusement subsidiary, then you will have no broadcasting, nobody will buy an instrument, nobody will pay a licence, and the thing will never begin.

(DD: 3 April 1924)

In early 1925 Walsh, whose title in the interim had been changed (he was now Minister for Posts and Telegraphs), brought the outline of his new scheme to parliament. There would be a main station in Dublin, and a subsidiary one in Cork (the previous year he had warned parliamentarians that he had had requests from almost every county for its own station). The licence fee, at £1, would be double the UK equivalent, and although some 2,800 licences had been purchased even before the new Irish station began broadcasting, the attempt to persuade the listening public to part with the finance necessary to support the new station was to be unremitting and frequently unsuccessful.

The technical work on the new service was carried out with considerable help from the BBC, and Reith actually sat on the first board charged with appointing a Station Director (Gorham 1967: 19). A 1 kilowatt transmission apparatus was set up in a military barracks close to the centre of the city (the site continued to be used for this purpose until 1980). The range at which the transmissions could be received depended on the sophistication of the receiver: a crystal set could pick up the signal up to 20 miles away, a one-valve set up to 50 miles away, and a two-valve set up to 80 miles away. Even a one-valve set, however, cost approximately £2, the best part of a week's wages for the average worker. An enterprising primary school teacher in Achill, some 181 miles from Dublin, reported proudly that he had received the test transmissions 'at good loudspeaker strength, and comparable with Daventry [the BBC 25 kw station] in every respect'. He added:

> It might not be too much to hope that in the near future the Education department would have receiving sets installed in all the national schools in the State, and thus bring into the otherwise colourless lives of many poor children the helpful and delightful influences connected with listening-in.
>
> (*II*: 30 December 1925)

The new station was allocated the call-sign 2RN (i.e. 'to Erin') and began broadcasting at 7.45 p.m. on Friday, 1 January 1926. The opening announcement was made by a non-political figure, Douglas Hyde, whose devotion to the Irish language (he was founder of the Gaelic League) was enhanced by the fact that he came from the country's religious minority. He was selected without opposition, in 1937, as the country's first president. His speech, the greater part of which was in Irish (after an introduction in English 'for any strangers who may be listening in') underscored an important theme in the station's early years, which was to become something of a battle-ground in Irish broadcasting later. This was the extent to which the national broadcasting service should – or could – be used as a key element in the official policy aimed at reviving Irish as the spoken language of the majority of Irishmen and Irishwomen, which it had not been for almost a century. There was one notable absence from the programmes broadcast on the opening night: news. The station had still to come to an acceptable financial arrangement with the news agencies (who were British) or with locally based newspapers, for the supply of this exotic commodity. The first advertised news bulletin, on 24 May, may have been a re-broadcast of British news about the general strike then in progress in the United Kingdom; more frequent news bulletins featured from the end of June but a regular daily news bulletin did not appear until 26 February 1927, when it was broadcast at 1.30 p.m.

2RN broadcast initially for six days a week, rapidly increasing to seven. The programme schedule, however, indicated at least a partial victory for Walsh. There were no broadcast lectures on animal husbandry or personal hygiene; instead, a solid diet of music, classical and traditional, the latter echoing the Victorian drawing-room rather more than the raw, untutored talent of the folk music which was a vibrant presence in the countryside.

There was as yet, however, no formal legislative framework to support the new station financially; and the tiny staff who ran 2RN, amounting to no more than a handful of people, were to find out, over and over again, that the dead hand of the Department of Finance acted to obstruct or deny the fulfilment of often very modest ambitions. This did not prevent costs from creeping up; but no matter how much these were restrained, they lagged increasingly behind licence fee revenue. With what sounded like desperation Walsh told the upper house of parliament, the Senate, in July 1926 that only 5,000 licences had been taken out among the estimated 25,000 people who actually owned sets, and the revenue from this source needed to be supplemented by a duty on imported sets and components (Gorham 1967: 33). The licence fee was halved in August of the same year, but there were few prosecutions for evasion, and district justices generally took a lenient view of offenders, which did not encourage compliance.

A legislative framework for the new system was provided with the introduction of the Wireless Telegraphy Bill in November 1926, Section 2 of which prophetically defined wireless telegraphy as any system capable of transmitting 'messages, spoken words, music, images, pictures, prints or other communications, sounds, signs or signals by means of radiated electro-magnetic waves'. It also put the collection of licence fees on a firmer footing: by the end of the following year, it was reported that the number of paid up licences had now risen to 15,000.

> It may be that the vigilance of the Civic Guard also must be thanked, in part, on account of the reduction of unlicensed users of 'wireless' receivers. It is likely that considerable numbers of unauthorised persons continue to tap the 'wireless' waves that roll through the free State, and we hope that these will be roused to a sense of the meanness of their conduct.
>
> (*IT*: 5 December 1927)

The perennial shortage of money did not necessarily stifle initiative. During 1926, 2RN pioneered the broadcast of live sports events (the BBC was prohibited from broadcasting news before 7 p.m., in order not to affect the sales of evening newspapers) and it is claimed that the live transmission of commentary on a hurling match in 1926 was the first live broadcast of a field game in the northern hemisphere. News made its delayed appearance after the conclusion of satisfactory arrangements with the providers. These included, not least, the BBC, which gave permission to excerpt some of its foreign bulletins, and in general the service was merely the re-circulation of material already published by print and other agencies, notably the *Evening Herald* and the *Evening Mail*. This could be supplemented from unusual sources: one of 2RN's technicians had been a ship's wireless operator, and used to listen to Morse transmissions from ships in the area for interesting snippets of information for re-broadcast (Clarke 1986: 50). The station's staff complement was increased by one to facilitate the introduction of this service. The employee concerned, known as the Station Announcer, was originally employed on a part-time basis, but by November 1926 he had become full time, and the planned extension of the broadcast news had become a reality. The minister told the Dail:

> Broadcasting will develop a line of Press dissemination very much wider than we find at present. Already a Press bulletin is being issued nightly. It includes news from half a dozen foreign capitals and sometimes local doings, and certain local markets. That bulletin occupies seven or eight

minutes of our time. It is the intention to extent that margin to perhaps fifteen or twenty minutes later on.

(DD: 30 November 1926: 369)

The context in which this announcement was made was a debate on an advertisement for the employment of an additional, part-time reporter. The fact that broadcasting was – and remained until 1961 – an integral part of a government department, was fully reflected in the job description. The unfortunate employee, who was to be employed initially on a part-time basis, was expected to record the proceedings of Dail and Senate, to obtain reports from police and fire brigades of 'important or sensational happenings', to obtain particulars of outstanding events from national cultural organisations, to prepare a bulletin of foreign news, stock market reports, provincial news and market prices. In addition to all of this, and on a part-time salary of £4 per week, he would be required:

> to furnish a guarantee that there will be no infringement of copyright, and shall provide a bond for £1,000 to be obtained from an approved insurance society or company indemnifying the Minister for Posts and Telegraphs as representative of the State against any action, claims or expenses caused ... by any infringement or alleged infringement of copyright.

(DD: 30 November 1926)

Another innovation was the broadcasting of specially arranged symphony concerts: at the first of these, in November 1927, working-class listeners were let in early, at a specially reduced price; middle-class patrons were not admitted until later, and had to pay more. But not all innovations were equally welcome: John Logie Baird, who visited Dublin in January 1927 to lecture on his new ideas about how pictures could be transmitted, offered to give a talk on 2RN about his invention, but withdrew his offer when he was offered a brief spot at a time when virtually no one would have been listening (Gorham 1967: 40, 44, 36).

By then, broadcasting was – surprisingly – paying for itself. But there was a potential flaw: the import duties, which were providing the bulk of the revenue, were to dwindle as more and more Irish companies began manufacturing sets within the boundaries of the state. Advertising had begun, but was yielding very little revenue, and there were the seeds of future controversy in arguments about whether more modern kinds of music might be permitted on the Irish airwaves. A critic in one of the four rival periodicals established to tell listeners about Irish and UK broadcast schedules issued a public warning about the new music – jazz – which had crossed the Atlantic at high speed and was sweeping through Europe. The popularity of these strange sounds, he sniffed, was:

not a very sound argument as to why we should not discard – if necessary by decrees – the music of the nigger in favour of products of our own artistic creation and the creation of cultured peoples.

(Fanning 1983: 22)

This was not an atmosphere receptive to new ideas, or technologies. A further brief negotiation between John Logie Baird, the inventor of television, and the new broadcasting station, came to nothing, although the *Irish Times* predicted hopefully in 1929 that experiments with television were just about to take place, and that 'there is a possibility that the transmission of pictures may be included in the nightly broadcasts' (20 November 1929). Few more optimistic forecasts can have been made.

Whatever the content, the popularity of the new service was evidenced by the flood of complaints about poor or inadequate reception from outlying areas of the state. The Dail in 1930 therefore agreed to a proposal by Walsh to establish a new high-power station at Athlone, more or less in the geographical centre of the country. This was at a time when the station finances were showing signs of strain. The Cork studios, which had been producing a weekly programme since 1927, were closed down in 1930 at a saving of £1,000 a year, and sale of licences appeared to have reached a plateau, with an increase of fewer than 1,000 bringing the total of licences issued to 26,000 by April 1931.

Faced with these financial problems, and with the apparent unattractiveness of advertising (it generated only £1,000 out of a total revenue of £45,000 in 1930–31), station managers embarked on a new ploy to ensure that the station should pay its way without assistance from general taxation. This was all the more necessary in that the new Athlone station was estimated to cost about £58,000, all of which would have to be found out of future revenues.

The commercial innovation spurred by these figures was the sponsored programme, as 'undiluted advertising talks as had previously been allowed were not a desirable form of broadcast advertising' (DD: 23 April 1931). A sponsored programme was one whose production was paid for in its entirety by a commercial undertaking, but in which the announcement of the sponsor's name was limited to a brief section at the beginning and the end of each programme. Preference was given to Irish manufacturers, and importers were not allowed to advertise items which were being sold in competition with those produced by Irish manufacturers. Until radio – and later television – came into its own as an advertising medium, these programmes, often produced with a high degree of professionalism, attracted a substantial and regular audience: they included drama serials, programmes produced by music retailers and – significantly – programmes produced by the Irish Hospitals Sweepstakes, a private company which had been given the power to run a national lottery on a monopoly basis, and which used the increased power of the Athlone station, particularly in the early 1930s, to inform listeners not only in Ireland but in Britain (where the lottery was illegal) of its attractions. In 1935, after advertisements for its lotteries had been banned in UK papers, it even offered to provide the government with a completely free radio station, if it were allowed to broadcast advertisements for its tickets into Britain. Despite the enthusiasm for this scheme of the Minister for Industry and Commerce, Sean Lemass, the government turned it down (NAI: Taoiseach: S 7095).

The quiet, almost placid world of mainstream print media was, however, now about to be disturbed. As already noted, Mr de Valera had been actively seeking support and money for his proposal to establish a new daily newspaper which would provide a platform for himself and his supporters: all the existing national dailies were opposed to his newly founded Fianna Fail party to one degree or another, not least because the civil war was still a fresh memory. The 1927 Ard Fheis (annual conference) of his party passed a resolution urging the Fianna Fail national executive to explore the possibility of starting a new paper, but it was a resolution which merely sanctioned work which had already been in progress for some time. Irish Press Ltd was formally established in Dublin as a limited company in September 1928, and 200,000 shares were offered at £1 each to encourage small investors. Battle lines were being drawn, in politics and journalism alike.

Northern Ireland: a divided media

In Northern Ireland, the newspapers read by Catholics and Protestants alike operated without any such restrictions; nor is there much evidence that British publications posed as great a threat to indigenous media as nationalists south of the new border tended to argue: the closely knit nature of both communities ensured that the cohesive, bulletin-board functions of both the *Irish News* and the *Newsletter* formed a bulwark against many of the diversions offered by the British press.

The case-hardened religious and political divisions in society had in any case been mirrored in the media for many years: the *Belfast Newsletter*, founded in 1737 (it was to drop 'Belfast' from its title in 1962) reflected mainstream Protestant and Unionist tradition, and it drew its readership from that community almost completely; the *Irish News*, founded in 1891 performed the same function for the Catholic and nationalist community. A partial exception was provided by the *Belfast Telegraph* (founded as the *Belfast Evening Telegraph* in 1870, dropping the word 'Evening' in 1918), which had, by virtue of its monopoly position in the evening newspaper market, a readership from both communities. In the same city, the *Northern Whig* (founded in 1824), intermittently espoused a more liberal version of Unionism. It never managed to establish a sound enough circulation base, and was eventually to close in 1963.

The *Irish News* itself was a product of the bitter political split over Parnell in the 1880s. The existing Belfast nationalist paper at that time was the *Morning News*, which had been founded as a tri-weekly in 1855 and had become a daily in 1872. The *Morning News* had supported Parnell, and Catholic lay and clerical support was quickly organised by the bishops in the cause of establishing a more orthodox voice. The *Irish News*, thus created, appeared for the first time on 15 August 1891, and rapidly overhauled the ailing *Morning News*, whose title it acquired in July 1892. In the aftermath of 1916 the *Irish News* had been a proponent of Home Rule for Ireland within the British Empire, and was deeply disappointed by the partition solution embodied in the Treaty. The establishment of the Northern Ireland parliament at Stormont in May 1921 was, it maintained 'a plan by unscrupulous politicians to assassinate Ireland's nationality'. It quickly came to the conclusion, after the territorial status quo had been effectively ratified by the Boundary Commission in 1925, that Northern Catholics and nationalists had to work out their own political salvation within the new constitutional arrangements, which angered nationalists (including some bishops) who felt that an all-Ireland solution was still a short-term possibility. Both strands were re-united in 1928 under the nationalist politician Joe Devlin, who had been managing director of the paper since 1923 (Phoenix 1995: 24–5), but circulation was weak and was revived only by the appointment of a new editor, Sydney Redwood, in 1929. He cut the price of the paper to a penny and, through a combination of aggressive marketing and journalistic flair, succeeded in substantially reviving its fortunes and making it an effective voice of mainstream Northern nationalism (Phoenix 1995: 27–8).

The *Newsletter*, founded in 1737, was one of the oldest newspapers in the two islands. Owned by the Henderson family, it was no less staunch in its defence of Unionism and, before the partition of the island, of the British connection. In November 1919, when the violence of the War of Independence was making itself keenly felt in the North, it allocated the blame unambiguously in religious terms:

> It is the bigotry of [the Catholic] Church, and its constant efforts, open and secret, to increase its power, which have brought a large part of Ireland to the lawlessness which is disgracing it today.
>
> (Kennedy 1988: 40)

When, after the April 1925 election in Northern Ireland, the president (as the head of government was then known) of the Irish Free State, W.T. Cosgrave, sent a telegram of congratulations to Northern nationalists who had been elected, the *Newsletter* castigated what it described as the 'direct influence by the head of one state in the internal affairs of another' (Keogh 1994: 26). The Unionist proclivities of the *Belfast Telegraph* were, if anything, reinforced by the dramatic events that surrounded the birth of the Irish Free State and the associated creation of Northern Ireland as a new constitutional entity with its own parliament. In the May 1921 election to this parliament the *Telegraph* printed Unionist candidates' speeches in full, accompanied by photographs captioned: 'Vote Only For These Candidates'. One of the Bairds, together with Trevor Henderson of the *Newsletter*, was knighted to coincide with the opening of the new parliament. Thomas Molles, who became editor in 1924 and retained that position until 1937, combined this responsibility with membership of both the Stormont and the Westminster parliaments (Brodie 1995: 41–4).

His strong pro-government sympathies were particularly in evidence during the 1926 British general strike when, having been told that the printers at the *Daily Mail* in London had refused to operate the presses because Harmsworth's paper had included an anti-trade union editorial, promptly printed the offending material in his own paper (Brodie 1995: 47). His paper also achieved the distinction of being the first Irish newspaper to be despatched by plane: copies were airlifted to Stranraer in Scotland in March 1925.

The *Northern Whig*, owned by a family named Cunningham, had been a radical paper in the nineteenth century, but the Home Rule controversies pushed it firmly into the Unionist camp after 1885. If it was solidly Unionist, however, it also gave vent from time to time to unusual views, in that it managed to define a stance which included occasional criticism of Northern Ireland's Unionist government without in any sense querying the constitutional arrangements. It represented itself as 'The people's popular paper – for the housewife, the farmer, for the labourer' (Kennedy 1988: 15) under its editor Robert Lynn who was, like Molles, a member of both parliaments. Lynn's successor in 1928, William Armour, was the son of a Presbyterian clergyman and supporter of Home Rule: his brief tenure of office was characterised by a subliminal sense of disenchantment with Unionism which did not encourage the Cunninghams to keep him for long.

The *Whig* claimed in the 1920s that it had the largest circulation of any Ulster morning newspaper – probably around 30,000 copies. But by 1922 the *Newsletter* was claiming daily sales of 34,000, and the *Telegraph* was probably selling well in excess of 70,000 copies at the same period. As the interests and policies of the two parts of Ireland diverged, so did the attitudes of their newspaper editors. As far as the Northern Unionist papers were concerned, the South was there primarily as a visual aid to illustrate the benefits of Unionism. They commented regularly on the 'unhappy plight' of the denizens of the Free State, and the even more unhappy plight of its Protestant or Unionist minority (Kennedy 1988: 20–21).

Broadcasting in Northern Ireland, both in its origins and in its modalities, reflected the political and social anomalies of the region. It was not called into being primarily as a response to the division of the island in 1922, but as a result of pressure from a group of enthusiastic radio amateurs. Once established, however, it was inevitable that this and related factors would become a major influence – sometimes hidden, sometimes overt – on its programming and policies.

As Rex Cathcart points out in his definitive history of the BBC in Northern Ireland up to 1984 (1984: 5) there was at first no compelling reason why Northern Ireland should have had a separate BBC presence: no other region of the United Kingdom had one, and Northern Ireland's population was only 1.5 million, much smaller than that of Scotland or Wales. Indeed, the initial exclusion of Belfast from the BBC's first list of areas which were to be served by regional transmitters may have owed something to political considerations. Local enthusiasm, however, carried the day; a decision to plan for the new station in Belfast was taken in December 1923 and announced publicly in February 1924. The first broadcast was transmitted on 15 September 1924 from a studio in an old linen warehouse in Belfast, where the opening announcement was made by Tyrone Guthrie. The formal opening did not take place until 24 October, when it was performed by the governor of Northern Ireland, Lord Abercorn, in the presence of Reith and other BBC executives. The station's transmitting aerial was slung between two 187 foot chimneys at the electrical power generating station in East Bridge Street, where the transmitter was housed (Clarke 1986: 12). The transmitter was of comparatively low power, with an effective range of not much more than 30 miles: until the power was enhanced, there were frequent complaints from would-be listeners outside this radius, notably in Derry.

An early station director, Gerald Beadle, noted that South Africa, where he had previously worked, and Northern Ireland, were both 'peoples divided against themselves' (Cathcart 1984: 2). Although this was principally reflected in a stipulation by the Unionist government of Northern Ireland that it should retain the right to terminate transmissions from the Belfast station at any time if it thought this necessary in the public interest, initial reaction to the programming from within both communities was broadly welcoming. Wireless enthusiasts who contacted the nationalist *Irish News* with their comments were, the paper reported on 16 September, 'loud in their praise of the efforts of the officials of the station to provide such interesting programmes'. An Advisory Committee was established (as Dublin was to do for its own station) and a number of positive initiatives were taken, particularly in relation to schools broadcasts.

The opening of 2RN in Dublin in January 1926 did not seem to raise the temperature perceptibly; indeed the Belfast and Dublin stations cooperated on a number of musical programmes which were generally the subject of favourable comment. The honeymoon, however – if this is what it was – was to come to an end for a number of reasons, some of them internal to Northern Ireland itself, others emanating from south of the border.

Despite the early enthusiasm of the *Irish News* for the new station, Northern Ireland nationalists, that third of the population which felt that it had been shanghaied into a constitutional arrangement to which it was fundamentally opposed, was slow to give even conditional allegiance to the new institutions. Teachers in Catholic schools at first refused to accept their state-paid salaries from Stormont, and looked to Dublin instead. This created a politically – and financially – embarrassing situation for Dublin, from which it extricated itself only with some difficulty. Similar considerations dictated that the Catholic Church in Northern Ireland decline to participate in the workings of the committee set up by the BBC to advise on religious broadcasts there, and the Church maintained this stance until 1944.

Similar tensions began to obtrude in the form of controversies about the arrangements made by BBC NI for St Patrick's Day each year. Neither community could ever be entirely satisfied; and Unionists, in particular, were more particularly exercised by the fact that these particular programmes were being transmitted for broadcast throughout the United Kingdom, and were therefore labelling them culturally in a manner of which they disapproved at some visceral level (Cathcart 1984: 44–5).

This was most marked in respect of the 1931 broadcasts, but the level of apprehension and resentment was to be further increased by two other, related factors. One was the accession to power in Dublin of Mr de Valera's Fianna Fail party in 1932; the other was the development of a feeling among Unionists that BBC NI needed to be more combative in order to counter the new high-power station broadcasting from Athlone. Plans to increase the level of cooperation in programming between Belfast and Dublin were an early casualty of this new atmosphere, and growing intra-communal tension in the mid-1930s sharpened a growing awareness of the political significance of broadcasting, especially where news was concerned. Although party political broadcasts were inaugurated in Britain for the 1933 general election, none were allowed in Northern Ireland before the war. There were serious disturbances in Belfast in 1935, involving several deaths, and the BBC's practice of reporting these without analysis or context provoked one Unionist politician to argue in the *Northern Whig* the following January that direct control of BBC NI by the Stormont government would make possible 'counter-propaganda to the republican stuff which comes over nightly from Athlone' (31 January 1936). To its credit, the *Whig* rejected this analysis, arguing that making BBC NI a purely local operation would not only reduce the level of resources to which it had access (leading to inferior programming), but would not guarantee any improvement in news broadcasts (1 February 1936).

Charles Siepmann, the BBC's Director of Regional Relations, was sent to Belfast from London in 1936, as preparations were being made for the establishment of a full regional service in Northern Ireland in that year. He wrote a much-quoted report in which he expressed his view that broadcasting in Northern Ireland was necessitated by political considerations, and was not justified by the availability of indigenous programme resources. He added:

> The bitterness of religious antagonism between Protestants and Catholics invades the life of the community at every point and for our purposes conditions almost everything we do (…) In the official life of Northern Ireland the Roman Catholic by virtue of his religious faith is at a discount (…) Politics and public administration conditioned by religious faction have about them an Alice-in-Wonderland-like unreality.
>
> (Cathcart 1984: 3)

A year later, Beadle's successor as Regional Director in Belfast, George Marshall, was to set out his own position in a quite uncompromising form when, objecting to a programme entitled 'The Irish' which had been produced by the BBC's Northern Region, he observed:

There is no such thing today as an Irishman. One is either a citizen of the Irish Free State or a citizen of the United Kingdom of Great Britain and Northern Ireland. Irishmen as such ceased to exist after the partition.

(Cathcart 1984: 6)

The stage was set: the play would have a long run.

2   Affairs of state, 1931–47

The sixteen years between 1932 and 1948 were a period of uninterrupted rule by Fianna Fail, the party which had not been founded until 1926 and had not entered the Dail until five years before it took power. It would be misleading, however, to assume that this extraordinarily long period of single-party government was synonymous with a period of quietism in the media. The establishment of the *Irish Press* in November 1931 by the leader of Fianna Fail, Eamon de Valera, served notice on the existing media establishment that things would never be the same again. The outbreak of war in 1939 created a whole new series of tensions between media generally and the government. Towards the end of the period, radio, for the first time, began to come into its own as a public service with a much broader remit than had hitherto been the case.

The establishment of the *Irish Press* was as seismic an event, in its own way, as the birth of 2RN. It was – and remained – unique in twentieth-century Ireland as the only national newspaper to have been established which had an overt relationship with a national political party. In this it mirrored similar newspapers in a number of Continental European countries, where the tradition of a party press, and of a press linked to trade unions, had in many cases been well established. The similarities, however, ended there: the *Irish Press* was in many respects a unique creation, born of the fertile and inventive mind of its progenitor, Eamon de Valera.

The principal objective of the paper was undoubtedly to focus and coordinate electoral support for Mr de Valera's party, Fianna Fail. But it was also to be a commercial enterprise: no party could or would support a dependent national newspaper for long. To achieve these two objectives, it had to acquire and maintain journalistic and commercial credibility within a structure that would also guarantee its political loyalty.

This balancing act found formal expression in the articles of association of the company established to publish the paper. The board of directors comprised de Valera himself and seven others – prominent businessmen, chosen not only because their companies operated in every part of Ireland, but also, in at least one case, on the basis of religion (one director was a prominent member of the Church of Ireland). These choices were intended to reassure the business community – whose advertisements would be needed to support the new publication – that the company was in sound hands, and to reassure Irish Protestants that modern Irish Republican journalism would not be in any way sectarian.

The political loyalty of the paper to Fianna Fail was underwritten by another, even more important structural element. This was the designation of Mr de Valera himself as controlling director, with the power to assume any or all of the functions associated with the management and control of the newspaper, should he choose to do so. This was a sophisticated formula. The paper would not be controlled by Mr de Valera's Fianna Fail Party; but, as leader of the party, he could whenever necessary act to ensure that it did not operate against the party's interests. Setting the paper at arm's length from the party in this way had two distinct advantages: it created at least a veneer of political independence, however transparent this might be in practice, and it protected the paper and its journalists from the type of constant interference by party committees which would have probably guaranteed its commercial ruin.

Its first issue, on 5 November 1931, carried an editorial which declared that the *Irish Press* was 'not the organ of an individual, a group, or a party' but would be 'a national organ in all that term conveys'. It added:

> We have given ourselves the motto: Truth in the News. We shall be faithful to it. Even where the news exposes a weakness of our own, or a short-coming in the policies we approve, or a criticism of the individuals with whom we are associated, we shall publish it if its inherent news values so demand ... Until today the Irish people have had no daily paper in which Irish interests were made predominant ... Henceforth other nations will have a means of knowing that Irish opinion is not merely an indistinct echo of the opinions of a section of the British press.

Its first editor, Frank Gallagher, had a pedigree in nationalist journalism that included a major role in the production of the Sinn Fein *Bulletin* during the War of Independence. In his instructions to reporters and sub-editors as the new paper prepared for its launch date, he made its ideological direction quite clear (NLI: MS 18336). Its hostility to the prevailing administration was embodied in a directive that it was not necessary to report every word of praise spoken by judges to policemen – courts and police alike were actively involved in the suppression of the remnants of the defeated Civil War forces and, frequently, the harassment of their sympathisers. At the same time, they were reminded not to make the *Irish Press* merely a Dublin paper, and to emphasise aspects of news stories that featured women and children. Sub-editors were warned that 'propagandist attacks on Russia and other countries should not be served up as news' – an indirect admonition to be wary of the value-systems embodied in the British and American news agencies, which were virtually the only available source of international news.

From the start, the new paper made it clear that its primary target readership was comprised of the two groups that provided Fianna Fail with most of its electoral support: the urban working class and small farmers. It developed an immediate expertise in reporting sport, particularly the traditional games of Gaelic football and hurling. It was virtually alone in publishing much writing in the Irish language (although this component was to shrink in the years ahead), and it provided an outlet for a generation of gifted and eager young journalists and writers who had been effectively excluded from employment in the media for years by virtue of their political views. It also broke new ground in that it was the first daily morning paper to put news on its front page.

Public reaction to the new paper was initially enthusiastic: its print run of 200,000 for the first edition sold out, and it eventually settled down to around 100,000. The government did not trouble to disguise its hostility, banning *Irish Press* reporters for a time from meetings organised by the government party (Cumann na nGael, later Fine Gael), and declining to supply it with information in the normal way. The existing newspapers responded in different ways to being described as 'a section of the British press'. The *Irish Times* gave it a patrician welcome, and even reprinted an extract from its first editorial. The *Irish Independent* carried on as if the *Irish Press* did not exist, and edited out references to the paper from its reports of speeches by Fianna Fail politicians.

More seriously, the Murphy family, the major shareholders in the Independent group of papers, also used their commercial muscle to veto a request by the *Irish Press* to be accommodated on the special newspaper trains which took early editions of all the morning newspapers to non-metropolitan destinations. This was facilitated by the interlocking directorships of the chairman of the Independent board, Dr Lombard Murphy, who was also a director of the Great Southern Railway Company (Irish railways were still privately owned at this time). The *Irish Press* appealed against this to the Railway Tribunal, an arbitration body, and the case dragged on into 1932 (*IP*: 22 April 1932). Although the *Irish Press* was eventually successful, its inability to use the special trains and the need to set up a completely independent distribution network involved it in heavy initial costs.

Although the head of the Irish government, W.T. Cosgrave, brushed aside suggestions from his more extreme followers that the new paper should be banned – it would, he thought, wither away naturally (Oram 1983: 175) – it rapidly became an irritant that could not be ignored. This was particularly because Gallagher, refreshing a technique he had employed to considerable effect during the War of Independence, began to publish articles containing cogent evidence that members of the Garda Siochana (literally: 'Guardians of the Peace', the new police force) had treated political opponents of the government roughly, even with brutality.

This was a new element in an already highly volatile political situation. The economy, which had been devastated by the Civil War, was in poor shape; the government went so far as to take a shilling off the state old age pension, and invoked wage cuts and freezes elsewhere in the public service. Fianna Fail, having abandoned its abstentionist policy, was now participating in constitutional politics, and aiming to replace the government at the next general election. Its commitment to the democratic process, however, was frequently questioned by the government, which reacted strongly to any publications which questioned its legitimacy or hinted at the validity of extra-parliamentary action. This led directly to the passage in October 1931 of the Constitution (Amendment No. 17) Act, establishing a Military Tribunal with wide powers to suppress publications. Although the Tribunal's proscriptions included the Republican newspaper *An Phoblacht*, its activities were directed to a greater extent against left-wing minority publications, such as the *Irish Worker*, edited by the trade union firebrand – and Communist – Jim Larkin, and the *Worker's Voice*, whose banned issue of 31 October 1931 declared that 'the form of the State is a secondary matter – the issue is which class rules' (NAI: Taoiseach: S 4669). The Tribunal's supervisory activity extended even beyond the boundaries of the State, to include bans on the *Irish World* and the *American Industrial Liberator*, both published in New York. Its zeal sometimes exposed its ineptness: one issue of the banned *Republican File* was comprised solely of quotations and excerpts from the *Irish Press*, the *Irish Independent*, Patrick Pearse (the revolutionary executed by the British in 1916) and W.E. Gladstone (Horgan 1984b: 53).

Gallagher's *Irish Press* articles, implying as they did that the police were acting considerably in excess of their legal authority, immediately came under official notice and, in December 1931, he was arraigned before the Tribunal on a charge of publishing seditious libel. He defended himself vigorously, but the election intervened before the case had been concluded. The outcome of the election was that Mr de Valera was able to form a minority government, but the newspaper of which he was controlling director was still undergoing due process before the Tribunal. Gallagher was eventually convicted, and fined £50. The fact that his trial was actually in progress during the election campaign helped to enhance support for Fianna Fail at the polls, but the role played by his newspaper itself was undoubtedly much more significant. The *Irish Independent* commented, with all the grace of a bad loser:

> Yesterday the Fianna Fail party's organ indulged in quite an orgy of abuse of other newspapers for what was termed 'misrepresentation' in regard to the elections ... On the same day that Fianna Fail worked itself into a paroxysm of vilification, that journal and its editor were convicted of publishing a seditious libel with intent to vilify the Irish government and the National Police Force.

> (*II*: 18 February 1932)

Political advertising in all the newspapers was a notable feature of the election. Despite having the *Irish Press* at its back, Fianna Fail advertised in both the *Irish Times* and the *Irish Independent*, even if this was mostly aimed at countering claims made by its political opponents in advertisements in the same papers. Neither of the two government-supporting papers allowed their editorial opinions to be swayed by the receipt of these funds: in its pre-election editorial, the *Irish Times* in particular warned the electorate that Fianna Fail's land policy was Marxist and would be tried in Ireland despite the fact that it had failed in Soviet Russia. After the election, the *Irish Times's* opposition to the new administration, unlike that of the *Irish Independent*, was qualified by a willingness at least to give Mr de Valera a chance to show that he might not live up to the picture of him as a socialist ogre, with which they had earlier regaled their readers. In effect, a double conversion was taking place: Mr de Valera was coming to terms with the compromises necessary in the administration of a country of whose constitutional arrangements he totally disapproved; and the *Irish Times* was coming to terms with a political party whose antecedents it regarded as radically subversive but which was now in government.

Although the work of government to a considerable extent kept de Valera away from the business of running the paper – his implicit trust in Gallagher was also relevant – this did not mean that controversy about the paper's political role abated. Indeed, it was centrally involved in three key sets of circumstances: the crisis involving the role of the governor-general (the legal representative of the Crown in Ireland under the Free State Constitution); the discovery by de Valera of a legislative device by which he could re-finance the paper; and a challenge by the paper's political correspondent to the still extant Military Tribunal. In the middle of all of these controversies, an attempt to create a rival for the *Evening Herald* failed; the new paper was called the *Evening Press* for the first six weeks of its existence, and was then renamed the *Evening Telegraph and Evening Press*. At this stage it was threatened with legal action by the Independent group, which owned the copyright in a paper called the *Evening Telegraph* which had once been published by the *Freeman's Journal* (Oram 1983: 180). This potentially expensive problem, which might have undermined the success of the daily paper, led to the closure of the evening paper on 26 October 1932. The *Irish Press* was not to publish a successful evening paper until 1954, when the *Evening Press* appeared.

The peculiar relationship between the head of government and his newspaper was further explored when the governor-general, a retired nationalist politician named Eoin McNeill, took umbrage at a report in the *Irish Press* of a diplomatic incident in which he was involved, and accused de Valera of having inspired the report. De Valera replied that the *Irish Press*:

> gathers its news as other newspapers do, and publishes what it gathers at the discretion of its editors. Any particular item of news would, it is true, be suppressed were I to issue an express rider to that effect, but ever since the paper was founded I have carefully refrained from giving any such orders.
>
> (*IP*: 12 July 1932)

It is important to note what was here being asserted, and what was not being denied. De Valera's interpretation of censorship was a narrow one, and negative: it did not include positive action by him to shape the content of the paper in a way which did not involve direct suppression.

As a political reporter in the old, barn-storming days of the *Press*, my father was close to Dev. He used to tell me stories about Dev phoning the news-room every night to know what was coming out in the paper the next day. He often had no hesitation in changing copy, in changing a whole front page.

(Kilfeather 1997: 22)

De Valera's biographers noted that he delegated work in plenty, but 'to what-ever he took personal charge of he gave the closest supervision'. This included, on the night of the first edition, supervising the despatch of the early editions to the rural areas. And they report his comment that if it ever came to a choice between leading the party and running the paper, he believed that he would choose the latter (Longford and O'Neill 1970: 270–71).

The crisis involving the governor-general reached a climax during the Eucharistic Congress, a major religious festival. De Valera had ensured that the governor-general, who according to protocol would have taken precedence over the head of government, was not invited to any of the functions associated with this event. After protesting ineffectually, McNeill released the correspondence to the press on the evening of 10 July 1932. In the early hours of the following morning, newspapers were informed that the government had declared the letters to be confidential state documents, which could not be published. Police intercepted British papers at the mail-boat, and Northern Ireland papers at border crossings. By the afternoon of 11 July, however, the government came to the view that, as the letters had already 'appeared in foreign newspapers, the Executive Council has decided to authorise publication in the Irish Free State of the entire correspondence' (*IP*: 12 July 1932).

The *Irish Press* drew the obvious moral from the story – obvious to its controlling director, at any rate – charging that McNeill was 'wholly unsuited to the position he occupies' (12 July 1932). The *Irish Times* chose to interpret it as an attempt to muzzle the governor-general, rather than as an exercise of press censorship. The *Irish Independent* described the government as resembling 'a lot of spiteful schoolgirls' and suggested that its attempt at censorship had been 'extraordinary and ineffective'. It was left to Northern Ireland and British papers to beat the drum loudest in defence of press freedom: the *Northern Whig* regaled its Protestant readers as they gathered for that day's Orange Order marches with a description of de Valera's action as 'an almost incredible display of peevish narrowness' and the *Mid-Ulster Mail* pictured him as 'donning the mantle of Lenin' (11 July 1932). It was left to the London *Star* to point the moral:

Even the sternest rebel could catch a hint of the world's laughter that was going to greet the fact that one of the letters which Mr de Valera was forbidding the press to publish was one written by himself in defence of the liberty of the press ... when that press happens to be his own.

(12 July 1932)

An equally anomalous position developed at the end of 1932, when the Military Tribunal, its activities now directed at the paramilitary supporters of the ousted government rather than towards Republicans, was hearing evidence from Joe Dennigan, the political correspondent of the *Irish Press*. Dennigan, after having refused to give the name of an anonymous informant whom he had quoted in an article on government policy towards illegal organisations, was found in contempt of the Tribunal and sentenced to a month's imprisonment – the first journalist in the modern Irish state to go to gaol for refusing to reveal a source. This evoked a rare display of unanimity among his fellow-journalists on all the main papers, who unsuccessfully petitioned Mr de Valera, in his capacity as head of government, to exercise the prerogative of clemency in respect of his employee. De Valera declined, but paid a cannily timed visit to Mountjoy Gaol, in which Dennigan had been incarcerated, after which, Dennigan subsequently reported, the prison diet improved considerably. On Dennigan's release after three weeks imprisonment (with remission for good behaviour), in January 1933 Dublin journalists organised a dinner of welcome for him, and even persuaded the notoriously parsimonious *Irish Press* management to pay for it.

De Valera was not slow to turn his new power and position to advantage in other ways, and now moved to put the final piece in place in a complicated jigsaw which had been created several years earlier. In the years 1919–21, Irish emigrants living in the United States had been invited to subscribe funds for bonds which would eventually be redeemed by an independent Irish government. A large amount of money was collected and lodged in a US bank, but, after the civil war, a dispute arose between de Valera (who had been involved in the original fund-raising) and the Free State government, about the ownership of the money. The US Supreme Court decided in 1927 that it belonged to neither, and determined that the money, less expenses, should be returned to the original subscribers.

In 1930, de Valera wrote to those Irish-Americans who had subscribed to the bonds, asking them to transfer their right to be reimbursed to him, in order that he could launch a national Irish newspaper. Many did so. Now in government, he moved financial legislation to repay all the American lenders – those who had transferred their rights to him as well as those who had not – with a premium, effectively returning $1.25 for every dollar they had lent. The funds for this operation came from the Irish exchequer, which his party now controlled. After a bitter parliamentary debate on 5–6 July 1933, in the course of which the opposition finance spokesman, Patrick McGilligan accused him of 'looting the public purse for a party organ' (DD: 5 July 1933), the measure was passed. A sum of £1.5 million was paid to the bondholders, £100,000 of which found its way directly back to the *Irish Press* on the basis of the transfers signed three years earlier.

De Valera also moved swiftly to improve the terms of trade for all Irish newspapers in a way which responded simultaneously to nationalist and to moral arguments, and reflected his government's strongly protectionist economic policy. Even before the establishment of the *Irish Press*, the controversialist Fr

R.S. Devane S.J. had been arguing in the Jesuit magazine *Studies* in 1927 (Devane 1927b) for a tariff on imported newspapers and magazines. Almost as soon as he assumed power, de Valera moved in precisely this sense: tariffs were imposed on imported newspapers and periodicals in the budgets of 1932 and 1933, affecting some 200 papers in all. The combined circulation of English daily newspapers in Ireland in this time would have been about 170,000, as against a circulation for Irish dailies of approximately 280,000. De Valera's measures, however, had a marked effect: the value of imported newspapers fell from £216,000 in 1932 to £99,000 in 1934 (O'Donnell 1945a: 392). What the moralists seem to have been particularly concerned about were the British Sunday newspapers, some 350,000 of which were sold in Ireland every week. The tariffs were maintained until July 1971, when they were eliminated as part of the general reduction of tariffs being carried out in preparation for membership of the Common Market.

The *Irish Independent*, unfazed by the upstart *Irish Press*, continued on its magisterial way. It was particularly conscious of the value of advertising, including advertising itself. Between the wars:

> all visible celebrities of reasonable rectitude were enticed into Middle Abbey Street and photographed receiving a suitable gift, usually a blackthorn stick, from the advertising manager. An opera star was hired to sing to the people from the roof of Independent House.
>
> (O'Donnell 1945a: 392)

No doubt partly as a result of these initiatives, the Independent shareholders' dividends rose from 7.5% in 1933 to 22.5% in 1940.

If de Valera's tariffs were indirect aid to the domestic media, more direct aid was also contemplated. In 1934 the cabinet authorised the establishment of an inter-departmental committee to examine, among other things, the development of a national periodical press, and whether it might be possible 'to restrict the importation of newspapers and periodicals'. The initiative in this particular case came from the Minister for Industry and Commerce, Sean Lemass, who based his arguments 'mainly on moral and cultural grounds, though the possible economic advantages, e.g. increased employment, have not been lost sight of' (NAI: Taoiseach: S 2919A). This initiative withered on the vine, and no direct subsidies of any kind were to be made available to any Irish publication for another fourteen years. The 1930s were in fact marked by another, more malign development: a rash of libel actions 'by writers and against writers', one of which snuffed out George Russell's journal, the *Irish Statesman*, and another of which crushed James Joyce's friend, the literary barrister Oliver St John Gogarty (de Vere White 1967: 26–7).

The Northern Ireland Unionist papers maintained a high level of watchfulness. The *Belfast Newsletter* greeted Mr de Valera's election with predictable dourness: 'It will be well if the people ringing their bells today are not found wringing their hands tomorrow' (Keogh 1994: 64). The *Northern Whig* had accurately discerned (4 October 1932), in the 1932 imbroglio between de Valera and McNeill and in the subsequent forced departure of McNeill, the seeds of the dissolution of the constitutional link between Ireland and Britain. Both it and the *Newsletter* (4 April 1935) continually drew their readers' attention to de Valera's step-by-step approach to dismantling the British connection. These developments – and the harsh economic climate, which was responsible for widespread unemployment and hunger – provoked in turn more dramatic events, as when, during this period, a large number of mourners at a Protestant funeral were incited to make an attack on the offices of the *Irish News*, and were prevented from carrying out their plans only by the sudden appearance of an armoured car sent by the police (Oram 1983: 183).

In Dublin, although the economy was in an almost equally deleterious state, in part because of the economic war between de Valera's government and that in Britain, the absence of sectarian tension, and the continuing haemorrhage of young workers to Britain in search of employment, ensured that social tensions did not find such violent expression. De Valera, however, remained conscious of the threat to his political position from Republican militants, many of whom now believed that he was as great a traitor to Irish nationalist aspirations as the government he had supplanted. For this reason – and in marked contrast to his predecessors, who had paid particular attention to left-wing minority publications – he ensured that a close watch was kept on Republican newsletters and magazines, most of which were under permanent scrutiny by the Department of Justice, and some of which were intermittently banned (NAI: Justice: S Files 1932–9). The IRA itself was proscribed in 1936, a development which was warmly welcomed by the *Irish Times* (Gray 1991: 65). Indeed, that paper now showed a warmth towards Mr de Valera that marked a distinct, if gradual, shift away from its earlier positions. Although it advised voters to support Fianna Fail's principal opponent, the Fine Gael party, in the 1937 election, a year later it was to be found describing the result of the snap election of 1938 as 'eminently satisfactory'. 'We are glad', it commented, 'that he [Mr de Valera] has been returned to power' (21 June 1938; Lee 1989: 215).

Given the expressed support of all the major political parties, but especially of Fianna Fail, for the Irish language, it is surprising that the creation of the Free State, and then Mr de Valera's accession to power, did not see a flowering of national or periodical journalism in the Irish language, which at that time was spoken habitually by no more than 10% of the population. Mr de Valera saw to it that his *Irish Press* frequently published material in Irish; but not even his enthusiasm could maintain the output at the level at which it was inaugurated, with a promise of half a page a day. One periodical, *An tUltach* ('The Ulsterman') had been in existence since 1924, but nationalism was always strongest in that province for political and historical reasons.

The task of reviving the language as the main medium of communication for the majority of the population – an ideological objective which was all too frequently advanced by people with little knowledge of psychology, linguistics or education – was entrusted chiefly to the schools, and above all to the primary schools. In these circumstances, the role, and the potential benefit, of Irish-language journalism was downplayed or even ignored. It is particularly surprising that no subsidy scheme existed until 1948: Irish-language journalism, a tender plant at the best of times, was expected to survive on its own in an increasingly hostile environment.

Given that support for the Irish language tended to be numerically strongest among the more conservative sections of the population, it is particularly interesting that the most vibrant expression of writing in Irish at this time came from the radical left. This was *An tÉireannach* ('The Irishman'), published weekly from 1935 to 1937. As a journal, it was unique in many ways. It drew its political inspiration from a small group of left-wing Republicans who had become discontented with the sterile opposition of the dwindling paramilitary IRA, and who were becoming interested and involved in social issues in the South of Ireland. In 1935, they formed an organisation known as the Republican Congress, which was a determined but ultimately unsuccessful attempt to win over militant Republicanism to the cause of socialism. *An tÉireannach*, their house organ to all intents and purposes, published lively articles excoriating Irish conservative politicians and – unusually for any Irish publication at the time – drawing attention to the increasing menace of continental fascism (Ó Cíosáin 1993: 100–4).

In the mainstream press, subtle but significant changes of personnel were taking place. In 1934, Gallagher resigned as editor of de Valera's own paper, frustrated by the penny-pinching attitude of his directors; de Valera found another position for him as head of the Government Information Bureau. A rapid succession of unsatisfactory successors was ended in 1937 by the appointment of the paper's London editor, Bill Sweetman, a tough journalist who was prepared to stand up to anyone, including, on occasion, Mr de Valera himself. At the *Irish Times*, the editor was John Healy, who had filled this position since before the establishment of the Free State and had engineered a relatively positive approach in his former proto-Unionist paper to the new constitutional arrangement, as well as a more lukewarm one to Mr de Valera's accession to power. He died in 1934, when he was succeeded by R.M. Smyllie, an ebullient journalist who had joined the paper in 1919. Smyllie had been working on a provincial paper in Co. Sligo and was on holiday in Germany when he found himself caught up in the war, and was interned by the Germans for its duration. Emerging unscathed at the end of hostilities, he was invited to report the Versailles peace conference for the *Irish Times*, and subsequently rose rapidly through the paper's ranks. He was a long-term observer of Germany, about which he wrote regularly and perceptively: on 3 July 1934, for instance, he remarked that: 'For the moment, Herr Hitler and Herr Goering control the situation, but the measure of their authority is the quickness of the "Black Shirts'" trigger fingers' (Schulz 1999: 119).

At the *Independent*, the new editor from 1935 was Frank Geary, who had joined his paper in 1922. He devoted his considerable journalistic talents to consolidating his newspaper's grip on the growing Irish Catholic middle classes, blending straightforward journalism with an unswerving loyalty to the Catholic Church and its moral values.

Editorial changes were made discreetly: Smyllie's appointment did not even figure in the pages of his own newspaper (Gray 1991: 57). He inherited, along with his editorial responsibilities, a necessary sinecure: like Healy, he was to be the Irish correspondent of the London *Times*, and in time also of *The Observer*. Although there was no commercial or organisational connection between these papers, this unofficial linkage had been established for many years. Nor was it merely *pietas*: Irish journalists were extremely badly paid and, given that Dublin in some respects shared an information ecology with London, senior editorial executives on Irish newspapers (with the exception of the *Irish Press*) tended to draw a significant part of their remuneration from these external activities. In many cases, it cost them little effort: occupying key positions in their own news organisations, they simply filtered the Irish news that was passing across their desks and recycled it, when suitable, for the UK editors. This financial nexus was to prove a major factor in the demise, many years later, of the Irish News Agency.

The one international issue of the later 1930s which excited general attention in Ireland was the Spanish Civil War. Here, interestingly, the newspapers were divided on unexpected lines. In the North, the *Belfast Telegraph* saw the war as overwhelmingly one with political rather than religious connotations, coming down firmly on the side of the British government's policy of neutrality. 'On the whole', it told its readers on 31 July 1936, 'it would not be right for any Power to take sides openly with either of the combatants.' By 31 August it was noting sourly, with a sideswipe at the Catholic Church, that 'there is little religion on either side, and it is a sad reflection on the influence of the Church … that so many of its members or nominal members should descend to deeds that are normally associated with the Middle Ages'. The *Irish News* also supported neutrality (which in essence was de Valera's position), but from an understandably different perspective, arguing on 30 September 1936 that 'Irishmen can gain for their own country a high reputation if they concentrate on their own and the country's needs and leave cloak-and-sword romance to the novelists' (Bell 1969: 152).

The *Irish Independent*, as might have been expected, adopted a strongly pro-Franco line, making much of reports of atrocities by Republican forces directed against priests and nuns, and sent a journalist to cover the war from the Franco side. 'All who stand for the ancient faith and the traditions of Spain', it announced on 22 July 1936, 'are behind the present revolt against the Marxist regime in Madrid.' Local newspapers tended to follow the *Independent*'s line. Small socialist papers like *The Worker* and the Communist party's *Irish Democrat* urged intervention on the side of the Spanish government, but without conspicuous success (although groups left Ireland to fight on both sides). The *Irish Times*, equally predictably in the light of Smyllie's strongly anti-fascist views, was much more measured, publishing 'some of the most factual, balanced editorial analyses to be found in Europe' (Bell 1969: 140), and continued to regard the legal Spanish government as deserving of support, at least until its final collapse. It sent a reporter, Lionel Fleming, to report from the Republican side: Fleming's even-handed despatches, which detailed the anti-religious campaign by the government but also described its actions as a legitimate struggle against fascism, generated a threat of a religiously inspired boycott by several prominent advertisers (Fleming 1965: 170). The threat materialised, to the point where all Catholic-owned schools withdrew their advertisements from the paper, and Smyllie (whom Mr Hugh Allen of the Catholic Truth Society described as acting 'in sympathy with his Masonic brethren in Barcelona') was forced to withdraw Fleming (Cooney 1999: 91).

What was intriguing was the attitude of the *Irish Press*. It did not hide its concern for the victims of atrocities, or for the welfare of the Catholic Church, but reported the conflict in a considerably more even-handed manner than the *Irish Independent*, which was remarkable given the fact that it was appealing, like the *Irish Independent*, to a largely conservative and Catholic readership. On occasion it even reminded those of its readers who were calling for intervention on Franco's side that the Vatican still maintained diplomatic relations with the Spanish government. Behind this was de Valera's political stance. Whatever his personal sympathies (and he was as devout a Catholic as any shareholder, director or reader of the *Irish Independent*) he was also, and in this case primarily, the head of a government which under international law recognised the Republicans as the legitimate government of Spain. This prompted support for a policy of neutrality, which he followed throughout the war in spite of the fulminations of the *Irish Independent*, and which found a ready echo in the pages of his own newspaper. In all probability this was no mere concern for diplomatic niceties, but a conscious decision that his newspaper would not lightly set aside the democratic decisions of the Spanish people. It also came easier to *Irish Press* journalists, many of whom came from a radical Irish Republican tradition whose political leaders had been excommunicated by the Irish Catholic bishops during the 1922–3 civil war. There was far more support for the republicans within Fianna Fail at this period than could have been determined from the newspapers, even the *Irish Press* (Bell 1969: 143).

This was not the only lapse from the standards which religious monitors, who had been hoping for better things in a newly independent Irish state, had been expecting.

From the secular point of view our newspapers are often little better than the English papers on which they are modelled. They have not the crude sensationalism of the English yellow Press, but great prominence is given to sensational features – murders, accidents, disasters and so forth. Like the English papers they devote a very large proportion of their space to sport. A Dublin daily paper intended for all Ireland will devote half a page to a dog show or a football match, and less than a quarter of a column to some meeting at which the leaders of intellectual life have spoken on a vital topic.

(Browne 1937: 262)

As rumours of wars darkened the European horizon, de Valera pushed forward doggedly with his policy of disengagement from Britain, most notably in his plan to give the country a new constitution. In the middle of the abdication crisis, he discovered a legislative loophole which enabled him to sever Ireland's connection with the Crown (though not with the Commonwealth). He then set about drafting a new constitution, which would be debated in parliament before being submitted to the people in a referendum.

The section of the draft constitution dealing with the liberty of the press provoked a lively debate, not least in the light of the controversy of four years earlier about the subvention of the *Irish Press*. The section guaranteed 'the right of the citizens to express freely their convictions and opinions' and added:

> The education of public opinion being, however, a matter of such grave public import to the common good, the State shall endeavour to ensure that the organs of public opinion, such as the radio, the press, the cinema, while preserving their rightful liberty of expression, including criticism of Government policy, shall not be used to undermine public order or morality or the authority of the State.
>
> (Article 40.6.i)

This aroused fierce opposition from members of parliament, not least from one of the parliamentary representatives of Trinity College, Dr Rowlette, who argued that it would preserve the right of a free press only 'as long as it does not differ with the opinion of the government' (DD: 2 June 1937). John A. Costello, a prominent opposition member and senior counsel, moved an amendment which would have deleted the entire sub-section as an unwarranted interference with liberty of expression.

De Valera portrayed himself, cannily, as a moderate between two extremes. The press, he reminded Costello (who would undoubtedly have agreed with him in this), could never be allowed total freedom.

> I say that the right of the citizens to express freely their convictions and opinions cannot, in fact, be permitted in any state. Are we going to have anarchical principles, for example, generally propagated here? I say no ... You should not give the proponents of what is wrong and unnatural the same liberty as would be accorded to the proponents of what is right.
>
> (DD: 2 June 1937)

Costello was forced into public agreement, even disclosing his personal view that 'the propagation of Communistic doctrine would be against public order and morality' (DD: 2 June 1937). A politically independent parliamentarian,

Frank McDermott, defended the draft constitution as a comparatively liberal document – which, in the circumstances of the time, and in the social and religious context of 1930s Ireland, it undoubtedly was – and used the debate to launch an attack on the illiberal attitudes on freedom of expression which had found a home in publications such as the *Irish Independent* and the *Irish Catholic*, and in neo-fascist organisations such as the Christian Front. The latter body, he noted, had been passing resolutions 'calling on the Government to make it a crime for a man to express Communistic opinions in his own home' (DD: 2 June 1937). The leader of the small Labour Party, William Norton, expressed the view that the article had 'a real Nazi ring about it' (*IT*: 4 June 1937). The fact that Norton was the only party leader without a national paper to support him shaped de Valera's reply: the purpose of the article, he said, was to provide safeguards against the emergence of 'wealthy people making still more wealth through the Press and making that wealth in a manner dangerous to the public good' (DD: 2 June 1937).

After a debate which evoked considerably more heat than light, the new section was passed. Almost immediately, it received an imprimatur from a prominent Catholic theologian, Dr Cornelius Lucey (later Bishop of Cork), who suggested that the constitution's outlawing of blasphemy might have been improved by the further proscription of 'anti-religious' matter, but that it was otherwise as close to perfect as was possible. In a contribution to the debate which blended a surprisingly contemporary suggestion that public figures should have less protection from the laws of libel than ordinary citizens (in order that wrongdoing could more readily be exposed) with a certain steeliness about the dangers of theological error, he observed:

> The right to publish what we may call 'the truth in the news' and 'the views in the news' has one essential limitation. It is subject to the general moral law. Now, the moral law forbids us to say or do anything, either wrong in itself or calculated to lead others into wrong-doing. And the reporter and editor are bound by this law just as strictly as the private individual is. Hence it is not permissible for them to write up what is immoral or uncharitable or otherwise wrong, even on the plea that it is true. For instance, they may not report all the lurid details of divorce proceedings, or set themselves out to promote class-antagonism, or give publicity to the secret failings of this or that private citizen ... There is good reason in this country why the State should tolerate all religions and allow them freedom of expression. but there is no reason why it should tolerate unbelief or, at any rate, open propaganda on behalf of unbelief.
>
> (Lucey 1937: 588–90)

He warned about the threats to press freedom in Italy and in Germany. The dangers he perceived there did not only affect the press; and the outbreak of the Second World War, which was not far away, presented government and media alike with another major problem: that of censorship.

The imminence of hostilities did not of itself prompt the government to legislate for censorship. Both the military and the bureaucracy had been nibbling away at the problem intermittently since the end of the civil war. In 1925, the army authorities prepared a detailed memorandum outlining a scheme for news censorship in the event of an outbreak of hostilities (O'Halpin 1999: 209), although it is not clear from the context who they thought the protagonists might be. In December 1930 the Executive Council (i.e. the cabinet of the Irish Free State) agreed to the establishment of a committee to create machinery for the operation of censorship in time of war, with representatives from the Departments of Defence, External Affairs, Justice, and Posts and Telegraphs (NAI: Taoiseach: S 8202). Again, the absence of actual conflict induced a certain lethargy, and in October 1935 the Executive Council was informed that the committee had ceased to function for a considerable time, and asked to revive it. This was agreed, and the attorney general was added to the committee, which finally produced a report in September 1938 (NAI: Taoiseach: S 10829). This, together with the Emergency Powers Act of 1939 – rather than the provisions of the 1937 Constitution, as Mr de Valera's political opponents had feared – was what formed the basis for the detailed policy that was to be introduced at the outbreak of the war. Both the Emergency Powers Act and the 1939 Offences Against the State Act, which proscribed the IRA (some of whose elements were pro-German) gave the state an extraordinary armoury of emergency powers under which many civil liberties, including the freedom of the press, could be subject to more or less arbitrary limitation.

Already in 1938 de Valera had put censorship third in a list of political priorities (after food and external trade, and before counter-espionage and military measures) designed to safeguard Ireland's neutrality in the coming conflict. The censorship he now instituted under Joseph Connolly, an ex-minister, and operated in close conjunction with military intelligence, was based on a carefully worked out, if occasionally inconsistent, set of imperatives, and was implemented with increasing severity until the very end of the war.

It was, first of all, primarily a censorship system aimed at the suppression of statements made within Ireland which might lead one or both of the belligerents to conclude that Ireland had abandoned its neutrality and could be classed as an enemy and therefore possibly even invaded. A secondary objective was to prevent the publication of information which might be of strategic use to the combatants. The censorship, however, operated in tandem with two other policies, at least one of which seriously compromised Irish neutrality, and the other of which made the domestic censorship appear laughable or sinister by turns.

The first of these policies was that of close cooperation with the Allies, in secret, on a range of subjects which were of prime importance to the war effort (O'Halpin 1999: 225–31). These included the exchange of vital intelligence information, meteorological information, and coastguard reports. The second, which had a more direct relevance to the question of censorship, was that the restrictions did not apply to incoming media. British newspapers circulated to all intents and purposes unhindered, although the *Daily Mirror* was banned for a brief period. The BBC and other radio stations (including Vatican Radio and, of course, German broadcasts in English and Irish) were not jammed, although, later in the war, the newspapers were prevented from printing the substance of Vatican Radio broadcasts about the persecution of the Catholic Church in Germany and in Poland. The US embassy freely circulated its *Letter from America* to Irish opinion-formers, giving, after US entry into the war, an understandably pro-Allied version of events the details of which had in many cases been rigorously excluded from the Irish print and broadcast media. Reports sent abroad by Irish journalists were not subject to censorship until 1941; and the censor's job was in any case made considerably easier because no Dublin newspaper maintained war correspondents in the European theatre during the hostilities. As a result of this, Irish readers were considerably more deprived than were, for instance, their contemporaries in other countries, notably neutral Sweden and Switzerland (Ó Drisceoil 1996b: 47).

The core rationale behind the censorship was expressed in a memorandum by Frank Aiken, the Minister for Coordination of Defensive Measures, in January 1940. In this, he faced up squarely to:

> some self-styled democrats who would hold onto the peace-time liberalistic trimmings of democracy while the fundamental basis of democracy was being swept from under their feet by foreign or domestic enemies of their democratic state. Wise men, however, discard these trimmings when necessary in order successfully to maintain the fundamental rights of the citizens freely to choose by whom they shall be governed.
>
> (NAI: Taoiseach: 11586)

Connolly's somewhat choleric temperament, and his general impatience with what he saw as the pro-British proclivities of the press (especially the *Irish Times*) was evidenced in a memorandum in November 1940, in which he observed that the censorship powers, although extensive, were still inadequate.

> For example, there is at the present time no express power to compel a newspaper to handle news in a particular way, that is to say, to prescribe the part of, or the space in the paper, and the manner or form in which a particular item must appear … Again, it is worth drawing attention to the fact that the Censorship is restricted to telling the papers what they must not publish – it has no power to insist on the publication of any particular matter.
>
> (NAI: Taoiseach: 10829)

His tidy bureaucratic mind went on to plan for the ultimate eventuality – an invasion of Ireland by one or other combatant, which would overrun Dublin. With this in mind, he drew up a grand design for a strategic withdrawal to Cork, whose two newspapers could continue to reflect official government thinking and priorities. The prohibitions were extraordinarily wide-ranging. One of Connolly's directives, for example, prevented the newspapers from publishing:

> matter which would or might be calculated to impair the financial stability of the State and in particular (a) matter reflecting adversely on the solvency of the exchequer; (b) statements or suggestions tending or likely to cause uneasiness or panic among depositors in banks; (c) reports or rumours of the intended imposition of new taxation; (d) matter likely to provoke discontent among servants of the State or that would be liable to cause a withdrawal of labour by any branch of the civil service.
>
> (NAI: Taoiseach: S 11586)

The big stick with which the government had armed itself was reserved for persistent offenders, notably the *Irish Times*, but also papers like the *Kilkenny People*, a weekly provincial newspaper whose editor, E.T. Keane, was at least as truculent as Smyllie in his dealings with the censorship authorities (Hannigan 1993: 15). The *Cork Examiner* got off relatively lightly: it was physically impossible, for all practical purposes, for that paper to submit proofs prior to publication as the other daily papers were required to do, and its conservative management operated a type of self-censorship, under the censor's benign but distant supervision.

There was a debate on the press censorship in the Senate in December 1940, but it fell rather flat, possibly because the worst excesses of the censorship had not by then manifested themselves. It was notable, however, for Aiken's enunciation in public of the hard line which he had earlier expressed in private.

> It is no change to the ordinary people of the country to have myself and my staff acting as Censor. It is only a change of function from the editor of the *Irish Times* to myself and my staff. It is we who have the final OK on what to cut out instead of the editors and in certain circumstances, when this country is in such grave danger as it is at the moment, I think the people are better pleased that the censorship should be in the hands of somebody who is responsible to the parliament elected by the people rather than of persons who are appointed by boards of directors and have no responsibility to the people, though normally they act in a decent way towards them.
>
> (NAI: Taoiseach: S 11586)

Connolly, and Knightly, who succeeded Connolly in late 1941, played a cat and mouse game with Smyllie for the duration of the war. References to any of the numerous Irishmen serving in the Allied forces were invariably deleted by the censor, encouraging Smyllie to devise a range of circumlocutions. In December 1941, when the *Prince of Wales* was sunk off Singapore, Smyllie managed to convey to his readers critical information about one of its crew – the *Irish Times* journalist Johnny Robinson, who had left the paper to join the navy at the outbreak of the war.

The many friends in Dublin of Mr. John A, Robinson, who was involved in a recent boating accident, will be pleased to learn that he is alive and well. He is a particularly good swimmer, and it is possible that he owes his life to this accomplishment.

(Gray 1991: 153–4)

Although the *Irish Times*, and the Protestant-owned *Evening Mail*, suffered substantially at the censor's hands (the *Irish Times* was forced to submit to complete pre-publication censorship from early in 1942), it would be incorrect to assume that other papers necessarily had an easier time of it. As Donal Ó Drisceoil points out in his definitive study of this topic, the editor of the *Irish Independent*, Frank Geary, was frequently as exasperated by the censors' activities as his counterpart in the *Irish Times*: as one censor wrote to another in late 1942: 'It has always been our strength that Smyllie and Geary cannot stand each other and I don't want to force them into an unholy alliance if I can possible avoid it' (Ó Drisceoil 1996a: 164). The *Sunday Independent* also suffered, while the *Irish Press* concealed its grievances, even to the extent of loyally supporting the government's censorship policy in an editorial at the end of the war. Geary's *Irish Independent* even resorted, on occasion, to publishing blank spaces where its editorials had been censored.

This sparring, for the most part carried on in private, concealed a number of other, more serious issues for the press. One of them was the maintenance of freedom of speech for members of parliament and, at election times, for parliamentary candidates. Chief among these – in both categories – was James Dillon, son of an old Irish Parliamentary Party politician, who was a forthright advocate of the Allied cause, and who resigned from Fine Gael early in the war because he could not support the policy of neutrality, to which all Irish parties were now committed. From then on, he was a marked man, and became 'the most censored of all politicians, with heavy treatment given to his letters to the press and reports of his speeches' (Ó Drisceoil 1996a: 264). This was so regardless of whether his speeches were made inside or outside parliament.

The censorship of Dillon's speeches was at least overt. In more subterranean ways, the censorship authorities resorted to discreet pressure including, for example, visits by members of the Gardaí to bookshops which were stocking offending publications. Connolly outlined the success of this policy in a memorandum in 1941.

There was a natural reluctance to alarm or antagonise either Dail or public by taking what might be regarded as excessive powers and, accordingly, an effort was made to secure the desired result as 'cheaply' as possible, and by indirect methods rather than full frontal attack. By this and similar devices we have up to the present achieved 90% of our objectives effectively, and often secretly.

(NAI: Taoiseach: S 11586)

The occasional casualties of this effective and secret policy included publications from right across the ideological spectrum, such as *The Leader*, an independent weekly (founded in 1900) which, unusually, combined enthusiasm for Gaelic culture with scorn for many of the official policies designed to protect it, and which had speculated unguardedly about the possible advantages to Ireland of a German victory. Another was the *Irish Workers' Weekly*, an organ of the minuscule Irish Communist organisation. *The Torch*, a Labour party publication which was frequently critical (or would have been if passed by the censor) of the government's economic policy and its effect on working-class voters, frequently fell foul of the censor, as did the oddly named *Penapa*, a short-lived pro-Nazi paper which appeared in 1941.

One of the problems facing the censors – and which the censorship operation paradoxically exacerbated rather than moderated – was 'the continuing insistence in many circles on viewing all oppression through the lens of the British record in Ireland' (Ó Drisceoil 1996b: 46). In this context, the ruthless suppression by the censorship of all atrocity stories meant that such rumours as filtered through to the public were largely discounted as yet further evidence of British propaganda. The *Irish Press* expressed the view openly in an editorial on 1 April 1943: 'There is no kind of oppression visited on any minority in Europe which the Six County nationalists have not also endured' (Lee 1989: 266). In the same year, all details of the massacre in the Katyn forest in Poland, where 12,000 Polish officers were murdered by Soviet forces, were rigorously suppressed. Aiken, the minister responsible, justified this course of action many years later, telling an interviewer: 'What was going in the [concentration] camps was pretty well known to us early on, but the Russians were as bad – you have only to look at what happened in Katyn forest. There are photographs to prove that' (Ó Drisceoil 1996b: 49).

The almost pathological even-handedness of the censorship left the mass of Irish readers of newspapers quite unprepared for the horrors that were revealed when the censorship was finally lifted on 11 May 1945. Although it was theoretically possible for Irish readers to obtain less censored war news from UK newspapers, most of which were technically unrestricted, shortage of newsprint, deteriorating public transport and other factors had led to a dramatic decline in their circulation in Ireland: as early as 1941, this was estimated to have dropped by as much as 60%. Many Irish readers, even when the facts of German genocide were unfolded, suspected that these stories were the product of British propaganda (in fairness it is worth pointing out that uninformed British and American readers assumed that Soviet propaganda was to blame) (Ó Drisceoil 1996b: 50). Even discounting the inevitable benefit conferred by hindsight, it is unarguable that the confusion between military and moral neutrality which was embodied in the censorship practices of the day was, in its worst excesses, completely unjustifiable.

The end of the war in 1945 saw an attempt by the Catholic Archbishop of Dublin to establish a Catholic Guild of Writers and Journalists but this initiative was never adopted by the profession with much enthusiasm, although some of its members were still active enough to protest against the production of a play by Sean O'Casey in Dublin in 1958 (Cooney 1999: 201). Journalism was never entirely cowed; indeed, a certain spirit of self-reliance engendered by the war was probably partly responsible for two initiatives which illuminated the media landscape. One was the creation of *The Bell*, edited by the writer Sean O Faoláin, in October 1940. This was partly an original creation, partly a response to the death in 1936 of D.P. Moran, the founder of *The Leader*, a quirky, irreverent centre-right journal of ideas which had been launched in 1900 (Inglis 1960: 108–77; Maume 1997), and which was to stagger on after Moran's death until 1970. *The Bell* acted as a powerful and effective focus for the scattered forces of literary and social liberalism in the country at the time: in its first editorial, it proclaimed itself a journal of the present and the future, not of the past.

> *The Bell* is quite clear about certain practical things and will, from time to time, deal with them – the Language, Partition, Education, and so forth. In general *The Bell* stands, in all such questions, for Life before any abstraction, in whatever magnificent words it may clothe itself. For we eschew abstractions, and will have nothing to do with generalisations that are not capable of proof by concrete experience. Generalisation (to make one) is like prophecy, the most egregious form of error, and abstractions are the luxury of people who enjoy befuddling themselves methodically. We prefer, likewise, the positive to the negative, the creative to the destructive. We ban only lunatics and sour-bellies.
>
> (*The Bell* 1 (1), 8–9)

Its virility even prompted one war-time Fianna Fail Cabinet minister, Sean MacEntee (who was given to writing somewhat mannered lyric poetry in his spare time) to respond favourably in 1942, when O Faoláin, approached the government for help. MacEntee, then Minister of Finance, was only persuaded against this course of action when colleagues pointed out to him that, if a subsidised publication chose to attack the government, the government could not withdraw the subsidy without being accused of censorship (UCD: MacEntee: P67/246). In its willingness to challenge established hegemonies, especially that of the Catholic Church, and in its embrace of cultural and political variety, *The Bell* played a major role in the emergence, not only of a newly vigorous Irish literary tradition, but of a willingness to take risks that was partly responsible for the defeat of the Fianna Fail government, after sixteen years of continuous rule, in 1948.

Another was the emergence of *Comhar* ('Co-operation') in May 1942. This monthly publication in Irish was the offspring of the Comhchaidrimh, the association of university societies dedicated to the promotion and advancement of Irish language and culture which had been founded seven years earlier. It maintained a consistently high standard of literary and political journalism, acting as a nursery for a number of activists who later became better known in national journalism and politics (Nic Pháidín 1987: 71). Its first issue carried an article by the youthful Conor Cruise O'Brien, defending his *alma mater*, Trinity College, Dublin, against charges of anti-Irishness. Contributors were to include the writers Frank O'Connor, Sean O Faoláin, Brendan Behan, and Myles na gCopaleen (the civil servant Brian O'Nolan) (Nic Pháidín 1987). Since 1941, O'Nolan had been afforded space in the *Irish Times* by Smyllie, for an irregular, multi-lingual column (Irish, English, Latin and Greek were among those employed) which poked devastating, literate fun at Irish pretensions of every kind. The same spirit led to the foundation in 1943 of *Inniú* ('Today'), an idiosyncratic weekly newspaper founded by Ciarán O Nualláin, a brother of the *Irish Times* columnist 'Myles na gCopaleen'. It was written in Dublin but – in order to help the economy of the underdeveloped Western areas – printed in Co. Mayo. During the war it was plagued by transport difficulties, and also by a well-intentioned but disastrous scheme aimed at boosting circulation by offering to correct essays in Irish by schoolchildren. This produced a huge workload, but very little finance, as the schools were slow to settle their bills.

Broadcasting: a new approach

The position of broadcasting in all of this was somewhat anomalous. Although it was carried out by a government department, rather than by an independent commercial organisation, its relationship with the censorship operation was at first poorly defined. Its news operation incurred official displeasure after it occasionally broadcast items which had been censored from the print media. Eventually, given the extreme sensitivity of the situation (its broadcasts could be heard outside Ireland, where the Irish print media were invisible) a regime was established within which news broadcasts had to be read over in advance to the head of the Government Information Bureau, Frank Gallagher, and on occasion to Mr de Valera himself. The most troublesome broadcasters were, on occasion, clerical: one preacher at a religious ceremony being broadcast by the station interpolated, without prior notice to the authorities, a passage highly critical of Hitler: this led to a brief stand-off between the station and the Catholic bishops, with the broadcasters demanding prior sight of sermons, and the ecclesiastical authorities declining on grounds of principle (Gorham 1967: 131).

For all its deficiencies as a conduit for news, however, the station's reputation was enhanced under an unusually sophisticated minister, P.J. Little, who was a devotee of classical music. Under his stewardship, the station's musical output increased, both in quantity and in quality. Music apart, the station's output consisted largely of well-established favourites, some of them borrowed from BBC-type formats, such as *Question Time*, and drama. A number of initiatives were also taken in an attempt to encourage the speaking of the Irish language, but any outreach in the most obvious direction – the schools – was stymied by the war-time difficulties in obtaining or repairing radio sets and batteries, as well as by the conservatism of the religious managers of the country's church-owned primary schools. Little was also responsible for the re-establishment in 1944 of the Broadcasting Advisory Committee, which had had a fitful existence up to 1953, and which had generally been regarded as a nuisance by the civil servants in control of broadcasting. Its second incarnation lasted for a full decade (Gorham 1967: 117–35).

The communications difficulties engendered by the war had a major impact on broadcasting in one sense: the country's isolation, and the perceived need to defend its neutral stance in every possible forum, led to the re-examination of a project which had been aired in one form or another since very shortly after the establishment of 2RN. This was the proposal to establish a short-wave radio service. Such a plan had already been proposed in the 1920s by Marconi and other operators anxious to break the monopoly of transatlantic communications controlled by the British Post Office and cable operators. Domestic financial stringencies, and political caution, meant that these proposals did not receive serious consideration, but the change of government in 1932, and the simultaneous launch of the BBC's Empire Service (later World Service), prompted a reconsideration, not least by the Department of Posts and Telegraphs Broadcasting Advisory Committee, which proposed in July 1932 that a short-wave station should be established for the benefit of 'the 4.54 million Irish people living abroad' (NAI: Communications: TW 8828). It was to be another five years before pressure from emigrants (and Irish newspapers) led to a serious study of the possibilities, and an inter-departmental committee was set up in 1937 to go into it in more detail (Cullen 1991: 13). No doubt hastened by the impending hostilities, installation of equipment for the new station near the existing medium-wave national station at Athlone was completed in February 1939, and the first short-wave broadcast was made on St Patrick's Day 1940.

Initial results were poor. The transmitter was under-powered, and reception reports from North America were sporadic. Increasingly desperate attempts were made by a committee which included the Nobel Prize winner for Physics, Professor E.T.S. Walton of Trinity College, Dublin, to improvise equipment that would boost the signal strength, but all ended in failure, and the attempts were effectively abandoned in September 1944. The equipment was recommissioned in May 1945 for a re-broadcast, in a French translation, of de Valera's reply to Churchill's VE-day attack on Irish neutrality, but this was largely symbolic.

The end of the war and the renewed availability of broadcast equipment rekindled the government's enthusiasm, and, under P.J. Little, one of the most enthusiastic – even visionary – Ministers for Posts and Telegraphs since the foundation of the Free State, planning proceeded apace. A new high-power transmitter was acquired, a forest of antennae covering 40 acres was erected, and – most importantly of all – government approval was secured for a huge level of expenditure, not only on capital but on current account.

In April 1946, Little announced a programme of enormous expansion to parliament. An increase in expenditure of almost 60% over the previous year was to be devoted to enlargement of the existing orchestra, the creation of a second orchestra (Little was a classical music enthusiast, and Ireland was a haven for many Central European orchestral players uprooted by the war), new positions were created for outside broadcast officers, and a repertory drama company was created, whose players formed the backbone of radio drama for many years thereafter. The news coverage was strengthened, and staff script writers and features producers were hired. Although the talents thus employed would be utilised across both the medium-wave domestic service and the proposed short-wave service, without the impetus of the short-wave plan few, if any of the improvements would have been made. Their primary purpose, as Little announced on radio, was to present the 'everyday story of the new Ireland, spoken with its own voice' (*IP*: 20 February 1947).

It was a false dawn, but for reasons none could have anticipated. A general election at the beginning of 1948 swept Fianna Fail from power, and put in its place a new government convinced of the financial profligacy of its predecessor. It could not rescind the staffing improvements but it could, and did, put the short-wave service (along with a projected transatlantic air service) into cold storage.

Northern Ireland: the divisions deepen

The political division between Northern Ireland and the South (which did not describe itself formally as a Republic until 1949) was echoed in the media on either side of the border. It was a border which few publications crossed from North to South, although the main Dublin newspapers would have had modest circulations in the North, particularly in Belfast. This did not mean that Northern papers were insensitive to political developments in the South: de Valera's election victory in 1932 had been greeted by the *Northern Whig* with an editorial (on 13 July) which declared that

> the destinies of the South today are in the hands of a coterie of Anglophobe agitators with no understanding or experience of government who are driven forward in their extremist policy by a secret organisation who seem quite prepared to go to any length to bring Ulster under the control of the Free State.
>
> (Kennedy 1988: 145–6)

The *Irish News*, for its part, greeted de Valera's 1932 election to power in Dublin with unrestrained enthusiasm. Later the same year, in a mirror-image of what happened to the *Irish Press* in the dying days of the Cosgrave government in Dublin, it found itself in the Belfast courts, prosecuted under the Special Powers Act for publishing a confidential circular issued to Orangemen, which, the prosecution alleged, was prejudicial to peace and order: its English editor, Sydney Redwood, was fined £100 (Phoenix 1995: 28–9). Even in these unpromising circumstances, however, Unionism occasionally appeared to be less of a monolith than was generally supposed. A small group of liberal Unionists, with links to Queen's University, coalesced in the late 1930s around a journal modestly entitled the *New Northman*, which criticised the Special Powers Act and what one of their number called in 1937 'the junta of self-seeking politicians who call themselves Ulster' (Kennedy 1988: 232). They were later to form the nucleus of the Irish Association for Cultural, Economic and Social Relations.

Within the North, the outbreak of the war provoked a degree of active disagreement between newspapers representing both sides of the community, particularly on the vexed question of conscription. This had been a running political sore in Ireland since 1918, and the prospect of its re-introduction on the eve of the Second World War inflamed editorial passions. The *Northern Whig* had in 1938 issued a caveat against conscription, but this was at a time when war was only a distant possibility. Early in 1939, when the British government reintroduced national military service, the Northern Ireland prime minister, Lord Craigavon, decided to provide dramatic evidence of his support for the cause by advocating the extension of conscription to that part of Ireland which his government controlled. Irish nationalists opposed the scheme, as Craigavon had no doubt confidently expected, and their views were faithfully echoed in the *Irish News*. The *Belfast Telegraph* declared on 26 April 1939 that this was 'ignoble and contemptible' and that those who refused national responsibilities 'should be denied all national rights' (Fisk 1983: 81). In the month in which war was declared, it stepped up its critique, declaring that 'many separatists in Ireland do not extend to other countries that zeal for the rights of small nations of which they talk so volubly when they themselves are concerned' (4 September 1939). The same paper showed its support for the cause in an even more practical way, by raising money for the construction of a number of Spitfires for the Royal Air Force; mere mention of this was enough to draw down on *The Progressive Printer and Newspaper Publisher*, a privately circulated trade magazine published in Dublin, the wrath of the Irish censor (Ó Drisceoil 1996a: 184). The fund was launched in August 1940, with a target of £5,000: the first day's total was more than £2,500 and the final total in May 1945 was more than £88,000, which built seventeen Spitfires, all named after Northern Ireland localities except for one, which was named after the Harland and Wolff shipyards (Brodie 1995: 73). The *Telegraph* offices in Belfast were damaged in a bomb attack in 1941: production was uninterrupted. The *Irish News*, whose offices had been severely damaged in the same attack, was helped by the *Newsletter* to put out a one-page emergency edition the following day; for the next six weeks, while repairs were in progress, the Nationalist newspaper was printed by the *Telegraph*. Later in the war, the *Telegraph* gave accommodation to – and the paper's presses printed – the Northern Ireland edition of the US Forces newsletter *Stars and Stripes* (Brodie 1995: 82, 87). Unlike Dublin newspapers, the *Telegraph* had its own war correspondents – one assigned to each branch of the services. Like all papers, North and South, it was subject to censorship, but the activities of the censorship office in Belfast, operated by the Minister of Information – by some reports draconian (Brodie 1995: 69) – have not been as well documented, as the censored stories were returned to the news-papers and not retained by them.

Censorship was not an issue at BBC NI, in large part because regional broad-casting from Belfast was suspended for the duration of the war. This was a decision based on military rather than on political considerations: broadcast wavelengths generally had to be synchronised so that enemy aircraft could not use them as beacons, and separate wavelengths for the regions were no longer possible. According to Cathcart (1984: 101) the British government carried this policy to the unusual length of re-broadcasting Radio Eireann for a considerable period into the war (without the knowledge of the Dublin authorities) to confuse German direction finding aids.

The dearth of censorable material did not mean that the Belfast organisation ceased to exist. If anything, Marshall (the regional director in Belfast) became even more active as the triangular relationship between Belfast, London and Dublin became ever more complex and fraught. Feelings in Belfast, or at least within the Unionist hierarchy, about Irish neutrality ran high, and attempts by Dublin to build even a modest base where common interests could be explored ran into dogged opposition from Marshall. The problem was that Unionist sentiment and British government policy were pulling in opposite directions (Cathcart 1984: 118–27). London – especially in the early years of the war, when the military situation was dauntingly serious – felt that promoting cooper-ation between Belfast and Dublin might add to the pressure on Ireland to abandon neutrality, whereas Belfast felt that any cooperation across the border was little short of treason. Few initiatives survived in this frosty climate, and the situation was not helped when an edition of the popular Radio Eireann programme, *Question Time*, was broadcast from Belfast in August 1942. When the quizmaster, Joe Linnane, asked a participant for the name of the world's most famous teller of fairy stories, the (nationalist) contestant cheerfully answered 'Winston Churchill', instead of 'Hans Christian Andersen'. The raucous applause which greeted this – uncorrected – sally ensured that this experiment in cross-border cooperation was not repeated.

By 1943, it was not only clear that Ireland would not lightly abandon its neutrality but – more relevantly – the British war effort was in less need of the assistance that might have been provided by access to the Irish ports, which had been surrendered in 1938. Pressure from London on BBC NI lessened and, although Marshall had his knuckles rapped by his superiors in July 1944, it was the end of a long period during which he had almost single-handedly ensured that many BBC broadcasts dealing with anything that happened on the island of Ireland were subject to his personal approval or veto.

The restoration of regional broadcasting from Belfast in July 1945 did not lessen the political pressure from Unionism. Basil Brooke, the Northern Ireland prime minister, proved as eager as his predecessor, J.M. Andrews, to interfere with broadcasting, either by making representations to London, or by making clear, as he did in April 1946, his belief that BBC NI should be controlled by Stormont (Cathcart 1984: 131). The BBC managed to fend off these attempts without much difficulty, but the price was paid internally in Northern Ireland, where open discussion of political issues, which had become increasingly common elsewhere since the end of the war and the election of the 1945 Labour government, was still conspicuous by its absence.

For all the differences between the two parts of the island, there were a number of organisations which operated on both sides of the border, and were concerned with journalism as a profession. These were the Institute of Journalists (IOJ) and the National Union of Journalists (NUJ), both of which were effectively British organisations which had established footholds in Ireland long before the Treaty of 1922. The IOJ, founded in 1884, was first in the field, and included in its membership proprietors as well as employees of newspapers. The NUJ was founded in 1907 for employees only, and was much more of a trade union: it established its first presence in Ireland in 1909.

The same year saw the first of a number of attempts to organise a separate journalists' organisation in Ireland. This was the Irish Journalists Association, whose weakness was evidenced by the fact that it did not publish its first newsletter until October 1914 (NLI: IR 07 g I). In October 1915 representatives of the NUJ had discussions in Dublin with IJA members about a possible merger, but IJA members resisted the adoption of trade union status and, by the time the NUJ formed its first formal branch in Dublin in 1926, the IJA had to all intents and purposes ceased to exist. The new NUJ branch quickly achieved a membership of about eighty, mainly from the national papers. A branch was formed in Belfast with seventeen members. The foundation of the *Irish Press* in 1931 provided a notable boost, as employees of that newspaper were strongly trade unionist in outlook, and a virtual closed shop was rapidly achieved there (Bundock 1957: 110). This did not mean that the NUJ had the field to itself. In 1938, prompted partly by a feeling of national self-reliance in the wake of the passage of the 1937 Constitution, and partly by a feeling that the NUJ's interests were too closely aligned with those of the national newspapers based in Dublin, a meeting was held in Thurles, Co. Tipperary, to found a new Irish Journalists Association (*II*: 12 April 1938). This initiative appears to have been short-lived, despite the attendance at the foundation meeting of journalists from the counties of Kerry, Limerick, Tipperary, Kilkenny, Galway, Laois and Offaly. The fact that some of its leading lights – for example its secretary T.P. Cleary and his assistant J.D. Hickey – not long afterwards secured employment with the national newspapers may have been relevant here.

Growing union militancy during the war years provoked a number of developments on either side of the border. In the South, the union faced a crisis decision following the passage of the 1941 Trade Union Act, which required all trade unions to register with the government and pay a large fee before being entitled to negotiate on behalf of their members. The NUJ central organisation was hostile to such a development – possibly influenced in part by Irish neutrality, but also because it objected to any government interference with trade union rights. Accordingly, it urged its Irish members to set up a separate organisation, and offered to pay the £1,000 required for a negotiating licence, as well as providing the new organisation with set-up grants in each of the following two years. This proposal, however, was defeated at the union's annual delegate conference in Leeds in 1942 after a plea from a Dublin delegate, the author and journalist R.M. Fox, who said that it amounted to abandonment of the Dublin branch. Later that year the union reluctantly complied with the registration procedures, while putting on record its determination 'to resist by every means in its power the application of these dangerous principles to the trade union movement' (Bundock 1957: 162).

In Belfast, there were problems with the employers, who revived the Belfast Newspaper Society, a formerly dormant proprietorial association, and rapidly came to an agreement on pay with the IOJ. By 1947, the NUJ's Belfast and District branch – an enlargement of the original Belfast branch – acquired members from the editorial staffs of all the newspapers, and approached managements (initially the *Belfast Telegraph*) for recognition. The proprietors, adopting a joint position, refused. The *Telegraph* decreed that 'no organisation, social or otherwise, can operate or function in any part of the company's premises unless with the direct and specific permission of the directors'. Any requests to meet management, they insisted, could come only through department heads (Brodie 1995: 93–4). In Dublin, the union was stronger and, in 1947, negotiated the first of a series of agreements which resulted in substantial improvements in pay and conditions (Bundock 1957: 223). Although this contributed in turn to the growth of the union, it was to be almost two decades before the Irish organisation had its own administrative structure, and indeed professional unity was to come under threat in the course of a number of controversies in the 1950s and 1980s.

In Dublin, the apprehension was even greater, driven partly by a communist 'scare' launched by Fianna Fail in the course of the general election in February 1948. The American legation in Dublin was particularly concerned about this, forwarding reports to Washington about communist activity in Ireland and, in particular, rumoured communist infiltration of the *Irish Press* and the National Union of Journalists. Just after the election, US officials in Dublin reported the views of a clerical friend of de Valera's about unwholesome influences in the paper the Fianna Fail leader controlled (USNA: 841D.OOB/2–1048: 10 February 1948). In December of the same year, they forwarded a report volunteered to them (and to the Irish security services), by an Irish journalist, the editor of the weekly *Catholic Standard*, which alleged that the Dublin branch of the NUJ 'contains quite a few active Communists', and specifically mentioned Michael McInerney, then a journalist on the *Irish Times* (later its Political Correspondent) who had previously been active in the Communist Party in Belfast (USNA: 841D.OOB/12–148: 1 December 1948). Some of these rumours reached Mr de Valera himself, who was concerned enough to seek reassurance from his editor, William Sweetman, about them, and in particular about the political loyalties of the *Irish Press*'s Foreign Editor, Sean O'Neill, whom the Americans thought 'systematically takes advantage of his position to slant the news ... minimises anti-Soviet statements and uses a series of journalistic devices to misrepresent the news as originally received' (USNA: 841D.00B/9–2349: 3 October 1949).

It was hardly coincidental that a serious attempt was made at about this time to set up a wholly Irish-based union for journalists, but the fear of communist infiltration would have been only a minor part of the motivation. More significant in the long term was the desire of the government to promote industrial organisation after the war, and its hostility towards UK-based unions generally. This had already been made manifest in a major split in the trade union movement, which now had one organisation for British-based trade unions, and another for purely Irish organisations. This general split now spread to journalism: in 1949 a number of journalists, with the active support of the Irish Transport and General Workers' Union, set up a new organisation known as the Guild of Irish Journalists, and issued its first press statement on 22 March asking bluntly: 'Why should Irish journalists be controlled from London?' (Horgan 1997: 144). Like its predecessor, the Irish Journalists Association, it eventually became moribund, although it experienced a brief revival in markedly different circumstances over thirty years later.

Events in Dublin continued to cast a long shadow northwards. Sometimes it was benign: the Radio Eireann short-wave initiative, which, as has been noted, produced a notable increase in resources and a second orchestra, may well have been one of the factors which released the purse-strings of the BBC to enable the creation of an orchestra for BBC NI a year later, in 1949. But more usually it was a cause for concern, and apprehension. This was particularly so when the constitutional issue raised its head, as it did in a marked manner after the election of a new, non-Fianna Fail government in Dublin in February 1948.

The head of that government, John A. Costello, shared power with a number of smaller parties, one of which, Clann na Poblachta, was at least as nationalist as Fianna Fail and on occasion considerably more so. This ensured that partition came again to the forefront of the political agenda, and, in his first St Patrick's Day address on Irish radio in March 1948, Costello made it plain that he yielded nothing to Mr de Valera in the matter of irredentism.

This would not have caused any problem had it not been for the fact that extracts from it were broadcast on the BBC World Service. This had a number of effects, some of which might have been anticipated. A Westminster Unionist MP immediately tabled a motion deploring the re-broadcasting of 'passages offensive to Northern Ireland' in Costello's speech. The irony was that Costello was almost equally offended, as the BBC, which had been given permission by him to edit his remarks for time reasons, had judiciously excised some of his more inflammatory statements about Irish unity (Cathcart 1984: 145). This perceived slight was to have one unforeseen consequence: the revival of the plan for a high-powered short-wave service in Athlone, which Costello's own government had killed off almost as soon as it came to power. In the South as well as in the North – and with notably more success, given the organic nature of the relationship between government and broadcasting – interventionist media strategies were still a popular option.

3 Coming of age, 1947–57

The end of the Second World War was not accompanied, in Ireland, by the rapid upsurge in living standards which many had confidently expected. Indeed, one of the major unanswered questions in Irish economic history is why Ireland did not benefit, to the extent that was apparent in other countries, from the economic growth that accompanied reconstruction in Europe. De Valera's grip on power was, partly as a result, beginning to weaken, and by the end of 1947 he was thinking in terms of a snap election which would catch his opponents unawares.

As part of his preparation for this contest, he moved to meet the claims of those who believed that his government was not doing enough for the Irish language, and to subsidise Irish-language periodicals for the first time. A grants system was devised by his Minister for Finance, Frank Aiken, and – although it was not implemented until after the change of government in February 1948 – put a number of key publications on a much sounder financial basis. *Inniú* received £4,900. *Comhar* got £1,150, with a further £750 if it was printed in Dublin, and *Feasta*, which was launched in 1948 by Conradh na Gaeilge (the Gaelic League) to replace its more modest journal *Glór* ('Voice'), received £1,800.

Neither this nor the other measures adopted by de Valera were sufficient to stave off defeat, but Fianna Fail's ejection from government for the first time in sixteen years had rapid consequences for Irish journalism in a number of different ways. The first was that the party moved almost immediately to establish another newspaper. This was the *Sunday Press*, seen as a less risky undertaking than an attempt to re-launch the failed evening newspaper. The Irish appetite for Sunday newspapers has always been substantial, and for years the proportion of British newspapers sold in the country on Sundays has been substantially higher than for the daily press on weekdays – on average, one paper out of three on Sunday, compared to one out of four on weekdays (Horgan 1993b). Planning for the paper began in 1948, and the first edition was published on 4 September 1949. Initially the project encountered problems similar to those which had been overcome by its morning stable-mate: the Independent group – whose *Sunday Independent* was of course threatened by the newcomer – let newsagents generally know that if they stocked the new Sunday paper, supplies of the *Sunday Independent* would be withheld.

In the circumstances, the *Irish Press* managing director, Sean Lemass (translated to this position from his former role as cabinet minister, and still a member of parliament), had to devise alternative strategies. These included approaching the proprietors of small shops in many rural towns and villages who had never sold newspapers before, but who were known to be loyal to the party and who would be prepared to open on Sunday to stock the new paper. In this way, a parallel distribution network was successfully organised. Rather more unusually, Catholic priests favourable to the cause were also invited to volunteer, and many did so, some agreeing to transport bundles of the newspaper in their cars to the churches, so that the crowds emerging from Mass could buy them immediately afterwards (Oram 1983: 239). The enterprise was immediately successful but not – interestingly – at the expense of the *Sunday Independent*, or at least not to any great extent. The circulation of the new paper – it was to reach a peak of more than 400,000 in the 1960s – did not appear to have been achieved at the expense of its main domestic competitor, suggesting that many of its readers were people who had previously bought a UK Sunday paper rather than the *Sunday Independent* (to which they would have objected on political grounds), or might not have bought a Sunday paper of any description.

As Irish journalists revelled in the opportunities offered by the emergence of a new national paper, and the major political changes that were taking place, they were also being faced by what many of them saw as unwarranted interference by the new government in the sphere proper to journalism. This was the government's plan to establish a new body, to be known as the Irish News Agency, which would be staffed by journalists but controlled by the government, and which would have an important role vis-à-vis foreign (principally British and American) publications.

This development had its origins in three major factors. One of them was political – the desire of Clann na Poblachta, a new political party (it had been founded only in 1946) and its leader, a barrister and former revolutionary and part-time journalist named Sean MacBride, to bring international pressure to bear on Britain to end the partition of the island. The second was the sense that the Irish case on partition had never been properly explained to the outside world, as virtually all news from Ireland went through a British news agency filter before reaching the international media. De Valera's early interest in the short-wave radio station had been based partly on a recognition of this factor. The third was a growing dissatisfaction with the work of the Government Information Bureau (GIB), which had been set up in 1934.

The GIB's role had always been an ill-defined one. It had been set up originally in an attempt to ensure that all ministerial statements would be issued to the press via a channel controlled by the head of government, thus avoiding embarrassing departures from government policy. A succession of strong cabinet ministers ensured that it never really fulfilled this role. Its secondary role, as a conduit for press queries to cabinet members and government departments, fell foul of civil servants' legendary observance of the Official Secrets Acts, and of the fairly transparent desire of the government to use its limited mechanisms for party political purposes. On 14 September 1935, the *Irish Times* complained, after a speech by de Valera had apparently been leaked by the GIB to the *Irish Press*, that the Bureau 'has divided most of its time between issuing no information at all and denying information that has already made its way into the papers'. During the war, the Bureau worked in close cooperation with the censor, ensuring that the government could release statements through the GIB to give its side of the argument on issues which were conveniently mired in the Censor's office. By 1948, the Bureau was discounted almost entirely by journalists, and deeply distrusted by the members of the government which had replaced Fianna Fail. Its head, the former *Irish Press* editor Frank Gallagher, was now a permanent civil servant and could not be dismissed, but he was despatched to what his new masters confidently, but mistakenly, assumed would be the quiet backwater of the Department of Health as an information officer. He was, in that capacity, to play a major role in publicising a controversial health scheme originated by the new minister for health, Dr Noel Browne.

The belief that Ireland was surrounded by a paper wall which had the effect of preventing Irish grievances against Britain from obtaining an international airing had some basis in fact. All the major international news agencies had their correspondents in Dublin, but these correspondents' reports were generally routed through London, where the desk editors who dealt with them had scant sympathy with Irish irredentism, or assumed that their international audiences would have little interest in it, or both (Horgan 1993a: 33).

The possibility that the world at large – outside the large Irish communities in Britain and the USA – might be relatively indifferent to Ireland's historic grievances, did not prevent the new government's Foreign Minister, Sean MacBride (who had once worked as a journalist for the French news agency Havas, and was leader of the Clann na Poblachta Party which was part of the coalition administration) from persuading the government to set up this new agency which would, he hoped, short-circuit the existing system and transmit Irish news directly to foreign outlets. He had been urging such a course of action on de Valera since at least 1945: now that he was in power, he had an opportunity to put his own ideas into practice and also to burnish his party's republican credentials. Irish journalists, however, had a different point of view, and put it to the government, directly through editorials in the newspapers, and indirectly through opposition members of parliament.

In May 1949 MacBride asked the government to set up an organisation to be known as the Irish News Agency (INA) whose publications 'should include reports of important pronouncements on partition. It should be strictly non-party and non-political in the sense that it should only deal with matters of foreign policy and matters that are non-controversial at home' (NAI: Taoiseach: S 14544). Early newspaper reports suggested that the agency's work would be confined to sending out articles by airmail, and to the use of short-wave radio, but as more details emerged, journalists became openly hostile. The *Irish Independent* suggested that the plan 'smacks too much of a plan to set up a propaganda department' (17 June 1949) and the *Irish Times* expressed the view that 'Mr MacBride's diminutive agency certainly will not galvanise the apathetic audiences of the great world into a state of appreciation' (15 July 1949).

A lot of this opposition was – and continued to be until the Agency's closure seven years later – substantially motivated by self-interest. This was openly admitted: an opposition member of parliament, himself a journalist, told the Dail that he was speaking on behalf of working journalists 'who feel that their livelihood is being attacked in this Bill' and that the Agency 'will be in competition with other journalists who send "copy" out of this country' (DD: 13 July 1949). Sensitive to this early threat to his plans, MacBride gave an undertaking that the Agency would not deal in 'hot' news, but solving one problem left him with another: how could an organisation which did not distribute news be legitimately described as a news agency?

Ill-starred though its birth may have been, the new Agency was given considerable resources and housed in MacBride's Department of External Affairs, where most of its day-to-day business was overseen by its managing director Conor Cruise O'Brien, then attached to that department as a civil servant. One of the first decisions of its board was to jettison MacBride's pledge that it would not deal in 'hot' news. This was on foot of a proposal from one of MacBride's close associates, Noel Hartnett, who was a member of the board. Although other board members assumed that this was being done with MacBride's covert approval, they were unaware of the fact that the relationship between MacBride and this particular associate had in fact soured, and that his proposal was made in the full knowledge that it would embarrass the minister, as indeed it did (O'Brien 1998: 148).

The Agency nonetheless got into its stride quickly, and within a year was generating about 9,000 words a day (Horgan 1993a: 35). Its staff, which rose to number almost fifty by 1952, included many of the country's brightest young journalists, who were paid at rather better rates than those offered by the national newspapers. It secured an agreement with the Hearst-controlled INS news services in the United States, whereby INS carried INA-generated stories for its American clients, while the INA had a monopoly on selling INS material (principally photographs) to the Irish media.

The more it succeeded in selling Irish news abroad, however, the more it aroused opposition among Irish journalists. It also fell foul of public sentiment when, as occasionally happened, it exported news which appeared to show Ireland in a bad light: this was particularly the case in relation to its reports in 1951 about a political controversy involving the appointment of a government supporter to a small rural post office, which became known as the 'Battle of Baltinglass'.

It combined attempts to become financially self-sufficient, through selling news, with the less publicised propaganda role which MacBride had originally envisaged for it. This uneasy dual role was defined by O'Brien in 1950 in a note to the Irish government's public relations officer in New York, when he said that the Agency:

> will function as a genuine news agency and not as a propaganda body. I must add for your own information that this will not prevent the agency from giving news and stories about Partition. This, however, will be thoroughly reliable and discreetly administered.
>
> (NAI: INA: 2)

The Agency's report for 1951–2 – not a public document – made considerable capital of its success in distributing to a claimed audience of 8.5 million people a photograph of policemen in Northern Ireland beating unarmed nationalist demonstrators in Derry with their batons. Almost two decades before television pictures of similar treatment being meted out to a civil rights march in the same city, propelling Northern Ireland on to the international agenda in a way that had never happened before, the photograph was already a potent instrument of political policy. This, the Agency proudly informed its political masters, was:

> probably the first time that a highly important political fact – viz that partition is maintained by force – has been so effectively brought across to an audience of large dimensions. The quasi-monopoly of the handling of Irish news for the world's press, once possessed by two or three of the great international news agencies, is now broken. Secondly ... the state of affairs whereby all Irish news was edited in London before issue ... is now a thing of the past.
>
> (NAI: Taoiseach: 14544 B)

This was one of a number of attempts by the Agency to avert attempts by the Department of Finance to close it down because it was consuming ever-increasing quantities of public funds. Its revenue-generating capacities had been seriously impaired when, at the end of 1951, the NUJ complained about its activities to de Valera, now Taoiseach again after three years in opposition, and secured an agreement that its distribution of 'hot' news would cease.

The journalists who had thus succeeded in clipping the fledgling Agency's wings were, the Department of External Affairs observed tartly in 1953:

> in large measure not engaged in the active collection of news. At least 90 per cent hold editorial positions on the Dublin daily newspapers and recast the news submitted to those newspapers by working journalists who receive no payment for the exported material. It is easy to see why such vested interests should be continuously and actively vocal in their opposition to a national news agency which pays cash for all news written.
>
> (NAI: Taoiseach: S 14544 B)

At the time this was written, the *Irish Independent* alone numbered among its staff the Dublin correspondents of the Press Association, Reuters, the Associated Press, the Exchange Telegraph financial newswire and a Canadian news agency.

The Agency limped along for a further three years and yet another change of government before being finally closed down in May 1957. Ironically – in the light of the guerrilla campaign which had been waged for the previous seven years – this provoked an immediate protest from the Irish Area Council of the NUJ, and even the General Secretary if the NUJ in London was moved to express his perturbation at the associated job losses. In the circumstances, they were unlikely pall-bearers.

Many years later its original managing director, by this time (1973) an Irish cabinet minister, spoke of its passing with some regret:

> Its ties to the State, and dependence on the State, were too close and too great. And it was aimed too much at the press outside this country, without being able adequately to fulfil the basic function of a normal news agency, which is to serve the press of its own country. I am convinced that a really viable Irish news agency must answer the needs of Irish newspapers, and must be controlled by them.
>
> (Horgan 1993a: 42)

For all its faults, the INA was probably one of the most exciting developments in Irish media during this period, which was otherwise marked by the regular expression of a crude political and cultural isolationism which was aimed particularly at foreign publications. As one historian commented (although his remarks are somewhat unfair, particularly to publications like *The Bell*):

> Regrettably most Irish journalism in this period [1932–58] had contented itself with the reportage of events and the propagandist reiteration of the familiar terms of Irish political and cultural debate until these categories became mere counters and slogans often remote from many actualities. Irish journalism therefore comfortably reinforced the prevailing sense that Ireland, marked as the nationalists constantly stressed by distinctive social, religious and linguistic forms, was somehow different from the rest of the world. It did not challenge Irishmen and women to reflect seriously on their own reality.
>
> (Brown 1981: 204–5)

From early in 1950, the government was deluged with a series of resolutions passed by local authorities in different parts of the country calling for action (NAI: Taoiseach: S 2919B). Leitrim County Council, for example, called on the government in February to prohibit the importation of Sunday newspapers 'in view of the offensive and obscene nature of articles continually appearing therein'; in April, Galway Corporation followed suit, charging that these publications were 'detrimental to the moral life, national aspirations and economy of the country'; in the same month, the Portlaoise Town Commissioners alleged that these publications were 'killing the soul of the nation'. In July, success was reported in the *Irish Catholic*, which noted that in the Irish-speaking parish of Annagry, in Co. Donegal, following an appeal by the local bishop, 'when the newspapers arrived in the parish and commenced distribution, the agents informed the carriers that they were not accepting delivery' (20 July 1950). The Taoiseach, John A. Costello, speaking not long before he lost office in the general election of May 1951, demurred: proposals for banning newspapers were, he said, a purely negative approach: 'the only way in which you can deal with matters of that kind is by raising the standard of taste of the people' (DD: 24 April 1951).

In spite of such opposition, the success of *The Bell* had shown that there was a constituency for the venturesome, even if the implied invitation was effectively taken up only by the *Irish Times*, where Smyllie continued as editor until his death in 1954. In July 1949 the latter paper published a series of articles on venereal disease which were 'greeted with dismay in higher Catholic circles, and the subject was almost completely boycotted by the Catholic press' (Blanshard 1953: 152). The following year, its correspondence columns became the venue for an extraordinary correspondence under the generic heading 'The Liberal Ethic', later published by the newspaper itself as a pamphlet, in which a wide range of literary and political figures elaborated, defended or attacked the ideology to which the paper was increasingly explicitly committed.

This found its most dramatic expression in April 1951, in the midst of a government crisis about a proposed new health scheme to which the Catholic hierarchy and the medical profession were resolutely opposed. After intense and fruitless negotiations with these interests behind closed doors the Minister for Health, Dr Noel Browne, was forced to resign. His last act before leaving office was to prepare a full dossier of the correspondence between himself and various bishops and politicians, which he released to the press. The newspapers were initially hesitant, as publication was technically a breach of the Official Secrets Act, and therefore a criminal offence, but Smyllie decided to publish regardless: the other papers, thus encouraged, did the same (12 April 1951). It was a remarkable breach, not only of the criminal law, but of the polite conventions of political journalism which had obtained hitherto. Nor were these events ignored in Northern Ireland: the *Belfast Newsletter*, long the unofficial organ of the Unionist party, gleefully reprinted the documents as a booklet – *Southern Ireland – Church or State?* – which was available thereafter from the Unionist party headquarters.

This was a brief blip: for the most part, the print media operated within boundaries which rarely overlapped. In March 1953, for example, the circulation of the major papers was as follows: *Irish Independent* 203,206; *Irish Press* 198,784; *Irish Times* 35,421; *Cork Examiner* 45,917. The largest selling Irish

Sunday newspaper was the *Sunday Independent* (395,507), followed by the *Sunday Press* (378,454) (DD: 19 March 1953).

The major problem faced by the *Irish Times* was the narrowness and vulnerability of its operations. Its presses, apart from a small amount of jobbing printing which it carried out, were idle for most of every day, and completely on Saturdays. It did not publish circulation information, unlike its main rival, the *Irish Independent*, which had been the first Irish national paper to submit its returns to the Audit Bureau of Circulation. Indeed, its circulation figures were not even made available to the board until the 1950s, on the grounds that it was commercially sensitive information which might cause the paper damage if it leaked into the public domain. The board was a group of five Protestant businessmen, who controlled all the voting shares: when one of their number died or wished to resign – which was infrequent – the remaining directors habitually purchased his shares, and redistributed them to the next Board appointee. The fact that many businesses in Dublin were Protestant-owned ensured a steady supply of commercial advertising, to an extent probably not warranted by the paper's circulation; but these factors could not be expected to continue into the indefinite future.

It had only two other small publications. One was the weekly *Irish Field*, dedicated to the horse-racing and breeding industries, which was a profitable niche publication but which did not really demand much of the company's printing resources. The other was the *Times Pictorial Weekly*, which had been started in 1941. All of its rivals had, since 1954, three substantial papers to keep their presses turning and their income steady. To remedy this dangerous reliance on a single product, and in what later came to be seen as over-optimism, the *Irish Times* in 1957 started a new Sunday paper, the *Sunday Review*, and in 1960 bought an existing evening newspaper – the *Evening Mail*. The *Mail*, like the *Irish Times* Protestant-owned, was an old-fashioned broadsheet newspaper with a declining circulation. Under its new owners, it became a bright and aggressive tabloid, but the experiment was a costly failure. The old readers did not like their paper in its new guise and, before it could attract a viable circulation among the younger urban readership at which it was aimed, mounting losses forced its closure in 1962. Until then, Dublin, with three evening newspapers, had if anything been over-supplied.

Even before the closure of the *Mail*, the *Pictorial Review* had gone to the wall in 1958. The closure of the *Sunday Review* in 1963, was an added blow. It suffered, like the *Evening Mail*, from the *Irish Times*'s small capital base, and might well have survived and prospered if its parent organisation had had a longer pocket. Like the *Mail*, it was a tabloid, as different from its parent in style and content as it is possible to imagine. (This did not prevent it sharing at least some writers: the *Irish Times* literary editor, the novelist and critic Terence de Vere White, wrote a humorous column for the review under a pseudonym.) Its chief innovation, however, was in the field of political journalism: its weekly feature 'Backbencher' evolved from a loose collection of anecdotes about politicians into an irreverent, hard-edged and demotic treatment of the political process characterised by inside information of a type and quality that journalism had not known until then. This was paralleled by, and to some extent dependent on, a loosening of the traditional disciplines which had ensured that cabinet leaks were to all intents and purposes unknown: now a new generation of younger politicians, particularly in Fianna Fail, were impatient at the slowness with which their elders were prepared to move aside, and began to use the media, and in particular the Backbencher column, to urge their claims for advancement. On the closure of the *Review*, the column was translated successfully to the *Irish Times*. Since the beginning of the 1950s, therefore, the *Irish Times* portfolio of publications had expanded to no fewer than five publications: the successive closure, from 1958 onwards, of the *Weekly Pictorial*, the *Evening Mail* and the *Sunday Review* left it economically shaken and apprehensive about the future.

No such doubts afflicted the *Irish Independent* and its associated evening and Sunday newspapers. Throughout this period it went from strength to strength, with a confident appeal to the increasingly prosperous Catholic middle classes. Its ownership had been to some extent diluted by marriage, so that the Murphy family, which had founded the paper, were now joined at board level by members of a Dublin medical family, the Chances. It was still, however, effectively a family business, whose shareholders paid little attention to the inner workings of the company and were content simply to receive their dividends, which were generally substantial. In some areas, the *Irish Independent* had a virtual monopoly of advertising. This was certainly true of the advertisements for teaching vacancies in Catholic primary schools (the majority of the country's primary schools), which were invariably advertised in the daily paper by the parish priests who were the managers of the schools. Another major source of advertising – in this case funded with public money – came from the vocational education committees, some thirty-eight of which administered public post-primary education across the country. These committees were politically controlled, in the sense that the bulk of their membership was made up of elected local authority representatives from the major parties. These committees organised their advertising budgets in such a way as to satisfy both the major political interests represented among their membership – Fianna Fail and Fine Gael. Fianna Fail councillors ensured that a slice of the advertising budget for teachers went to the *Sunday Press*; in return, they facilitated their Fine Gael colleagues who wanted similar advertisements to appear in the *Sunday Independent*.

To suggest, on the basis of this, that the Independent group papers were closely linked to one political party would be an overstatement. They had been intermittently critical of the Free State government in the 1920s and, insofar as they came to support that administration in a general way, it was more because they were alarmed by the threat to the civic and political hegemony of the middle classes which it discerned in Fianna Fail than because of any inherent conviction about the correctness of Fine Gael policies, which it continued to criticise from time to time, particularly when it perceived them to be hostile to business interests. To the extent to which it supported Fine Gael, it was primarily because it supported the Catholic middle-class and commercial group-ings, of which Fine Gael happened to be the most coherent and conservative political expression. Even this is to some extent a generalisation: some of the group's editors – notably Hector Legge, who became editor of the *Sunday Independent* during the war – had a fairly robust attitude towards, and main-tained strong journalistic links with, the main figures in all the political parties.

There was one interesting anomaly in all of this. In 1951, the young and impulsive Minister for Health, Dr Noel Browne, launched a scheme which would have provided free medical care for all mothers and for all children up to the age of 16. This scheme was bitterly opposed by the Irish medical profession, who enlisted the Catholic bishops in their support. Browne was forced to resign, and the government fell. The *Irish Independent*, which might have been expected to weigh in heavily behind the bishops and the medical profession, maintained an unexpected editorial silence. Although it would not have been widely known or remarked on at the time, the reason for this was in all proba-bility the fact that the Chance family, which was represented on the board, had some fifteen years earlier informally adopted the young Noel Browne, then an orphan, and paid for his university education. Ideology and practical politics dictated that they could not support the stand he had taken; but neither would they allow their papers to attack him.

As the controversy reached its climax, the *Irish Independent* sailed serenely on: in the issue which published the dramatic correspondence, it contented itself with regaling its loyal readers with the thirty-fourth in a fifty-part series of articles on 'The Lives of the Popes'. This was very much in character. Its Sunday stable-mate provided a platform for the last article by the redoubtable controversialist Fr R.S. Devane, on the evil influence of crime comics (*SI*: 22 March 1951): he was to die two months later (*II*: 24 May 1951). Part of his legacy was the organisation known as Cosg ar Fhoilseachain Gallda ('Ban on Foreign Publications') which, at a mass meeting in Dublin in 1952, announced plans to establish committees in every parish to boycott foreign (i.e. generally British) magazines and newspapers. These committees were presumably respon-sible for the appearance in many parts of Dublin, early in 1953, of posters declaring in heavy black type: 'THE FOREIGN PRESS IS A NATIONAL MENACE' (Blanshard 1953: 102).The organisation even secured a meeting with the Taoiseach, Eamon de Valera, to press its point of view on him, but without success (Adams 1968: 164). Mr de Valera continued to maintain that the correct response to all but the most objectionable foreign publications was to tax them rather than ban them (NAI: Finance: FO22/0021/33). When the tariff was finally ended in 1971, as part of Ireland's preparation for entry into the EEC, it was producing an annual revenue of £305,000. There was in fact little evidence that Ireland was in danger of being swamped by foreign news-paper imports, either in moral or in economic terms: the combined circulations of the three national morning papers in 1953 was almost 450,000 (*IT*: 19 March 1953), and per capita distribution of newspapers was still low – about a third that of the UK, and less than half that of Australia, Norway, Denmark and Sweden (*IT*: 19 August 1953).

In 1954, as the *Irish Independent* prepared to celebrate its fiftieth year in existence, it wrote to a number of senior Catholic churchmen inviting them to contribute special messages for an anniversary supplement (churchmen of other denominations do not appear to have been similarly invited, such was the narrowness of the paper's cultural and social focus). The cardinal archbishop of Armagh and primate of all Ireland, Dr d'Alton, told the paper that it could:

> justly claim that during the 50 years of its existence it has maintained a high standard of journalism and respected the decencies of life. It appeals to a wide circle of readers because it is usually varied in content, interesting, informative, without exploiting the cheap or sensational. It has always endeavoured to promote the best interests of the nation.
>
> (*II*: 22 December 1954)

D'Alton's counterpart in Dublin, the powerful Archbishop John Charles McQuaid, was more succinct but equally to the point. The paper had been marked, he told the editor, Frank Geary, by 'your policy of distinctive loyalty towards the Church' (31 December 1954). Geary responded in an editorial on 3 January 1955, in terms which could well have been published fifty years earlier:

> In the future, as in the past, we shall endeavour to live up to our title, to be both Irish and independent, allied to no party, free to criticise or to help any or all as the interests of the nation may demand, using the mechanism of progressive newspaper production and the power of honest, sober journalists to enlighten, educate and serve the Irish people.

This period marked the high point of conservatism so far as the *Irish Independent* was concerned; and it was echoed in other, commercially owned publications such as the weekly *Standard* and *Irish Catholic*. Neither of these publications had a circulation even remotely resembling that of the secular papers. They were 'strong points on an ideological frontier, and the average Irishman, not feeling the frontier to be menaced, nor much desiring to put it forward, is not particularly interested in them' (O'Donnell 1945b: 38–9). But even these publications had their differences: on the occasion of the abdication of Edward VIII in 1936, the *Standard* confined itself to a few well-chosen phrases about English immorality. The *Irish Catholic*, however, printed on its front page an article which made this the occasion for advancing the claim to the English crown of no less a personage than (the Catholic) Rupert I of Bavaria. Practically unnoticed by such trenchant defenders of the faith, however, there were stirrings in the clerical undergrowth – more particularly in the field of religious magazines, which had been for decades the repository of ultra-orthodox thinking and writing (Adams 1968: 65–8). One of the most notorious of these was the *Catholic Bulletin*, which greeted the news of W.B.

Yeats's award of the Nobel Prize in 1924 with the jaundiced comment: 'It is common knowledge that the line of recipients of the Nobel Prize shows that a reputation for paganism in thought and word is a very considerable advantage in the sordid annual race for money' (Brown 1981: 72). There was no official Church-owned Catholic newspaper, although the Catholic hierarchy had entertained the idea of starting such a paper in 1927, eventually deciding to support the foundation of the lay-owned *Standard* rather than initiating a publication under its direct control. The Church of Ireland had the *Church of Ireland Gazette* (founded 1856); the Presbyterians had the *Presbyterian Herald*, the Methodists had the *Methodist Newsletter*.

The generally obsequious approach of the mainstream media, notably the *Irish Independent*, towards the Catholic Church, had presumably made the creation of a specifically Church-owned newspaper an unnecessary extravagance. However, change was on the way, and in 1953, this had been noticed even by as fierce a critic as the American Paul Blanshard, who wrote that:

> Occasionally in clerical journals one can find among the writings of the younger priests a few faint intimations of the love of freedom, a few oblique suggestions that they are suffering pain and humiliation because they have been asked in an age of democracy to dedicate their lives to a system of power in which they have no voice or vote.
>
> (1953: 69)

Although he did not mention it by name, the probability is that Blanshard was referring to *The Furrow*, a monthly pastoral journal launched in Maynooth, the country's largest Catholic seminary, in February 1950. The association with Maynooth, long regarded as the seat of episcopal power in Ireland, could be misleading: the journal's progenitor, the Revd J.G. McGarry, was a pastoral theologian who realised, before many of his peers, that the Catholic Church in Ireland had become increasingly calcified and arthritic, and that there was a need for a fresh new voice on religious and theological affairs.

On the other side of the River Liffey from the *Irish Independent*, the *Irish Press* was also consolidating and expanding. It may have been no more than coincidence, but it is certainly striking that Fianna Fail, which lost power in the general election of May 1954, launched yet another newspaper later the same year. This was the *Evening Press*, which appeared for the first time on 1 September.

The *Evening Press* was launched with a sense of aggressiveness which shook up the newspaper business in Dublin considerably. Its news-hungry editorial style was paralleled in the commercial department, which canvassed advertisements – particularly small ads, the staple of the evening newspapers for many years – from advertisers in other papers, notably the *Evening Herald*. It bought a fleet of motor-scooters which made possible the delivery of papers to the outlying Dublin suburbs much faster than the other papers' vans, which struggled through the capital's increasing traffic, and it pioneered the 'bush' system –

a method of adding late news to previously blank spaces on the front and back pages of the paper at provincial distribution centres which had been equipped with primitive printing equipment (Oram 1983: 262–4). Its drive into the Dublin suburbs was further enhanced by an editorial policy which targeted a particular suburb every week, running selected news stories from these areas prominently and supporting sales with a poster blitz in the localities concerned. Its well-deserved reputation for hard news received an extraordinary boost when, on three separate occasions in its first five months in existence, it tracked down no fewer than three babies who had been taken from their prams by mentally distressed women, and saw them triumphantly returned to their mothers.

More serious business was afoot at its stable-mate, the *Irish Press*. The appointment of the novelist Benedict Kiely as its literary editor in 1951 made the daily *Irish Press*'s weekly literary pages a haven, particularly for younger Irish writers, and the paper's politics were also undergoing a discreet change. Although the paper was to remain under the control of Eamon de Valera until his retirement from active politics in 1959, his surveillance was becoming more remote, and his deputy Sean Lemass's tenure of office as the paper's managing director in 1948–51 had left its mark. Specifically, the paper was now beginning to take sides in an internal argument which was developing inside Fianna Fail. That party's old guard were firmly convinced that the best programme for economic development in Ireland was one based on native industries, protected by tariff walls and using native raw materials. This policy, which had been endorsed by Fianna Fail in government since 1932, was running into the sand in the post-war years. The native industries which had grown up shielded by protection were lazy and inefficient, and given to taking easy profits; some of them were near-monopolies. Imports, because of the tariffs and a licensing system, became the preserve of another coterie of comfortable agencies. Economic growth was stagnating and emigration increasing.

Lemass, who had overseen this policy during most of his party's tenure of office, now recognised its inadequacy and challenged his party's prevailing orthodoxy in a number of provocative speeches, notably in 1954, in which he chastised the shortcomings of native industry and warned that they could not expect protection to continue indefinitely. This provoked a subterranean ideological dispute within the party, in which the *Irish Press* played a significant role (Curran 1994). It did so by subtly endorsing Lemass's side of the argument, highlighting his attacks on the weaknesses of Irish industry, and sidelining or minimising contrasting party views.

The late 1940s and early 1950s were marked by a number of significant changes in radio broadcasting from Dublin (and Cork), based partly, though not exclusively, on the increase in resources allocated for the doomed short-wave station. Technically, there was a vitally important change from disk to tape-recording; financially, there was a considerable improvement in licence fee revenue after a tough enforcement campaign (about a quarter of listeners had refused, or neglected, to pay the fee). Restrictions on advertising were considerably relaxed after 1949; and content was changing, to admit not only the dreaded sounds of jazz – a new series on this topic was launched in January 1948 – but a whole series of new programmes for sports fans, children and undiscovered artistic talent (Gorham 1967: 183–5).

Radio Eireann was still, however, primarily a public service organisation, structured along sub-Reithian lines, in that it was much more closely controlled than the BBC, and used for ideological ends which were primarily politically driven. The latter factor was primarily in evidence in relation to the Irish language. The new government, which had come into power in 1948, was determined not to allow itself to be outflanked on a number of issues which its predecessors had made peculiarly their own, notably those of Partition and the Irish language. It moved, for example, to increase the time allocation on the radio station for the daily broadcast of news in Irish but – in hindsight at least – the way in which it did so provided as much evidence of inability to tackle the problem as of undoubted enthusiasm for the cause.

Part of this inability was systemic. Since independence in 1922, the Irish political and administrative system, though based on a network of local authorities to complement national government, was in fact one in which power was highly – and increasingly – centralised. Local authorities had – and still have – relatively little control over resources (one of their few revenue-raising functions, that of levying rates on domestic housing, was removed in 1977). These factors militated against a proactive approach to the revival of Irish which would have involved not only the type of subsidy to the Irish-language print media which was inaugurated in 1948, but even possibly the establishment of a radio station dedicated to the needs of those who spoke the Irish language, and who lived, for the most part in the Gaeltacht communities. This was an idea which had been mooted for at least two decades but which had always been rejected.

This political bias against decentralisation in broadcasting was buttressed by other factors which militated against the effective use of radio as a tool in the struggle to revive the Irish language. One was undoubtedly financial: the Department of Finance, always apprehensive of expenditure in the area of broadcasting, would have put up stout resistance against further extravagance (as it would have described it) on this modern luxury. Another was ideological: the maintenance of intensive language instruction in the schools allowed the perpetuation of the notion that the entire population was, at least potentially, Irish-speaking, and to allow or encourage the establishment of a separate Irish-language station would have amounted to a damaging admission that this was not the case. This was coupled with the danger that the English-speaking population, who would undoubtedly direct their programme choices away from Irish if allowed to do so, would no longer have the compulsory exposure to the ancestral language which was intrinsic to a single-channel, bilingual monopoly. The third was geographical: Ireland's Irish-speaking population was – and continues to be – geographically scattered, as the language retreated before the advance of commerce and was weakened by emigration, which differentially affected the

Irish-speaking areas in the north-west, west and south. There were therefore three strong regional dialects, each with its political and academic defenders, who fought vigorously to establish pre-eminence over each other even as the number of speakers (in any dialect) dwindled inexorably. By 1950, as the 1975 report of the Committee on Irish Language Attitudes Research pointed out, even though the census reports indicated a spread of Irish outside these traditional areas, 'the number of Irish-speaking mono-lingual, already small at the turn of the century, was ... non-existent' (Committee on Irish Language Attitudes 1975: 4).

This led to the situation in which Radio Eireann had no separate service for Irish-language listeners; its news in Irish was in fact written in English and then translated into Irish; and different dialects were used on successive days in order to assuage the sensibilities of the champions of each. It was to be more than another decade before any degree of standardisation was achieved.

Other, more political issues were also beginning to surface. From 1932 to 1948, it had been tacitly accepted that Radio Eireann was effectively a government mouthpiece, at least insofar as news and current affairs were concerned. Ritual complaints about this were made from time to time, but without any evident expectation that things would change. Opposition spokesmen were allowed on the radio at certain times, but in a context which spoke of concession rather than of right. There were no live political discussions.

The sensitivity of the situation was exemplified in a controversy which broke surface only after the change of government. One of the station executives, C.E. Kelly, was also the proprietor and editor of *Dublin Opinion*, the humorous monthly journal. His mild, even affectionate poking of fun at political figures was seen by Fianna Fail as *lèse-majesté* of a high order, and his political motivation was publicly queried in the Dail. The new government retaliated by making him Director of Broadcasting when a vacancy arose. Although he was even-handed throughout – a cartoon he published in June 1948 depicted the new Minister for Finance taking a large axe to the transmitting antennae for Radio Eireann's short-wave station – Fianna Fail re-deployed him rapidly away from direct involvement in broadcasting after its return to power in 1951.

The 1948–51 period, although marked by financial and technological advances, was not notable for much in the way of innovation in broadcasting; indeed, with the exception of an unprecedented excursion to Rome in September 1950 to record the Holy Year celebrations – the opposite was the case. Plans for schools broadcasting were aborted, and the advice of the Broadcasting Advisory Committee, which recommended in 1950 that broadcasting should be removed from direct government control, was studiously ignored. The change of government in 1951, however, saw the appointment of a new minister, Erskine Childers (he was to be elected President of Ireland in 1973, at the end of a lengthy political career), whose vision for the station, adumbrated in some detail in a major speech in the Dail in November 1952, gave a completely new tone and impetus to the direction, content and control of Irish broadcasting.

Childers was a moderniser, although – in the view of his critics, to some degree supported by archival evidence – much given to direct interference in broadcasting. He was certainly among the few Irish politicians of his era who saw broadcasting as an opportunity rather than a threat, and his structural changes, although in many respects tentative, were a sign of things to come. He effected a good working relationship with the new secretary of the Department of Posts and Telegraphs, Leon O Broin, from whom, unusually in the case of a civil servant, many of the decentralising ideas had emanated. Childers took ownership of these ideas, although his enthusiasms have to be put in the context of his sometimes overweening interest in minutiae: broadcasting or administrative staff would on occasion receive memos from him containing up to twenty-two separate queries, each requiring a specific answer (Gorham 1967: 222).

His structural changes to some extent fitted the general view of his character as well as his objectives. What he proposed to the Dail was the establishment of a Comhairle (Council) of five people who would advise and assist the minister, and be responsible under him for the general control and supervision of the service, now to be known formally as Radio Eireann. The downstream effects of this decision had to be worked out in practice: they included the relationship between this new Council and the old Advisory Council, which the minister had a statutory obligation to maintain, and the financial and staffing relationships between the Department of Finance, the Department of Posts and Telegraphs, and the reorganised broadcasting service. One thing remained indisputably clear: the new Comhairle would have only as much power and responsibility as the minister felt it should have, and the minister retained overall control, including direct control if necessary.

Although the minister now had two Councils, the old one and the new one, the relationship between them was never satisfactorily clarified. In practice, the minister planned to constitute the old Council more as a listeners' representative body, and the new one as a management body; but the possible flaws in this model led to a decision not to reappoint the old council when its mandate expired in November 1964, despite the statutory requirement to do so.

The changes in staffing and financial arrangements were substantial by contemporary standards. Large numbers of staff were transferred from the Department of Posts and Telegraphs to work under the general supervision of the new Council. Some made the transition from being traditional civil servants to administrators of a broadcasting system with more difficulty than others. But the new arrangement also gave a far greater degree of financial autonomy and clarity in relation to broadcasting budgets than had existed under the previous somewhat scrimping regime, monitored down to the smallest detail by the Department of Finance.

Childers showed his personal style in two areas in particular. One was in his encouragement of advertising and sponsored programmes. In a previous incarnation – before he became a member of parliament in 1944 – he had worked for a time as advertising manager of the *Irish Press*, and also as secretary to the

Federation of Irish Manufacturers – and he had a long-standing acquaintance with many industrial and commercial concerns. In March 1952, Irish companies which imported goods for sale in the Republic were allowed to advertise for the first time, as long as their products were not in competition with any Irish-made articles. The finances were further improved by an increase in the licence fee, although the costs of collection were (and remained) inordinately high, and there was a level of evasion which was substantial in relation to that obtaining in other countries, notably Britain.

The second was in relation to content. Like P.J. Little, Childers was a music enthusiast, and this was evident in his continuing support for the station's orchestral output. Other cultural innovations included the inauguration, in September 1953, of a public lecture series, the Thomas Davis Lectures (named after the nineteenth-century Protestant nationalist leader), more programming for children, more programming from the regions, and the first broadcasts of news in the mornings (in the middle of a newspaper strike in July 1952). In the absence of an effective short-wave service, an unexpected substitute was found: Brazzaville, in the French Congo, was prepared to re-broadcast Irish programmes, particularly sports reports, which were avidly listened to by a very select sub-group of the Irish diaspora – Irish missionaries working in Africa. It was a long way from Eamon de Valera's project of a primitive world-wide web for Irish emigrants everywhere on the globe, but it at least met an identifiable, if limited need with rare precision.

Political broadcasting, however, was the area on which most new ground was being broken. Under Childers, permission was given for the first time for unscripted political discussions; the ban on members of parliament participating in broadcasts was removed; and, in the run-up to the 1954 general election, party political broadcasts were introduced for the first time. The political parties themselves reacted to some of these initiatives with suspicion, and the larger parties discovered that, by refusing to participate in political discussion programmes, they could stymie discussion on any topic on which they felt uncomfortable – and did so frequently.

Under Childers' new Council, broadcasting also moved into the scientific age, with the inauguration of listener research, carried out in a number of surveys in 1953, 1954 and 1955. The first enquiries revealed that 85% of the potential audience listened to Radio Eireann, compared with 53% for Radio Luxembourg and 49% for the BBC Light Programme (Gorham 1967: 229), and that there was an unexpectedly large audience for Irish dance music programmes. This was an oddity – Irish dancing on radio seems an unusual attraction at best – but the popularity was in all probability due largely to the personality of one its best known presenters, known as 'Din Joe'.

Audiences for programmes in the Irish language rarely achieved double figures, but this was perhaps to be expected. As Maurice Gorham noted mildly, Radio Eireann was:

expected to revive the speaking of Irish; to foster a taste for classical music; to revive Irish traditional music; to keep people on the farms, to sell goods and services of all kinds, from sausages to sweep tickets; to provide a living and a career for writers and musicians; to reunite the Irish people at home with those overseas; to end Partition. All this in addition to broadcasting's normal duty to inform, educate and entertain. And all in a programme time amounting (if advertising time was excluded) to some five and a half hours a day.

(Gorham 1967: 222)

As the audience figures for Radio Luxembourg and the BBC plainly indicated, Radio Eireann did not have the luxury of attempting to achieve these objectives in a vacuum. Its potential radio rivals, however, were now to be crowded almost off the stage by the arrival of a new and even more potent competitor: television. In 1950, the secretary of the Department of Posts and Telegraphs, Leon O Broin, had inaugurated a long war of attrition with his colleagues in the Department of Finance in an attempt to get them to take television seriously: initially, suspecting costly empire-building on the part of O Broin, Finance rebuffed his attempts brusquely. In April 1951, a commercial manufacturer of television sets, the Pye company, organised a demonstration of television at the Royal Dublin Society, which created immense public interest. Despite Finance's disapproval, O Broin inaugurated small-scale explorations of the topic.

By 1953, BBC television from Wales and Yorkshire was already capable of being received on parts of the Irish eastern seaboard. When the BBC opened its first transmitter in Belfast late in that year, the social and political reverberations were beginning to make themselves felt in Dublin (where viewing was free, as no television licence scheme was in existence). O Broin had set up a small departmental committee to study the whole problem, but Childers, for once, found this an innovation to which he did not readily warm. Too much television, he warned the Dail, would kill the art of conversation, and he would never recommend the establishment of any Irish television service 'that is not absolutely first class and directed towards the preservation of the national culture as well as for entertainment purposes' (DD: 10 November 1953). Positions were being prepared for the lengthy and complicated ideological and financial arguments that were to frame the eventual introduction of an Irish television service eight years later.

Northern Ireland: challenging the status quo

In the Northern Ireland print media, the post-war years changed little in the *Irish News* or the *Belfast Newsletter*. Technological developments were few or non-existent, and staffs remained small: the entire editorial staff of the *Irish News* during this period amounted to less than a dozen journalists (Phoenix 1995: 34). The most dramatic event of the period was the launching of an IRA campaign against Northern Ireland police barracks and other facilities in 1956, which lasted until 1962, and which attracted the attention of Northern Ireland newspapers in a by now wholly predictable way.

The context was broadly political in that the government which had come to power in Dublin in 1948 launched, in 1949, an organisation called the Anti-Partition League, an all-party body designed at least in part to remove the partition issue from the sphere of domestic politics. This organisation, funded by the government, became more proactive than Southern politicians had been hitherto, and established branches abroad as well as subventing political activity by nationalists within Northern Ireland. It also had a journalistic context. The *Sunday Press*, founded in 1949, regularly published features extolling the lives and exploits of the IRA during the war of independence. Noel Browne, Minister for Health in 1948–51 and a thorn in the side of almost every other government thereafter, accused de Valera in his autobiography of 'shamelessly fostering the cult of the warrior and the soldier' in his papers during this period (Browne 1986: 232). Certainly, the governments between 1948 and 1956 had to some extent put themselves in a cleft stick by increasing the ideological and political pressure for a removal of the border, and then finding themselves having to deal with the paramilitary expression of entirely similar sentiments. There was an equal dilemma for nationalist newspapers such as the *Irish News*, which was to some extent alleviated by the prompt action of the Catholic bishops in condemning the new IRA campaign. The *News* was as even-handed as any Catholic and nationalist newspaper could be in the circumstances, declaring in an editorial on 27 December 1956 that 'much unhappiness in Ireland springs from the British-made border ... But the unhappiness will be increased by acts that defy the instruction of the bishops and weaken Ireland's position as a Catholic nation' (Phoenix 1995: 33).

The *Belfast Telegraph*, however, was undergoing something like a transformation, at least in relative terms. Its managing director, Bobbie Baird, who was also an enthusiastic amateur racing driver, died in a racetrack accident in July 1953, necessitating a re-shuffle of responsibilities (and, incidentally, touching off a series of financial problems which was to end, nine years later, with the purchase of the paper by the Thomson organisation). The editor, Robert Sayers, was appointed chairman as Baird's successor; he was succeeded as editor by his nephew Jack Sayers, whose own father had edited the paper in the 1930s. At one level a merely dynastic change, it also heralded a somewhat unexpected change of style and tone. Hitherto impeccably Unionist in its general outlook and editorial line, the *Telegraph* now became a paper considerably more open to other agendas. John Cole, who worked on the *Telegraph* as a young journalist under Sayers and was later to rise to eminence in London journalism, summed him up:

> Sayers wanted to make the paper more politically serious and intelligent, a purpose with which I strongly agreed, though I was sometimes out of line on some issues. He was determined to influence politics in Northern

Ireland. He had returned from the navy to be appalled by the narrowness of political attitudes. He was a liberal unionist, and wanted to build bridges with the nationalist community. His editorial policy was eventually to alienate some influential Unionists, businessmen and others, and various management figures, I gather, made alarmed noises about the dangers of losing advertising. But Jack held firm, knowing that the advertisers needed the Telegraph as much as it needed them.

(Brodie 1995: 105–6)

Sayers was also the Northern Ireland correspondent of *The Round Table*, an influential journal of Commonwealth affairs. Here, shielded by anonymity, he appealed in vain to Unionists to cultivate the middle-class Catholic vote (Gailey 1995: 47). His belief in the possibility of progress was only briefly shaken by the eruption of the IRA border campaign in 1956, and, by the time of the Stormont general election of 1958, he was emboldened to open the feature pages of the newspaper to opposition parties. He welcomed the election of four Labour MPs on that occasion as a sign of the coming normalisation of Northern Ireland politics and, in his post-election editorial of 1 April, noted:

The Unionist Party must re-emphasise that it is a party of the centre. There is being created a body of moderates, Catholics among them, whose votes are being mobilised and will go, outside the most industrial constituencies, to the party that offers reasonable discussion and impartial dealing, true civil and religious liberty and equality of citizenship.

Official Unionism was not impressed, but the gamble – if indeed it was a gamble – paid off handsomely. Profits increased, allowing the purchase of state-of-the-art printing machinery in 1955, and by 1957 average daily sales were reaching between 195,000 and 200,000 copies, an extraordinary performance which made the *Telegraph* easily the largest-selling daily newspaper on the island. Sayers continued to preach his brand of liberal Unionism – even resigning in protest from the Orange Order in 1959 at a time when Unionism had officially set its face against even the possibility that Catholics might be allowed to join the Unionist Party (Gailey 1995: 57–8). But his paper missed one vital trick. When the introduction of commercial television was mooted in 1957, it became involved in negotiations with a number of newspaper and other interests with a view to joining a consortium to bid for the Northern Ireland independent television franchise. The board, however, was divided, and in December 1958 opted out of the consortium: the franchise eventually went to another consortium headed by the *Belfast Newsletter* (Brodie 1995: 119–20). It was to prove an expensive decision.

The arrival of Ulster Television (UTV) – the Northern Ireland franchise-holder in the Independent Television Network – at Halloween 1959 was an important staging post in a series of developments which had been initiated almost a decade earlier (Cathcart 1984: 156–89). BBC radio in Northern

Ireland had been settling down, and even breaking new ground: its radio drama series, *The McCooeys*, acquired an audience of some half a million listeners for its unique recipe of Ulster folksiness which contrived to avoid all references to religion, so that nobody could actually ascertain the religious or political affiliations of the eponymous family. A discussion programme entitled *Ulster Commentary* explored new territory, including discussion of the constitutional issue, initially tentatively and then with greater confidence. In 1953, moving into a slightly higher gear, BBC Northern Ireland invited Professor Theo Moody, a Quaker, who was professor of Irish history at Trinity College, Dublin, to be one of the organisers of a series of historical lectures which was broadcast (and subsequently published) under the title *Ulster since 1800*. This series, while it stayed clear of the potentially explosive more recent past, certainly involved a serious attempt to tackle contentious subjects. Moody, according to Cathcart (1984: 176), actually used this experience to persuade the Dublin broadcasting authorities to inaugurate their regular Thomas Davis lecture series, mentioned earlier, later the same year.

In January 1954 an unscripted discussion programme, *Your Questions*, showed that people could disagree politically on the airwaves in a civilised manner. In the same year, just after Radio Eireann, BBC Northern Ireland began scientific audience research, which was to show that – in sharp contrast with the other BBC regions – local programming was actually more popular than the network output (Cathcart 1984: 182). In 1956, a BBC radio studio in Derry was blown up by the IRA at the beginning of their armed campaign against Northern Ireland institutions, which was to proceed fitfully until its abandonment in 1962: the Derry explosion, like other aspects of that campaign, had no discernible result on broadcasting policy, although it contributed substantially and understandably to Unionist defensiveness in general.

If anyone had doubted the nature or extent of the sensitivities involved, the ongoing controversies about politics on the radio would have enlightened them. In 1949, 1952 and 1953, successive elections, either to the Stormont parliament or to Westminster, provided fruitful ground for disagreement in this area. The BBC wanted to extend the practice of party political broadcasts at election times to Northern Ireland, but there were two significant problems. One was the difficulty of taking on board the fact that – unlike elsewhere in the United Kingdom – one party to the election (the nationalists) would be arguing not just for political, but for constitutional change. The second was more predictable, but equally intractable: disagreement between the parties about the appropriate share-out of broadcast time. The combination of these two problems created stalemate until the election of 1958, when the nationalists, realising that generosity was the price of access to the airwaves, agreed to accept only one of the two non-Unionist broadcasts, allowing the other to go the Northern Ireland Labour Party, which at that time had no elected members in Stormont. The Unionists, who had been allocated five broadcasts, accepted, without noticeable enthusiasm, that this innovation would be unlikely to plunge the province headlong into a constitutional crisis.

The arrival of television, however, was to re-open a number of old sores, and even create a few new ones. The debate had begun as early as 1951, with the publication of the Beveridge Report on new structures for the BBC in the era of television; but the Beveridge proposal for each region to have its own commission, broadly representative of its community, was bedevilled by the deep nature of the divisions in Northern Ireland society, to such an extent that such a model was seen as clearly inoperable there, even by local interests. A broadcasting service designed for the whole community, the *Northern Whig* succinctly pointed out on 12 June 1952:

> should preserve a greater aloofness from possibly controversial matters, should not only be aloof but should be known to be aloof, and though in the result it may be less representative of the province than might otherwise be wished the gain must outweigh the loss.
>
> (Cathcart 1984: 167)

BBC television arrived in Northern Ireland in the spring of 1953, but the coverage of the booster station was initially small. It was not until a new transmitter on Divis Mountain outside Belfast came into operation in July 1955 that coverage reached some 80% of the Northern Ireland population. The first live broadcast from the Belfast studio – including an interview with the Northern Ireland prime minister, Lord Brookeborough, took place in November 1955. Coincidentally, this was also the year in which the first live television broadcast took place on the other side of the border. This was again organised by the BBC, and was of an Ireland v. England boxing tournament, which was relayed via Belfast and Scotland to a number of other European countries (Fisher 1978: 23). In the North, technical standards were again improved by the adoption of VHF in 1956.

The advent of BBC television to Northern Ireland, and the fact that it was followed in 1959 by ITV, not only created a new set of tensions within Northern Ireland itself, but had a demonstrable effect on the other side of the border where, as we have seen, the Secretary of the Department of Posts and Telegraphs, Leon O Broin, had been trying since 1953 to persuade the government to adopt a realistic attitude to the new medium. Political competition between the two parts of the Ireland was to give his campaign the fillip it desperately needed.

4 Television, 1957–73

The late 1950s in Ireland, North and South, gave rise to critical debates about the nature, control and function of television in both parts of Ireland. Initially, and especially in the South, the debates were primarily about structures and control: in the late 1960s, questions of content began to assume greater significance, partly because of the developing Northern Ireland political crisis, partly because of social and other changes which were ruffling old certainties.

In the Republic, the Posts and Telegraphs committee referred to in the previous chapter presented its report to government in September 1953. It was a subtly written document, pushing for the establishment of a limited television service, which would be confined initially to Dublin, partly on the grounds that the republic could not be seen to be lagging behind Northern Ireland. This carefully understated political agenda was buttressed by the suggestion that a wholly private, profit-driven service would have incalculably negative effects on the protection and development of traditional Irish culture. Given that the new service would be a monopoly, it argued that it should be under state control; given that it would be expensive, it should be financed by advertisements as well as by a licence fee; and, given that direct governmental control was inappropriate, it should be run by a government-appointed body (Savage 1996: 21–7).

The initial arguments about this report were coloured by the Department of Finance's misapprehension about what exactly Leon O Broin, secretary of the Department of Posts and Telegraphs, was proposing. They assumed that he envisaged a television service run by Posts and Telegraphs; but O Broin, as has been seen in relation to his dealings with Childers and the development of Radio Eireann, had for some time believed in the need to give broadcasting a measure of autonomy. All these arguments were, however, to some extent carried out in a vacuum, partly because of Finance's opposition, but partly also because of a generally negative attitude towards the electronic media – Dublin's politicians tended to mirror the belief of their Belfast counterparts that broadcasting was a necessary evil.

By early 1954, Childers had had a change of heart. His initial hesitancy overcome, he began to argue positively for the development of television, or at least for a planning process to begin. Before his enthusiasm could gather momentum, however, he and his government lost power in the 1954 general election, and were succeeded by a second inter-party or coalition government whose Minister for Posts and Telegraphs, Michael Keyes, was cool towards the idea. Pressure was building up, however, especially after the enhancement of the BBC signal strength in Northern Ireland in 1955, and the reception of the first ITV signals from mainland Britain. Politicians and journalists alike began to question the government's lethargy. As an editorial in *Comhar* asked in September 1953: 'Can we afford ... to do nothing to minimise this baneful influence? Are we satisfied to let England win the last fight so easily?' Private companies were also beginning to nibble at the edges of what appeared, to some of them at least, to be a potentially highly profitable proposition. Politicians were being drawn into the action: a senior member of Fine Gael, Sean Mac Eoin, acted as a lobbyist for one group; Childers himself, now in opposition, was arguing enthusiastically for the interests of a competitor, the UK firm Pye Ltd.

All these developments prompted O Broin and his committee to submit a further report to government in March 1956. To the arguments already adduced in favour of establishing a native television service, a new one was now added: the danger to Irish morals emanating from foreign broadcasts. Even the BBC's television output, the committee argued, was governed by concepts which were 'wholly alien to the ordinary Irish home'. Some offending programmes were:

> brazen, some 'frank' in sex matters, some merely inspired by the desire to exalt the British royal family and the British way of life ... [T]here is constant emphasis on ... the British view of world affairs, and the British (including Six County) achievements. The BBC's resources are lavishly expended on reporting every movement of the royal family at home and on tour.
>
> (Savage 1996: 46)

Robert Savage's seminal study of the origins of Irish television suggests that this argument was a natural expression of the sexual conservatism and political isolationism frequently regarded as characteristic of the Ireland of the 1950s. A longer perspective suggests that this may be to some extent unfair to O Broin and his committee, and presupposes an unusual degree of personal prudery on their part. It should be remembered that O Broin was first and foremost an exceptionally intelligent and literate civil servant (he wrote excellent history in his spare time) who was skilled, like most civil servants of his generation, in identifying and emphasising those arguments which might be expected to appeal best to ministers. The cabinets to which he addressed these reports were, for the most part, composed of ageing men, some of whom had been in politics for the best part of thirty years and were close to retirement. In addition, the 1954–7 coalition cabinet was notably more clericalist than its Fianna Fail predecessor, and might have been expected to pay serious attention to the warning of Pope Pius XII in 1955 that:

It is impossible not to be horrified at the thought that through the medium of television it may be possible for that atmosphere poisoned by materialism, fatuity and hedonism, which is too often breathed in many cinemas, to penetrate within the very walls of the home.

(Savage 1996: 110)

On the other hand, there was a central fallacy in the argument, of which O Broin and the other committee members could hardly have been unaware, and which supports the possibility that their emphasis on the moral issue may have been as much tactical as ideological. British television broadcasts were already, by the late 1950s, available to about 40% of the population of the Republic. To suggest that the advent of an Irish television service would eliminate or even dramatically reduce the attractiveness to the Irish audience of British television, with its huge budgets and sophisticated production values, would be extraordinarily unrealistic. And this is even more problematic in the case of broadcasts featuring British popular culture. The Irish mass audience for television has never found it difficult to combine a deeply rooted, and at times even visceral Republicanism, with a deep fascination with the activities of the house of Windsor. Common experience alone suggests that during the wedding between Prince Charles and Diana Spencer, social activity outside the workplace almost came to a complete halt in many parts of Ireland for a period of several hours. In this respect, at least, the possibility is that O Broin and his colleagues knew that, even if they could not turn back the tide, they could harness some of its power to their own purposes.

O Broin was prepared to seek allies anywhere, even in the BBC, whose programming he had so pungently criticised. Realising that the costs of a new Irish television service could be sharply reduced if some BBC programming – presumably not the sort to which he had objected – could be purchased at discounted rates, he tried unsuccessfully to get a commitment from the BBC in this regard. The BBC was, however, impressed by one of his key arguments – that letting the BBC influence the content of a new Irish television service would be a valuable quid pro quo for an Irish political decision to reject the American suitors who were promised to give the Irish government television for nothing. This, from O Broin's point of view, would have been the worst of all possible options, and his apprehension would have been increased by his knowledge that the Tanaiste, Sean Lemass, who was to succeed de Valera as Taoiseach in 1959, was a supporter of the private option (Horgan 1997: 310).

After the change of government in March 1957, the cabinet began to discuss the problem in an earnest, but apparently confused way. It decided in October to establish a television service 'as early as practicable … under public control … [and] so far as possible, without cost to the Exchequer' (NAI: Taoiseach: S 1499B). Less than a fortnight later the new Minister for Posts and Telegraphs, Neil Blaney, made a somewhat ambiguous announcement in which he intimated that the new service would be largely commercial in character, and that its entire capital and maintenance costs would be met by a promoting group or groups in consideration of a licence which would allow them to operate commercial programmes for a term of years (*IT*: 7 November 1957). It would be a condition of the licence, he added, that a certain proportion of the schedule would be available for programmes of a public service character.

This announcement touched off a major controversy. Senior broadcasting executives threatened resignation, an (unrelated) cabinet reshuffle moved Blaney elsewhere, and O Broin redoubled his efforts. His position received invaluable support from a senior political figure, the Minister for Finance, Sean MacEntee, who secured his colleagues' agreement early in 1958 for the establishment of a commission to look at the whole question, but whose terms of reference were expressly written to ensure:

> that no charge shall fall on the exchequer, either on capital or on current account, and that effective control of television programmes must be exercisable by an Irish public authority to be established as a television authority.
>
> (Keogh 1995: 33)

It was, in effect, an impossible task. The only way to ensure that television would be cost-free would be to entrust it to a commercial organisation; but no commercial organisation would be prepared to take it on board with the restrictions envisaged. Initially, this did not dissuade would-be suitors. They included a number of British and American and other interests from abroad, including Pye, and the Canadian media magnate Roy Thomson. Internally, Gael Linn, the Irish cultural and language organisation, offered to run the new service. After the publication of the report, but before the government had taken its decision, there was a late and indirect approach from the Vatican, where the Pope had apparently overcome his dislike of television to the extent that he was prepared to accept that, in safe, Catholic and Irish hands it could be used as a medium for the re-evangelisation of Continental Europe (Savage 1996: 154–5).

The difficulties encountered by the commission in reconciling its brief with the political and economic realities of the situation were evident in its final report, which was submitted to the government in May 1959. Four out of twenty members submitted a minority report, and some of those who signed the main report expressed personal reservations about aspects of it.

The commission concluded that handing over television to a private monopoly was the lesser of two evils or – given the way in which its terms of reference had been drafted – the only way in which no charge would fall on the exchequer. It advised the government that:

> if Ireland is to have a television service, and under the existing circumstances the commission does not accept that Ireland can afford to be without its own television service, it follows that the service must for the present be provided by private enterprise, notwithstanding the considerable

difficulties that are attendant on the establishment of a commercial service by private enterprise.

(Report of the Television Commission 1959: 23)

It also – and this is where its attempt to square the circle became most obvious – suggested that the public authority envisaged in its terms of reference should be appointed by, and answerable to, the government, and should have important programming functions. And it recommended that radio and television should be under two separate public authorities.

The completion and submission of the commission's report evoked a last, desperate throw from O Broin. In a memorandum to the government, written ostensibly on behalf of his minister as a commentary on an interim report from another government commission, which had been set up to recommend ways of protecting the Irish language, he combined criticism of some of that commission's more unrealistic suggestions with a subtle appeal to the known cultural proclivities of the cabinet. A programme contractor of the type envisaged, he argued, would be motivated solely by the prospect of private profit, and would by definition ignore national objectives – including the most important objective of all, the revival of the Irish language.

If television is to be used positively for national objectives, the proper procedure in the Minister's view is that the Television Authority should itself operate the programmes – that is – all the programmes.

(NAI: Communications: T007/57)

Two months later the Taoiseach, Eamon de Valera, had resigned, and his place had been taken by his deputy Sean Lemass, who favoured the privatisation option. It is all the more remarkable, therefore, that one of the first cabinet meetings over which Lemass presided, on 31 July 1959, rejected the commission's core proposal, and decided instead that the new service should be provided under a public statutory authority alone.

On the face of it, this was an extraordinary *volte face* by Lemass, but there is strong circumstantial evidence that he was an unwilling convert. In the first place, he tried to keep the door open for one of the unsuccessful foreign bidders even after the decision had been taken, attempting unsuccessfully to persuade his Minister for Posts and Telegraphs to interest the disappointed businessman in the prospect of establishing 'profitable' international sound broadcasting from Ireland (NAI: Communications: T007/57). Second, he allowed it to be known after his retirement, through a political journalist who was a confidant of his, that his cabinet colleagues had out-voted him on the issue (*IP*: 18 January 1969). De Valera had departed; but Lemass had inherited, and made only minimal changes in, the cabinet which de Valera had appointed, and which contained a strong majority favouring the older man's point of view. They would also have been far more receptive than Lemass to O Broin's final, successful plea (Horgan 1997: 312).

The broadcasting legislation which was eventually drafted on the basis of this government decision became law as the 1960 Broadcasting Act. By now, the number of radio licences had increased to some 500,000, but the number of television sets, though increasing rapidly, was still probably less than 50,000. The Act set up a new Authority, known as the Radio Eireann Authority (it later became the Radio Telefis Eireann Authority), whose members were appointed by the government. In general terms, the Authority was given a relatively free hand in managing the new service, but the government retained a number of functions. One of these was to decide on the length of the broadcasting day, and the amount of advertising permitted; another was the licensing of broadcast stations. Section 17 of the Act required the Authority to 'bear constantly in mind the national aims of restoring the Irish language and preserving and developing the national culture'; Section 18 laid down that, in news, current affairs and matters which were the subject of controversy, the station should present material objectively and impartially and without any expression of the Authority's own views.

The only other section of the Act dealing in any way with programming, and which was to prove one of its most controversial aspects (although not thought so at the time) was Section 31, which empowered the government to issue a directive to the Authority in writing at any time prohibiting the broadcast of specified material, or insisting on the broadcasting of specified material. It was to be a decade before this provision was first implemented, at the height of the conflict which was to erupt in Northern Ireland in 1968. Although an IRA paramilitary campaign against the British presence in Northern Ireland had started in 1956 and was still in progress in 1960 (it was abandoned formally in 1962, although it had been of very low intensity for some years prior to that date), at the time the Act was passed in 1960, it was not even considered relevant to the debate about broadcasting.

The 1960 Act was, according to one authority, a relatively forward-looking piece of legislation, given the era in which it was drafted.

> It gave the broadcasting authority a great measure of autonomy, protected by legislation, and it ensured that any government directives which would affect programming had to be served on the Authority in writing. Given the particular circumstances of Ireland, still a comparatively young state, born in violence and immediately afterwards torn by civil war, with a continuing internal security threat, an unsolved problem as regards Northern Ireland, economically under-developed and sociologically unsettled, it was a remarkably liberal piece of legislation and, by and large, provided a sound statutory framework for the first fifteen years of the restructured broadcasting service as it entered the television age.
>
> (Fisher 1978: 27)

The context within which the Act was introduced, however, was more volatile than either government or broadcasters knew. De Valera's resignation in 1959, after more than thirty years as leader of his party – twenty-one of them as Taoiseach – was widely seen as symbolic of the departure of the political old guard. Leadership in the other major political parties was changing, too. The economy was improving, with the introduction of Keynesian economic planning in 1958; the level of popular education was rising; the emigration which had drained the country of some of its most vital human resources, especially in the 1950s, was lessening; urbanisation was increasing; and – whether prompted by the pernicious television programmes identified a few years earlier or not – social attitudes were undergoing an accelerated process of challenge and change.

Lemass, although himself a moderniser, was conscious of the dangers inherent in the new medium, and at one stage, even before the new service had been inaugurated, contemplated issuing a formal directive under Section 31 ordering the Authority, among other things, to pay particular attention to the 'image' of Ireland which would be presented, 'including the avoidance of stage-Irishisms, playboyisms', etc. Insofar as social problems were concerned, he thought, the desirable course would be to encourage objective presentation of facts and constructive comment. 'The "God-help-us" approach should be ruled out', he instructed. He had originally planned to codify these instructions as part of a formal government directive to the new station, but was dissuaded from this course of action by a senior civil servant who warned him that this approach might be seen as illiberal (Keogh 1995: 32).

The inauguration of the new service, on New Year's Eve 1961, was notable for a number of things. One was the gloomy attitude of the former Taoiseach, Eamon de Valera, now President of Ireland, who warned his audience about the dangers of the new medium even as he inaugurated its first broadcast: 'I must admit that sometimes when I think of television and radio and their immense power I feel somewhat afraid ... [it] can lead through demoralisation to decadence and dissolution' (*IP*: 1 January 1962). Another was the broad welcome from the print media, apparently as yet unaware of the threat it would pose to their advertising revenues. Critics wrote a daily review of the programming and, although some of it was criticised for having 'very little protein content' (*II*: 2 January 1962), there was a general air of excitement and celebration.

Under these circumstances, television immediately became a battleground in a way radio had never been. Some of the critics gave the appearance of having been lying in wait in the long grass: the Revd P. O'Higgins, S.J., Assistant Director of the Pioneer Total Abstinence Association, was quickly off the mark to say that he was 'appalled to see on one of the commercials very young people making whoopee with drinks in their hands' (*II*: 18 January 1962). Other conflicts were more intense, and of longer duration. They were principally in the areas of politics, of culture and of religion.

By simultaneously setting up a new service – television – and removing all broadcasting from the direct control of government, the cabinet had effectively taken two large steps in one. They had given themselves a residual right of control under Section 31, and they also retained the right to dismiss the

Authority, but these were guns that could each be fired only once. There were no formal channels through which they could communicate their views to the Authority, short of issuing a directive, and if they were dissatisfied with or annoyed by the station's output they were required (short of dismissing the Authority) to suffer in silence.

Suffering in silence does not come naturally to the average cabinet minister, and the early forays by Irish television commentators and presenters into politics and current affairs made many of them bristle. The tentative but – relatively speaking – venturesome initiatives of some broadcasters were in turn fuelled by a desire to hold politicians to account in a way that the media had rarely done up to now. This desire was accentuated by the weakness of orthodox political opposition: there was no prospect of an alternative government unless the two major opposition parties were to combine, and the smaller of these, the Labour Party, had set its face firmly against going into government with any other party. Under these circumstances, the eager young graduates in politics and history who filled the new positions in the current affairs programme slots found themselves often making an opposition case by default. Government ministers, unused to the journalistic conventions that sometimes make interviewers ask provocative questions which do not necessarily reflect their own point of view, sometimes mistook liveliness for wholesale subversion. The RTE current affairs programme *Broadsheet* was regarded as a prime offender. Lemass, as Taoiseach, frequently intervened privately with the director-general of the broadcasting station in attempts to secure what he believed would be a fairer hearing for government policy on this particular programme (Horgan 1997: 316). It was, he told an aide in 1962, becoming increasingly 'a medium for the uncritical presentation of the views of persons associated with various ramps and crank projects', and broadcasters should 'take the whine out of their voice' (NAI: Taoiseach: S 3532 C/63).

The most dramatic conflict in this area took place in 1966, shortly before Lemass retired. The government was in conflict with the National Farmers' Association about agricultural policy, and it became known that a cabinet minister had contacted the television station unofficially to complain about an alleged lack of balance on the issue in one of its news broadcasts. Queried about this in the Dail, Lemass made no bones about it: the government, he said, would take such action by way of making representations or otherwise as might be necessary to ensure that Radio Telefis Eireann (RTE) did not deviate from the due performance of its duty. And he defined the duty:

> Radio Telefis Eireann was set up by legislation as an instrument of public policy and as such is responsible to the Government. The Government have over-all responsibility for its conduct and especially the obligation to ensure that its programmes do not offend against the public interest or conflict with national policy as defined in legislation. To this extent the Government reject the view that RTE should be, either generally or in regard to its current affairs and news programmes, completely independent

of Government supervision. As a public institution supported by public funds and operating under statute, it has the duty, while maintaining impartiality between political parties, to present programmes which inform the public regarding current affairs, to sustain public respect for the institutions of Government and, where appropriate, to assist public understanding of the policies enshrined in legislation enacted by the Oireachtas.

(DD: 12 October 1966)

This gloss on the Broadcasting Act provoked widespread controversy. Although it might be going too far to say, as some of his critics did, that Lemass was here equating 'public policy' with 'government policy' (Doolan 1969: 205), it was unmistakably the first public exchange in a war that had been subterranean but was now assuming a much more open character. RTE's broadcasters retaliated spiritedly, with a week of programmes dedicated to the issue of media freedom, and even managed to internationalise it to some extent, by securing an airing for their views on US television. The government, for its part, was not greatly discommoded: in 1967, it intervened directly to prevent the station sending a television crew to North Vietnam (NAI: Taoiseach: 98/6/19) and, in January 1968, to prevent another crew being sent to the breakaway state of Biafra, which was attempting to secede from the Federal Republic of Nigeria, and in which many Irish Catholic missionaries were working. The dangers of a clash between the broadcasting agenda and Irish foreign policy, which did not want to offend the legal Nigerian government unnecessarily (even though it was a military dictatorship), and which favoured the US role in world affairs, was the prime motivating factor in each case. In 1969, there was another major controversy involving a current affairs programme on illegal money-lending in Dublin. The Garda Siochana were outraged at a suggestion in the programme that they were not doing enough to stamp out this activity, and put pressure on the government, which led to the establishment of a lengthy judicial tribunal to enquire, not into illegal money-lending, but into the *bona fides* of the programme itself. Unsurprisingly, this tribunal came to the conclusion that the programme had not provided legally convincing evidence for its allegations. Television was still, at this stage, a primarily urban phenomenon: a 1967 survey found that the proportion of rural households with television was as low as 25% in some areas; by 1978, only just over half of the households (54%) in Connacht had television, compared with 92% in Dublin (Brown 1981: 261).

There were further controversies about the role of current affairs broadcasting in political affairs, involving lengthy negotiations between party whips and producers about the ratio between participants from government parties and those from the opposition. These skirmishes resulted, by and large and not without tension and disagreement, in an incremental improvement in the freedom of the station and in the willingness of politicians to accept a measure of accountability. The basic mood has been accurately described as one in which current affairs broadcasters 'have generally aligned themselves with a middle ground which is progressive and social democratic' (Kelly 1984: 98).

In the area of culture, the Irish language was at the centre of controversy. The Authority was criticised from both ends of the spectrum. Irish-language organisations took up the running initially, claiming that the Authority was failing to fulfil its obligations under the Act because it did not broadcast enough programming in Irish. Later, and especially after the foundation in 1964 of an organisation called the Language Freedom Movement, dedicated to abolishing compulsory Irish in schools and as a requirement for positions in the public service, it found itself criticised for broadcasting too much.

In its first annual report for 1960–61, the Authority declared that it had set out to provide a programme service which:

> as far as possible would have a distinctively Irish quality, would reflect traditional Irish values and would recognise Radio Eireann's responsibility as a public service concerned with cultural and educational matters as well as with the provision of news and entertainment.
>
> (Fisher 1978: 31)

The unspoken argument was that it was also a station which had to pay its own way in the world, and leaning too far in the direction of a proactive policy on Irish would, in a medium where the competition for viewers (and hence advertisers) was becoming daily more intense, undermine its position in the marketplace. In the circumstances, it had to steer an unsteady middle course, which ended up by satisfying no one. It rejected the idea of ghettoising Irish-language programming, devoted substantial resources to children's programmes in Irish in particular, and probably played a substantial part in the popularisation of Irish traditional music that was to achieve an international dimension in the 1970s and 1980s. Although each of the first two Authorities had been well-freighted with enthusiasts for the language, the second authority adopted a more interventionist approach than its predecessor. After the publication of the report of the Commission on the Restoration of the Irish Language in 1964, the pressure from this group for the state broadcasting service to play an even larger role in the language revival movement became so strong that it led eventually to the resignation of the Authority's chairman, the broadcaster Eamonn Andrews (Horgan 1997: 320).

Pressure continued to mount, and the formation in 1969 of an organisation to campaign for greater rights for Irish speakers – Gluaiseacht ar Son Cearta Sibhialta na Gaeltachta ('Movement on behalf of Civil Rights for the Irish-speaking Areas') saw an intensification of protests against what were seen as RTE's inadequacies in this area. A pirate Irish-language radio station, Saor Raidio Chonamara ('Connemara Free Radio') was established on 28 March 1970 (Ó Glaisne 1982: 29), but was quickly snuffed out by the police. Political pressure followed, with questions in parliament, and RTE then moved swiftly in 1970 to obviate any challenge to its monopoly by accepting the need for a separate Gaeltacht station, and setting it up within the existing RTE structures. It began broadcasting in April 1972 from purpose-built studios in Casla in Connemara, and its function was originally envisaged as providing a service from a number of subsidiary studios, purely for the Gaeltacht communities, dispersed as they were between the non-contiguous areas of Connemara, Donegal, Munster and Meath. The first interlinked broadcast from these studios took place in 1973. As the service has been nationally available for many years, it also has an audience outside the Gaeltacht areas: a 1994 survey suggested that it had succeeded in attracting and retaining some 15% of the national radio audience, on a regular or occasional basis, during the preceding decade (Watson 1997: 218).

The question of religion was another, almost equally sensitive area. In 1962, three of the country's Catholic bishops took the unusual step of seeking – and obtaining – a private meeting with Lemass in which they complained about the religious views (or lack of views) of three named broadcasters (Horgan 1997: 317–18). Lemass defused the situation, and the station moved towards appointing an adviser on religious programmes. Here too the bishops suffered a setback. Archbishop John Charles McQuaid of Dublin, in whose diocese the broadcasting studios were situated and who was an advocate of the doctrine of episcopal territoriality, had trained one of his younger priests in television and film techniques, in the confident expectation that this man would be appointed to the new position. The Authority, however, looked elsewhere, and employed instead a genial Dominican priest who, as a member of a religious order, was not subject directly to the Archbishop's authority, and who played a delicate and important role during the formative years of Irish television with great tact and good humour. The Archbishop's loss, as it turned out, was broadcasting's gain: Dr McQuaid established an independent studio for the young priest, Fr Joe Dunn, who, over the next three decades, with a team of clerical and lay people whom he himself recruited and trained, created a series of some 400 television documentaries under the Radharc ('View') label. Many of these were broadcast on RTE itself and indeed also on foreign stations: taken together, they represent a remarkable contribution to the genre, and to the social and media history of modern Ireland. The decision to keep RTE, and indeed Irish broadcasting generally, at some distance from the power of the Catholic Church was further exemplified in 1965 when Lemass responded negatively to a proposal (which had been made to him by Pope Paul VI during an audience in Rome) that Ireland should establish a Catholic radio station capable of transmitting programmes to Britain and further afield. This refusal, however, may be regarded as somewhat qualified by the view of the Minister for Posts and Telegraphs, Michael Hilliard. 'I have always felt', he wrote to Lemass on 9 April 1965, 'that the proper answer to suggestions for a Catholic station is that we have one already in Radio Eireann' (NAI: DFA: 96/2/14).

It was outside the area of direct religious broadcasting, however, that tensions were sharpest. The advent of a new entertainment programme in the summer of 1962 – it was originally designed as a 'filler' programme, to be taken off again after the summer was over – heralded a new talent, and a new approach which was to have a profound effect on Irish social mores. This was the *Late Late Show*, moderated by Gay Byrne, who had left a career in insurance for one in light entertainment. Byrne's deft choice of topics, and even defter handling of a wide range of personalities (many of them controversial, some of them wild, others dedicated to the art of public confession) immediately set a stamp on the new station which was peculiarly its own. The programme, which was broadcast on Saturday evenings, became – for an Irish public unaccustomed to the public flouting of taboos – an unmissable weekly occasion. One of the biggest single taboos, as might be expected, related to the public discussion of sexual matters, and here the tension was often not just social, but inter-generational. It has been captured expertly by the novelist Colm Toibín.

> In Enniscorthy when I was a lad we all sat glued to it. We were often embarrassed that someone was talking about sex: there were older people in the room who didn't like sex being talked about … If any other programme talked about sex, it would have been turned off. Turn that rubbish off. But nobody ever turned the *Late Late Show* off. The show was too unpre-dictable: you just never knew what you might miss.
>
> (Toibín 1990: 87)

But the programme was about more than sex. It was also about politics. Politicians initially rejected its attempts to inveigle them in front of the cameras in such a highly unstructured, and therefore risky, format, and continued to do so until the early 1970s (NAI: Taoiseach: 98/6/20); but they could not resist the lure of such huge exposure to the electorate indefinitely. And it was also about religion: its reputation, never seriously in doubt after the early months, grew exponentially when, in 1966, an angry bishop publicly criti-cised the programme. It was also, incrementally, about the development of a new orthodoxy, which challenged the old, Gaelic and somewhat authoritarian one, or at least constructed an alternative lens through which it might be viewed, and presented that orthodoxy attractively interleaved with a wide variety of traditional, pop and on occasion even classical music. That new orthodoxy was not without its own questionable aspects: but television, and Byrne, created a dynamic where before there had been stasis, or at best tortoise-like movement. As one of Ireland's foremost cultural historians put it:

> The apparently unscripted nature of the show, which moved abruptly from levity to gravity, from frivolity to major social issues, without any warning, made it compulsive viewing for audiences. The paradoxical manner with which the programme combined a home-spun intimacy with 'Brechtian' television techniques (displaying studio technology, the presenter himself calling the shots at times) gave it a place in life not unlike that of the provincial newspaper: people watched it if only because they were afraid they might miss out on something.
>
> (Gibbons 1996: 79)

Another view was that the reasons for the popularity of Byrne's programmes (he had an influential morning programme on radio as well) were related primarily to the social context, to the silence about issues which had become an all-enveloping fog. 'Surrounded by that silence, we wanted, in the 1960s, to hear ourselves speak in a charming, sophisticated and worldly-wise voice' (O'Toole 1990: 168). This incremental, sometimes contested attempt to modify the context within which Irish social issues were discussed, was not confined to news, current affairs and the *Late Late Show*, but extended into other entertainment areas, notably drama (Sheehan 1987). One study tracing the development of Irish television drama from its inception in 1961 to the 1980s, and concentrating on the long-running serials *The Riordans* and *Tolka Row* (rural and urban respectively), suggested that the former programme, in particular, 'made deep inroads on a dominant ideology which looked on the family – and indeed the family farm – as the basic unit of Irish society' (Gibbons 1984: 43). The same serial has been endorsed for the way in which it gave women a central and progressive role in television drama (O'Connor 1984: 130). A related essay, focusing more sharply on the urban *Tolka Row* drama, although critical of what it described as the series' tendency to confirm rural stereotypes of city life, argued that it was 'an attempt at re-inserting the missing discourse of the urban working class into Irish culture and, as such, can be seen as an important element in television's wider ideological project' (McLoone 1984: 63). RTE, however, did not always represent a uniformly liberal agenda: in 1967, it incurred odium and ridicule in almost equal proportions after instituting its own ban on the broadcasting of a ballad by the Dubliners, 'Seven Drunken Nights', because of its references to alcohol and adultery (NAI: Taoiseach: 98/6/83).

Many of these arguments, however, rapidly took second place to the overarching debate about television's role in the developing crisis in Northern Ireland, which began to take shape in 1968 and, by 1969, erupted into political violence of an intensity and on a scale not seen for at least three decades. What happened was as unexpected for the media as it was for the political establishments in Dublin, Belfast and London. RTE, for example, had no permanent office or studio facilities in Belfast in 1968.

In May 1970 there was a political crisis in Dublin, when two cabinet ministers were dismissed from the cabinet and subsequently charged with an attempt to import arms illegally for use by nationalists in Northern Ireland. Neither was convicted, but the government was deeply shaken, and the media excitement about what was going on was intense. There was an initial stand-off between government and broadcasters in June 1971, when the Taoiseach, Jack Lynch (since 1966), expressed the view that it was unsuitable to use a publicly funded broadcasting system to interview for transmission members of an illegal organisation, i.e. the IRA (DD: 24 June 1971). RTE responded that the programme would be amended only if a directive was received under Section 31 of the Broadcasting Act: no directive was issued.

Not long afterwards, on 28 September, the current affairs RTE Programme *Seven Days* carried interviews with leading members of both branches of the IRA (which had become divided along ideological lines, with one group emphasising a military solution, the other social radicalism). This, evidently seen by the government as a direct challenge to its authority, prompted the issue on 1 October, by the Minister for Posts and Telegraphs, of the first directive under Section 31, which instructed the Authority to:

> refrain from broadcasting any matter that could be calculated to promote the aims or activities of any organisation which engages in, promotes, encourages or advocates the attaining of any political objective by violent means.
>
> (MacDermott 1995: 31)

This directive, which by law had to be re-issued annually, was to remain in force in one guise or another until January 1994. It is certainly significant that neither in 1970 nor in any subsequent year did any member of parliament raise any objection, in parliament, to its imposition or renewal. Procedurally, the renewal of the directive did not need to be debated unless a member of either house of the Oireachtas (Dail or Seanad) put down a motion to reject it: no such motion was ever tabled. At this remove in time from the events concerned, such a lack of concern with a major restriction on freedom of speech is difficult to understand, but the historical context suggests a number of reasons. These include a fear among politicians of all parties that the Northern conflict might spill over the border into the Republic (as, on occasion, it did); strict party discipline; and an unwillingness on the part of any elected representative to take an action which could be interpreted as supporting the IRA. It is also noteworthy that the newspapers offered scant comfort to their colleagues in broadcasting: the *Irish Times*, for instance, suggested on 2 October, in the immediate aftermath of the government's action, that RTE's coverage of the Northern conflict had been marked by 'too much breathlessness' and even suggested that its lack of judgement might lead to staff changes.

The wording of the directive, despite its apparent clarity, offered little in the way of concrete operational guidance to RTE. Its breadth – theoretically, it could have operated to ban all reports of organisations everywhere in the world, including for example the African National Congress in South Africa – was enhanced by a studied ambiguity, which may well have been designed for intimidatory effect. The RTE Authority sought clarification, which was refused. The government put on further pressure in June 1972, when it met the authority to complain about its broadcast of mute film of IRA members. Later the same year, the situation escalated out of control when RTE broadcast on 19 November a radio report based on an interview by one of its reporters, Kevin O'Kelly, with a senior IRA figure, Sean Mac Stiofain, who, as it happened, was not publicly named in the course of the report. The government demanded an explanation and the Authority responded that although they agreed that in retrospect the interview had been a lapse of editorial judgement, they felt it was an internal RTE matter. The government rejected this explanation as unsatisfactory, dismissed the Authority in its entirety on 24 November, and appointed a new one. Subsequently, the IRA leader who had been interviewed was arrested and put on trial. RTE were forced to surrender the tape of the interview but, in court, the journalist who had carried out the interview, Kevin O'Kelly, refused to identify the defendant as his interviewee and was sentenced to a prison term – later reduced to a fine – for contempt of court.

These events created widespread public controversy, including protests by journalists employed by RTE. One distinguished commentator, Basil Chubb, professor of Politics at Trinity College, Dublin, went so far as to call for news and current affairs to be separated from the rest of broadcasting 'under the control of an independent board that … has the will and the courage to insist that Government interference be formal and public and to resist covert pressure' (*IT*: 31 August 1972). Later, he was to observe that this increasingly lengthy list of instances of government involvement in the affairs of the national broadcaster 'were seen as a sinister catalogue of events by some, and could hardly be viewed with equanimity by anyone' (Chubb 1974: 81).

The Northern situation generally ensured that the government was already suffering from some instability and so, early in 1973, Lynch called a snap general election to secure his position. He succeeded in increasing his party's vote, but a decision by the two opposition parties to join forces for the first time since 1954 saw him lose office. The new Minister for Telegraphs was Dr Conor Cruise O'Brien, who had been a Labour member of the Dail since 1969.

Mainstream national print media in the Republic experienced the late 1950s and early 1960s as a period of relative calm. The *Irish Times* was undergoing a process of retrenchment, especially with the closure of the *Evening Mail* and the *Sunday Review*, but board changes at that paper were paving the way for developments which would see it expand considerably towards the end of the decade. Douglas Gageby, a Dublin-born but Belfast-raised Protestant nationalist, who had played a key role in the establishment and promotion of both the *Sunday Press* and the *Evening Press*, accepted an invitation to join the *Irish Times* board in 1959. Between then and 1963 he attempted, without a great deal of success, to broaden the paper's appeal, and then an unexpected editorial vacancy in the latter year saw him assume full editorial control. For the next decade, he consciously moved to expand the paper's boundaries, northward and westward, and away from the Dublin metropolitan area, which at that time accounted for a large proportion of the paper's total sales. Major T.B. McDowell, the paper's managing director, who had originally invited him on to the board, facilitated this process by creating new financial systems within the paper, giving editorial executives much greater budgetary control.

Like RTE, none of the Dublin newspapers had a substantial presence in Northern Ireland in the early 1960s. The *Irish Times* broke new ground in this area, not only by reporting the Northern Ireland parliament at Stormont at considerable length (its new Belfast correspondent, Fergus Pyle, was to become editor of the paper for a period in the 1970s) but by sending reporters, feature writers and others North of the border to interview the younger generation of Northern Ireland politicians and to assess the situation.

This enlargement of the newspaper's agenda was complemented, geographically, by the development of a key interest – and appropriate editorial coverage – in non-metropolitan Ireland, particularly the West. Intellectually and journalistically, it was accompanied by the development of a cadre of specialist writers. These were – unusually for the time – given their own by-lines, and their work, focusing on areas like education, religion and women's affairs, to some extent reflected, and to some extent informed, the changes that were then taking place in Irish society. It pioneered, too, investigative features on controversial topics, most notably as written by Michael Viney, a gifted young English journalist whose lengthy, fully researched series on topics such as divorce, illegitimacy and adoption broke important new ground, and contributed substantially to growth in the paper's circulation as they were extensively promoted and ran in the newspaper on successive days for up to a week each.

Changes were slower to take place elsewhere, but they were happening nonetheless. At the *Irish Press*, revenues and circulation were healthy, but there was an underlying sense of stasis, created by the still-dominant presence of Eamon de Valera, now nearing the end of his active political career. As he prepared to leave office and inaugurated his campaign for the presidency, which he was to fill for the next fourteen years, he was harried mercilessly in the Dail by Noel Browne and a colleague, Jack McQuillan, the only members of the tiny National Progressive Democrat Political Party, who had done research into the ownership structure of the *Irish Press*. In a withering attack timed to do maximum damage to de Valera's campaign for the presidency, they accused him directly of a conflict of interest – a charge which stung, even in those relatively laissez-faire days, and which would have been even more damaging if directed with as much evidence against a public figure in the 1990s (Coogan 1993a: 674–7). But there was, at the *Irish Press*, another malaise, mostly on the industrial relations front, which boded ill for the future. For the time being, this was concealed by the fact that the Press group formed part of a consortium of Dublin newspaper managers, who met trade unions as a group and who operated a 'one out, all out' policy which meant that unions (which to all intents and purposes meant the print unions, the strongest in the industry) could not pick off employers one by one.

The strength of this arrangement was evident in the course of a major strike by printers in the summer of 1965, which closed down all the capital's newspapers. That strike was settled, partly because of the firmness of the employers, but also because of a factor which underlined the commercial role of newspapers in the city's life. The *Evening Press*, at that time, was the primary vehicle for full-page advertisements by major retail stores, in which the availability and prices of a wide range of items, from kitchen utensils to clothing, would be spelt out in great detail. This was not primarily for the benefit of urban dwellers, who could ascertain prices and availability for themselves, but for non-metropolitan readers, who used these advertisements as essential information on their carefully planned excursions to the capital.

At the height of the strike, a deputation of centre city traders came to see the *Irish Press* management to explain that, since the strike had begun, their turnover had fallen by between 30% and 40%. The newspaper's managers explained that the cost of settling the strike on the printers' terms was prohibitive; and the traders agreed to subvent the cost of settlement by increasing their display advertising by a guaranteed percentage for a period after the papers came back on the street.

The daily *Irish Press* also secured a new editor in 1968. This was Tim Pat Coogan: his appointment was unusual for a Fianna Fail paper in that he was the son of a former Garda Commissioner whose allegiance to the Fine Gael party had been well-known. But Coogan, who had served his apprenticeship on the *Evening Press*, was an editor of considerable dynamism. The founder of the *Irish Press*, Eamon de Valera, was now president of Ireland and long removed from any active involvement in the running of the paper. His son Vivion, who had taken over the reins, was also a back-bench government member of the Dail. The paper was still starved of resources and capital: it would run issues of 16 pages when its rivals, the *Irish Times* and *Irish Independent*, were producing 30- or 40-page papers – but editorially Coogan had a measure of freedom, which he used to good effect. He enhanced the work of the paper's independent political correspondent, Michael Mills, by preventing sub-editors from shortening his reports unnecessarily; he employed a corps of effervescent young women journalists, some of whom – like Mary Kenny and Anne Harris – went on to greater heights in Irish and British journalism; and he encouraged his literary editor, David Marcus, in the production in 1968 of a regular page of 'New Irish Writing' in which many young writers who became deservedly famous in the 1970s and 1980s first cut their teeth.

The 1965 strike, already noted, seemed on the surface to represent a victory for the employers over the printers. But it had been bought at a high price and, when the printers again went on strike in 1973, the employers' line wavered. As it happened, the strike coincided with a general election. On the day the new government was formed, the *Irish Times* broke the one out, all out agreement with the other newspaper managements, and appeared on the streets on its own. It published a front page explanation for its decision, adding that it would not capitalise on the situation by printing additional newspapers. The next day, the *Irish Independent* and the *Irish Press* settled with the printers and followed suit.

This was to have long-term consequences for the *Irish Press* in particular. Shorn of the protection of the other managements, and bedevilled by a long history of poor industrial relations, it was now in an exceptionally weak position to face the long period of readjustment that was to accompany the arrival of the new generation of newspaper technology. Although the drama and controversy of events in the North from 1968 were to enhance its circulation sporadically, this was not enough to prevent the erosion of its readership and commercial bases by other factors which are dealt with in more detail in Chapter 5.

The *Irish Independent* and its associated evening and Sunday newspapers were to change little, so far as a casual outside observer might notice during the 1960s, but the daily newspaper in particular was changing internally in ways which began to set a question mark against its stereotype as a Fine Gael-supporting, conservative Catholic newspaper. Its editor, Frank Geary, was a newspaperman of the old school, in that comprehensiveness and accuracy were his two core values. Although this made him to some extent indifferent to the new journalism of opinion and investigation that was developing elsewhere, particularly in the *Irish Times*, he gave some of his younger staff a relatively free hand, particularly in the area of editorials and features: the feature department was effectively controlled by a small group of leader-writers, in a way which was structurally different from the other national papers, which had editorial executives with specific responsibility for feature areas.

Its innovations in this area included a regular weekly survey of the Continental European press, which it inaugurated in the wake of Ireland's first – and unsuccessful – application to join the Common Market in 1963. It became probably the first Irish newspaper from the nationalist tradition to salute the memory of those Irishmen who had died in the First World War: one of its editorials, on the fiftieth anniversary of the outbreak of that war, consisted in its entirety of the well-known poem 'For a Dream', written by the Irish poet and patriot, Tom Kettle, shortly before he died on the Somme (4 August 1964).

In June 1965, it became the only national newspaper to express specifically editorial support for the writer John McGahern, whose book *The Dark* had been banned by the Censorship Board. Although it was to some extent critical of the book, it commented:

> What matters is that Mr. McGahern has taken a most serious topic, the misery that assails an adolescent mind; he tackles it seriously, with sympathy and sincerity; he sets it in a framework which, we believe, undermines the value of what he has tried to do but which has no bearing whatever on the author's intention or his effect.
>
> (3 June 1965)

In April 1966, it not only mended its ideological fences with some finality by saluting the fiftieth anniversary of the Easter Rising (which it had roundly condemned at the time, going so far as to urge the British authorities to execute – but without naming him – the socialist leader James Connolly) but marked a significant break with its stance during the Spanish civil war by publishing, in May, an editorial condemning Franco's repression of striking miners in the Asturias.

Geary was succeeded in 1968 by Louis MacRedmond, a young barrister who had been in charge of these editorial writers, and whose editorial stance embodied a more open and sometimes critical, though always loyal, attitude towards the Catholic Church than had been customary under his predecessors.

In 1969, however, following a momentary downturn in the paper's profits, he was dismissed (technically, the board said that they wanted him to assume other responsibilities, but there was little doubt but that a dismissal was what actually occurred). Unusually, all his journalistic staff made a token protest by leaving the building during the production process and parading around the block, after he had dissuaded them from actually going on strike. Even more unusually for Irish journalism, his principal rival, the editor of the *Irish Times*, Douglas Gageby, immediately put him on a retainer, and published frequent articles by him until he again secured permanent employment.

Outside the mainstream media, increasing economic activity, the new volatility in political life and the wider availability of higher education was producing a potential market among literate young readers, and this was met at least in part with the publication of a fortnightly current affairs magazine, *Hibernia*. The magazine as such had existed since 1937 as a monthly paper aimed at the Catholic middle classes, and contained a smattering of current affairs. In 1968, however, one of its contributors, John Mulcahy, acquired the paper from its proprietor, and turned it into a lively, irreverent and often well-informed magazine which specialised in an eclectic but highly marketable mix of political gossip and features, book reviews, and authoritative business and financial journalism. Its tone was crusading and investigative: by 1973 it was already carrying articles alleging conflicts of interest and possible corruption in relation to the activities of local politicians in the Greater Dublin area – an issue which resurfaced, with dramatic effect, at the end of the 1990s. After an expensive libel action in 1976, and a risky expansion to weekly publication in 1977, Mulcahy closed it in 1980 to make way for his *Sunday Tribune*.

Northern Ireland: lifting the lid

In Northern Ireland, the late 1950s and early 1960s saw changes in broadcasting of two kinds. One, structural change, was the establishment of Ulster Television (UTV) in 1959, under the aegis of a group of Northern Ireland business interests, not least the *Belfast Newsletter* and its owners, the Henderson family. The second, however, was more problematic, politically speaking. This was the development of a greater interest, by both the BBC and ITV, in the internal political arrangements and circumstances of Northern Ireland.

Towards the end of 1958, the BBC presenter Alan Whicker came to Northern Ireland to prepare a programme for the BBC current affairs slot, *Tonight*. His televisual essay, when it was broadcast on 9 January 1959, was a presentation to the national British audience of a part of their own state with which they would, at best, have been only dimly familiar – certainly far less familiar than they would have been with, for example, Wales or Scotland. It was not a flattering portrait, and although it caused little comment elsewhere in the UK, it evoked widespread Unionist protest in Northern Ireland, particularly through the newspapers, which did their best to turn the BBC into a whipping-post for its slights, real or imagined, on Northern Ireland's character, people and habits. At the height of the controversy Robert McCall, the BBC's regional controller in Northern Ireland, wrote to his superior in London, Grace Wyndham Goldie:

I will fight like a cat, as always in the past, to protect the integrity and independence of the BBC – no pressure from Government PROs, tourist boards, and the rest. But I must confess that this area needs special treatment.

(Cathcart 1984: 193)

Whicker had prepared further reports on Northern Ireland: they were never broadcast. Only three months later, however, controversy erupted again when the BBC broadcast a US series in which the American journalist, Ed Murrow, interviewed celebrities, one of whom was the Irish actress Siobhan McKenna. McKenna, who was born in the West of Ireland and evidently had strong nationalist views, made a number of comments on the current political situation (it should be remembered that an IRA campaign against Northern Ireland installations had been fitfully in progress since 1956) in which she described IRA men as 'idealists' and asked why the British government, if it believed that partition was no solution in Cyprus, continued to maintain it in Northern Ireland (Cathcart 1984: 194).

Within days of the broadcast on 25 April, Brian Faulkner, the Unionist politician who was later to become prime minister of Northern Ireland, resigned from the province's BBC Advisory Council in protest. A scheduled showing of the second part of the interview with McKenna was cancelled: the BBC in London had been effectively warned off the turf.

This acute sensitivity to outside observers and broadcasters, incubated for decades in the less public, but equally sensitive environment of radio, was to be accentuated by television, and remained a feature of Northern Ireland politics and broadcasting for many years to come. Although the BBC internally did make attempts from time to time to broach contentious subjects in a framework in which Unionists in particular would not feel that their alleged misdeeds were being paraded before a wider audience, it operated by and large in a protective rather than provocative mode. One programme, on religious discrimination in employment in Northern Ireland, which was broadcast in 1962, was, according to Rex Cathcart's authoritative study, 'not typical' (1984: 197).

But the BBC no longer had the playing field to itself. The first broadcast from the new Ulster Television Network, the ITV franchisee, took place on Halloween 1959. The new service could acquire viewers from only one source – the BBC – and it did precisely that, rapidly achieving some 60% of the total viewing figures. This paralleled developments in Britain where the more public-service oriented BBC inevitably found itself at a disadvantage when matched against the profit-oriented, commercial character of ITV. The competition between the two networks in Northern Ireland had a beneficial effect in that neither could ignore the need to build constituencies and audiences within each of the major religious and political traditions: UTV explicitly stated that it was in the business of community reconciliation (Cathcart 1984: 187). The dynamics of the situation, however, were to ensure that, even with this added impetus, developments would be slow, and few major risks would be taken.

The political crisis in Northern Ireland broke, for its media, rather earlier than it did in the Republic. Coming events cast their shadow before them in October 1962, when a news clip of the Revd Ian Paisley attacking the Catholic Church – he was on his way to protest in Rome against the presence of delegates from the World Council of Churches at the Second Vatican Council – led immediately to a rare BBC disclaimer. This was also the first month in which UTV had a full-fledged operational newsroom. The events of the next few years seemed to indicate at first that this was no more than a flash in the pan: relationships in broadcasting between Dublin and Belfast became more cordial, and a land-line was established between the two stations, enabling them to share sports broadcasts as well as news and current affairs. The visit to Belfast in January 1965 by the Taoiseach, Sean Lemass, to meet the Northern prime minister, Terence O'Neill, gave rise to a flurry of cross-border meetings between civil servants, politicians, and – inevitably – BBC and RTE personnel.

In 1966, however, there was a series of events which, although they did not provoke the kind of political violence that was to break out in 1968–9, reawakened community tensions which had never been buried very far beneath the surface. The year 1966 was the fiftieth anniversary of the 1916 Rising in Dublin, the cradle of the nationalist revolt which led, via the War of Independence, to the Anglo-Irish Treaty of 1921 which partitioned the island and gave it two separate parliaments and jurisdictions. The anniversary was marked, in the South, by state-led celebrations, and by a considerable amount of irredentist rhetoric.

The same anniversary was marked, in Northern Ireland, by an outbreak of nationalist sentiment and by the display of nationalist flags (illegal under legislation passed by Stormont). BBC and UTV bulletins which reported these events were seen by Unionists as evidence of network bias: not even a visit to Belfast by Queen Elizabeth, evidently designed to reassure Unionists, managed to calm the situation. Broadcasters in Northern Ireland, still taking their cue to a certain extent from the *rapprochement* between Lemass and O'Neill, continued to broaden their agenda to include more programming reflecting the different cultural and political traditions. As ever, it was network attention, rather than the regional output, which provoked most Unionist concern: a programme on Derry broadcast in the national *Twenty-Four Hours* series prompted one prominent Unionist to declare in late 1966 that both BBC and UTV were guilty of 'a veiled sympathy with the anti-Partition conspiracy' (Cathcart 1984: 207).

The emergence of the civil rights movement in Northern Ireland in 1968 created a new situation in which the media in general, but particularly television, played a new and central role. There had been sporadic disturbances in Northern Ireland for many years, but the political convention that Northern Ireland affairs could not be discussed in the Westminster parliament meant that nationalist grievances lacked an effective sounding-board (the Stormont parliament was effectively under the permanent control of their Unionist opponents). Television now became that sounding-board, amplifying both the protests against the political status quo in Northern Ireland, and the Unionist government's ham-fisted and often brutal attempt to suppress them. This was particularly true of dramatic footage secured by an RTE cameraman, Gay O'Brien, of a civil rights march in Derry in October 1968 which was met by water-cannon and baton charges. When the BBC used this footage in preference to their own, television itself became an extension of the battleground, as both sides jousted for control of the medium, or at least for an effective input into its coverage.

Unionists in particular were prone to interpret all coverage of the disturbances as subversive, regardless of the fact that the civil rights movement, as such, did not have a constitutional agenda. The broadcasters did their best to elaborate an ethic in the middle of a rapidly intensifying conflict, not often with conspicuous success. Particular exception was taken to BBC reports of serious civil disorder in Belfast in August 1969, when whole streets of Catholic houses were torched by Loyalist vigilantes: the BBC reported what had happened without making any effort to identify the source of the attacks, and subsequently defended its decontextualised report. Eight years later, Martin Bell, who had been seconded from London to join the BBC team in Northern Ireland, charged that this had been a grave mistake and was 'the only time when I was stopped by the powers above from saying what I wanted to say' (Cathcart 1984: 212).

Northern Ireland broadcasters shared one dilemma with their counterparts in the Republic – at least until the issuing of the directive under Section 31 of the Irish government's Broadcasting Act: what modalities should govern the portraying of, or interviews with, paramilitary forces? This became particularly relevant after the Provisional IRA re-emerged as a force in 1970, and the Northern Ireland Civil Rights Association's campaign for legal changes within the existing constitutional framework began to take second place to a conflict which was increasingly being expressed in terms of the traditional Unionist/Nationalist cleavage. The BBC showed a number of films of IRA personnel on both sides of the border (Loyalist paramilitaries were, until 1974, a much less potent reality). This led to considerable controversy, and even – in April 1971 – to the imprisonment for four days of a BBC reporter, Bernard Falk, for refusing to identify a defendant charged with IRA membership as someone he had previously interviewed for television. This in turn produced a system of referring such critical questions upwards to higher authority.

There were, inevitably, increasing differences of opinion between BBC Northern Ireland, whose controllers and editorial staff were hyper-sensitive to local pressures and protests, and the national network, newly gripped by a major political and constitutional crisis on its own doorstep and indeed within its own territory. This was evidenced most sharply in the controversy over a major discussion programme scheduled by the national network and entitled *The Question of Ulster* which the BBC successfully broadcast in January 1972 despite strong political pressure from the then Conservative Home Secretary, Reginald Maudling. The BBC's major crime on this occasion was to include, among the participants, two politicians from the Republic. Two months later, the Stormont parliament was suspended, and the political and media landscapes changed simultaneously: increasingly, from now on, London was to figure more prominently in both areas.

These events left their mark in the print media too, but here developments in editorial policy were being paralleled, at least in the cases of the *Irish News* and the *Belfast Telegraph*, by changes in ownership and direction. In 1964, Dr Daniel McSparran, who had controlled the *Irish News* for three decades, retired: his place was taken by his son, also Daniel McSparran. Two years later, the paper had a new editor, Terence O'Keeffe, a Liverpool-born, Jesuit-educated journalist who nudged the paper away from its Catholic bulletin board image and in the direction of openness towards other traditions (Phoenix 1995: 35). Its editorials, nonetheless, mirrored both the rising hopes and the subsequent disillusion of Northern nationalists when the promise of 1965 gave way to the conflicts of the late 1960s. On 10 October 1968, in the aftermath of the civil rights march in Derry, it came editorially to the conclusion that Unionism would never really change its spots, and that the nationalists, in accepting the role of official opposition at Stormont (as they had done in 1965 at the urging of the Dublin government) had made a fatal political mistake.

Ironically, the initiation and spread of civil conflict helped the circulation of all Northern Ireland newspapers, as each side consumed news and information avidly. There was a growth in political cartooning, in which a divide rapidly appeared between UK-based and some Irish media. Whereas Irish-based cartoonists could occasionally rise to a sophisticated, sometimes black humour, UK cartoonists in the mainstream (and especially the tabloid) press

> tended to avoid those aspects of the Ulster issue which would normally emphasise the differences between the political left and right ... it was tempting to regard events in the province as a struggle between the British virtues of reason, decency and moderation and the Irish antitheses of these.
>
> (Darby 1983: 120–21)

All the papers had now been modernised to a considerable extent: when the *Newsletter* put news on its front page for the first time in 1961, it was the last of the three Belfast daily papers to do so. And the deepening divisions did not preclude some commonality of interest: in 1969, when an unfounded rumour circulated suggesting that the BBC broadcasting operations in Northern Ireland were about to be closed down because of a shortage of money, not only the *Irish News*, but the *Belfast Telegraph* and the *Newsletter* published trenchant editorials condemning the idea (Cathcart 1984: 211).

So far as offering an analysis of the Northern Ireland problem was concerned, the *Newsletter* did its best to suggest that the cause was less Unionist intransigence or discrimination, more a desire, on the part of militant Republicans, to recapture the political support that had been seeping away from them since partition in 1921. The *Newsletter* pointed out that, although in 1921 more than 30% of the electorate in Northern Ireland had voted for nationalist candidates, between 1929 and 1969 that percentage had been halved (Shearman 1987: 47). These arguments did not impress more militant elements within nationalism. During the 1970s, there were nine bomb incidents at or in the vicinity of the newspaper's offices: one bomb in 1972 injured twenty-one of the company's employees, and another in 1973 damaged a strong-room containing bound volumes of the paper going back to 1738.

Risks of a different kind affected the *Belfast Telegraph*. As already noted, the paper's management had been wrestling with the problem caused by the untimely death of Bobbie Baird, the managing director, in 1953: death duties on his estate (which included the *Telegraph*) were enormous, and although the directors lent money to cover this debt, it rapidly became evident that the paper itself would have to be sold. It was eventually purchased, after a lengthy legal case, by the Canadian newspaper magnate Roy Thomson in September 1961 for £1.25 million. The closure of the *Northern Whig* in September 1963, in the wake of a strike by the National Union of Journalists, cleared the field of at least one competitor (although the *Whig* was a morning paper). Thomson's canniness in making the purchase was richly rewarded in subsequent years: the profits on the *Belfast Telegraph* approximately covered his losses on the London *Times*, which he had purchased earlier.

With the *Telegraph*, of course, he had also inherited Jack Sayers, one of the most influential – and disappointed – editors of his era. Over most of the following decade, until his retirement in 1969, Sayers supported moderate Unionism in its attempt – belated and ultimately unsuccessful – to find common ground with moderate nationalism, and did so with a single-mindedness that sometimes blinded him to the power of the forces ranged against it. As Ian Paisley became part of the movement aimed at unseating Terence O'Neill in 1966, he wrote starkly about the dilemma facing Northern Ireland in his editorial of 12 July: the choice was 'between responsible government through the present Unionist leadership or a form of dictatorship through a religious war led by a latter-day "Mad Mullah"' (Gailey 1995: 108). Throughout 1967 and 1968 he worked in public and private to bring about a *rapprochement* between the leaders of both communities, most notably Cardinal Conway, the Archbishop of Armagh, and the Northern Ireland Minister of Education, William Long. The Dublin journal, *Hibernia*, described him as O'Neill's 'doppelgänger' (3 January 1969). In the circumstances, he almost certainly under-estimated the threat to orthodox Unionism from its fundamentalist wing, and over-estimated O'Neill's electoral strength, and the influence that the *Telegraph* could bring to bear to support him. Two months later, however, his worsening health and the rapidly deteriorating political situation finally exacted their price, and he retired.

His biographer noted:

> Through him, liberal Unionism was made acceptable, even fashionable, for the first time since 1903. By adopting an independent media line he broke the stranglehold of Glengall Street [the address of the Unionist Party

headquarters] on the media and revitalised political debate in the province. This development was part of the wider collapse of the political press in Britain, but with the fierce control exercised by the party through the Hendersons at the *Newsletter*, the Cunninghams of the *Northern Whig* and Harry McMullan at the BBC, it took enormous courage.

(Gailey 1995: 164–5)

The media consumption habits of nationalists and Unionists in Northern Ireland remained sharply divided. In 1970, 87% of the *Newsletter's* readership was Protestant; 93% of the *Irish News's* readers were Catholic. The *Belfast Telegraph* readership mirrored this divide – 68% Protestant and 32% Catholic, a proportion reflecting the sociological breakdown of the two main allegiances in the province. Interestingly, the *Belfast Telegraph*, despite its editorial stance, did not alienate the more extreme supporters of both sides: up to half of its Protestant and Catholic readers supported a Loyalist or strongly Republican viewpoint respectively. Only 5% read a newspaper edited in Dublin, and 32% read a British paper. Perhaps unsurprisingly, and in spite of the frequent criticisms to which the public broadcast media were subjected, they were thought to be the most reliable source of news by twice as many people as awarded the print media that role (Rose 1971: 343–5). Catholics were more likely than Protestants to read a UK-published paper, indicating that they did so probably because of their coverage of sport and entertainment rather than for political reasons. It is also relevant that although UK tabloids were noted for their anti-Republican and pro-British army attitudes for the duration of the conflict, a certain level of editionising ensured that the more jingoistic headlines were, on occasion, confined to the editions circulated on the larger island.

The more extreme Unionists, against whom Sayers had been inveighing, now even had a paper of their own. This was the Revd Ian Paisley's *Protestant Telegraph* – the name itself undoubtedly a back-handed compliment to the *Belfast Telegraph* – which was founded in April 1966 and which provided its readers with a potent mixture of anti-Catholic invective and proto-Unionist political sentiment. Paisley's Free Presbyterian Church, of which it was effectively the mouthpiece, was to grow substantially, both in the number of its adherents and in the resources it had available, over the next three decades. The *Protestant Telegraph* now has a circulation of about 15,000.

But the era also produced a novelty of a different kind in the shape of *Fortnight*, a magazine was established in 1970 (the first issue was 30 September) by a group of young Queen's University lecturers and others with the aim of recognising and then working to accommodate community differences through rational discussion. The name *Fortnight* was chosen because it was the only option, among many others considered, which was totally free of any sectarian or political undertones. Its first editor, Tom Hadden, was a lawyer, and this may have led to an emphasis on legal and civil rights issues in the early years of its existence. Its even-handedness was not always welcome. When it opposed internment without trial in 1971, its printers in Northern Ireland refused to handle it, and it was printed in Dublin for three months until a grant from the Rowntree Trust enabled it to buy its own press. After going through various vicissitudes, it established a rare reputation as a journal in whose pages politicians and writers of every political persuasion could find a home, and its current circulation is about 3,500: despite its name, it now appears monthly, yet another of Northern Ireland's anomalies.

5   Crossing a watershed, 1973–85

The decade or so from 1972 onwards saw major changes in Irish media, particularly in the Republic. The North was more immune to major structural and ownership changes for some time after the purchase of the *Belfast Telegraph* by the Thomson Organisation, but even here the decade saw the emergence of new titles and the sharpening of competition. In Dublin, the somewhat old-fashioned and complacent ownership and management systems were being reformed or broken up as a more aggressive and modern form of capitalism took shape. New titles were appearing; the influence of UK media was becoming a subject of debate, particularly in relation to their treatment of the Northern Ireland issue; and the evolution of broadcasting reflected not only the all-pervasive influence of the Northern conflict but recurrent controversies about national identity, programme choice and political interference.

By early 1973, the economy of the Republic had been on an upswing for some years. Even the *Irish Times* balance sheet had improved under the influence of a number of variables: economic growth, political controversy and venturesome editing. A number of significant developments then took place in rapid succession. On 2 March Major T.B. McDowell, who had been chief executive of the company for eleven years, also became chairman. Twelve days later, the newspaper – then in the middle of a printers' strike – broke the one out, all out agreement between the Dublin newspaper managements to publish news of the formation of the new government the previous day. It did so, it said, because 'the Directors consider that they have an obligation to the public which overrides all other considerations' (*IT*: 14 March 1973). Simultaneously, three of the five directors who controlled the voting shares in the company were coming to the conclusion that they wanted to retire: they had received little or nothing by way of dividend for years, and indeed had to borrow to invest further in the paper from time to time. The shares were now acquiring some value – so much so that it would have been, in practical terms, difficult for the other two directors to purchase them all prior to re-constituting the board. There were also rumours that Roy Thomson, already the owner of the *Belfast Telegraph*, might be interested in adding to his Irish portfolio.

This possibility was averted by a major restructuring of the organisation devised by the chairman. A trust was set up on 5 April 1974, which acquired the shares of all the directors on the basis of borrowings of more than £2 million from the Bank of Ireland; and this trust was given the power to appoint a majority of members of the board of the company which now controlled the *Irish Times* directly. Douglas Gageby, who had been a director as well as editor, retired as editor.

Changes of a similar magnitude, although not of the same kind, were taking place simultaneously at the Independent newspapers. The company was still controlled by the Murphy and Chance families, and for some time rumours had been circulating to the effect that the company was ripe for a takeover. The country's first financial weekly, *Business and Finance*, declared on 1 March 1973 that it was 'grossly undervalued'. Its pre-tax profits in 1972 were over £0.75 million, and it had been extending steadily and profitably into the provincial newspaper field. On the east coast, where, generally speaking, the population had a higher disposable income, and where more commercial activity took place, it had acquired a number of titles in a wide swathe running from Drogheda in the north to Wicklow in the south, as well as the *Kerryman*, one of the largest and most prosperous of all Irish provincial papers.

The *Kerryman* had fallen into the Independent's hands on the death of its long-time owner, Dan Nolan; the Independent group was to suffer a similar fate as its founding share-holding families began to lose interest in continuing the business. Speculation as to who would take over at first centred on the wealthy McGrath family, which had built an industrial and business empire on the foundation of a franchise, which they had been granted by an accommodating government in 1930, to run a national sweepstake to benefit Irish hospitals. On 21 January 1973, however, this possibility evaporated in the wake of the publication, in the *Sunday Independent* of that date, of one of the most remarkable pieces of investigative journalism that had ever appeared in an Irish newspaper up to that time, and indeed for many years afterwards. This was an *exposé*, by the journalist Joe MacAnthony, of the activities by McGrath's sweepstake company, many of them illegal in the foreign jurisdictions in which sweepstake tickets were sold.

The article, which ran to some 8,000 words and over three pages of the paper, had been planned originally as a two-part series. The editor of the paper, Conor O'Brien, realised, however, that if the first half was published, the second half would in all probability never see the light of day; accordingly, he decided to run it all in one article. The McGraths were incensed, and withdrew all their lucrative advertising from the group for some weeks. MacAnthony resigned not long afterwards, after it had been made clear to him by a regretful O'Brien that his career within that organisation had effectively reached a full stop, at least in terms of promotion; and other potential purchasers began to eye the company.

On 17 March 1973 it was announced that a young Irish financier and businessman, Tony O'Reilly, had taken a large stake in the company, together with an associate of his named Nicholas Leonard, a former financial editor of the *Irish Times*. Leonard had earlier attempted to buy into the shares of the *Irish Press's* holding company in the United States: his efforts had been met with stiff resistance, and he had retreated (Walsh 1992: 220). He and O'Reilly were part of a new generation of Irish entrepreneurs which was reshaping the face of Irish business and industry. O'Reilly, who was an industrial chemist by training, had joined the Irish Sugar Company as a young man and helped to organise its diversification and growth. He moved from there to the US Heinz company, initially in charge of its UK operations, all the time maintaining an Irish base through a publicly quoted holding company called FitzWilton. O'Reilly's initial purchase amounted to no more than 20% of the controlling shares, but he persuaded the Independent group board, of which he was now a member, to agree to a performance-related formula in which he would be permitted to increase his equity holding in the company if it achieved certain specified commercial targets. In this way, he increased his equity incrementally: by 1980, when he was appointed chairman of Independent Newspapers, his initial investment of about £1 million was worth more than £5 million.

These changes, none of which had been predicted, threw the normally placid world of Irish journalism into a turmoil. There were rumours that the changes in share ownership at both newspapers had taken place against the background of the possible introduction, by the new government which took office in 1973, of a capital gains tax: such a tax, which had been mooted publicly during the general election campaign, was in fact introduced by the government later the same year. Simultaneously with O'Reilly's move into the Independent group, there was industrial trouble at the *Sunday Press*, whose journalistic staff had been summarily dismissed for refusing a management instruction to process for publication an opinion column by the broadcaster Gay Byrne, who was not a member of the NUJ. Alarmed by the suddenness of the change at the *Independent*, the group's 200 journalists took emergency action, effectively occupying the premises until they received a management guarantee that their jobs were not in jeopardy. The problem at the *Sunday Press* was also resolved, but the general air of nervousness and uncertainty was palpable.

Even these difficulties were to be rapidly overshadowed by other, more global factors. In the middle of 1973, the Organisation of Petroleum Exporting Companies (OPEC) began remorselessly to increase the price of crude oil. Ireland, as a small open economy, was more than usually vulnerable to the resulting downturn in the world economy. As the price of oil and oil-related products soared, manufacturing went into recession, consumer confidence evaporated and Irish inflation escalated – to a rate of 26% in 1976, the worst year of the crisis.

All these factors led to a collapse of the media advertising market, particularly in the newspapers (with restricted budgets, many advertisers preferred to concentrate their resources on television and radio where appropriate). This collapse in advertising revenue reduced both the size and quality of newspapers, as editorial and production budgets were in turn affected. The *Irish Times*, which had launched a new paper designed to tap a niche market in 1973 – a weekly called the *Education Times* – failed to make it pay its way and had to close it in

1976 as the company's reserves dipped to dangerous levels, a visible casualty of the overall economic situation.

The Independent group was experiencing similar problems, but was better equipped to deal with them. For one thing, it had a three-newspaper base. For another, it began to look outside Ireland for profitable investment opportunities: O'Reilly's international connections – he became Chairman of Heinz in 1973, and joined the board of Mobil Oil in 1979 – prompted a policy of diversification in media-related industries in Britain, the United States, Germany and Mexico: by the end of the 1970s, more than half the group's profits were being generated by subsidiaries or from investments strategically located outside Ireland.

In addition, a number of editorial changes were beginning to reap dividends in terms of circulation. Vincent Doyle, the editor of the daily *Irish Independent* from February 1981, brought to his position a tough – some would say ruthless – approach to news, and a determination to beat the opposition on all major stories. This was allied to changes in layout, typography and design which made the *Irish Independent*, although a broadsheet, assume at least some of the display characteristics of a tabloid. Its front page became more and more striking, and this hybridization of style not only helped it to fend off, to some degree, the competition from imported UK papers, but attracted younger and female readers away from the still more typographically staid *Irish Press*. The *Sunday Independent*, edited from January 1984 by Aengus Fanning, had adopted different tactics but with similar results: its new emphasis on pungent opinion columns, gossip and fashion enabled it to cut the circulation lead of the *Sunday Press* from 100,000 to 30,000: it was to overhaul it finally in 1989.

If the Independent group had a firm grip on middle Ireland, buttressed by an increasing range of profitable foreign investments, the economic and readership base of the Irish Press newspapers was less secure. Although the group appeared to survive the mid-1970s relatively unscathed, this was in large part because the Fianna Fail party was in opposition between 1973 and 1977. Attacking a government generally makes for better, or at least more lively, journalism than supporting one, and the *Irish Press* re-adopted this role with gusto: for sixteen years up to 1973, in effect, it had been a pro-government paper. But its apparent success in weathering the financial turbulence of that period masked other, long-term changes which were seriously to affect its future. Its readership profile was changing. At a time when advertisers were becoming increasingly sophisticated, and when the stratification of media consumers was increasingly being used to guide advertising decisions, the Irish Press group papers' readership (with the possible exception of the *Evening Press*), though substantial, was beginning to assume characteristics which did not generate much commercial enthusiasm. The readers – by contrast with those of other papers – tended to be older, were more likely to be male, to live in non-urban environments, and to have relatively smaller amounts of disposable income.

Nonetheless, in 1980, its last good year, the company reported profits of £715,000 before tax. The *Evening Press* was out-selling the *Evening Herald* by

30,000 copies a day, with a total of 172,000; and the *Sunday Press* had 55% of the domestic Sunday newspaper market with a circulation of just under 400,000 copies a week. The daily *Irish Press* was selling a respectable 100,000.

The death of Vivion de Valera in 1982, however, meant that control now passed to the founder's grandson, Dr Eamon de Valera, and this change was accompanied by management plans to make the long-awaited technological changes which were necessary if the group was to meet the challenges of the powerful Independent group with any confidence. The attempts to introduce these changes were accompanied by mounting financial losses and sharply deteriorating staff relations. In the summer of 1983 journalists held a lengthy meeting to discuss management's proposals on new technology and, after their wages had been reduced for taking time off work for this meeting, went on strike. The titles were off the streets for three weeks, but it was only the first in a series of similar disputes. Mounting losses – £1.5 million in 1983 and £3.5 million the following year – prompted a drastic management decision to switch from hot metal to computerised typesetting in 1985 without first securing union agreement. This led to a 12-week stoppage, which hugely damaged circulation: industrial peace was restored in the end only at a very high price, so high that it effectively cancelled out any potential savings that the new technology might have brought in its train: under the agreement, text for the newspaper had to be entered on two keyboards in succession – first by journalists, who typed it, and then by printers, who re-typed it from the reporters' copy on to a terminal keyboard. All three titles were now intensely vulnerable to both domestic and foreign competition.

One of the few initiatives to run counter to the general trend of retrenchment was a new Sunday newspaper, the *Sunday World*. The market for Sunday newspapers in Ireland, North and South, has always been a fiercely contested one. The British tabloid newspapers, in particular, were unopposed in the Sunday sector: their only Irish competitors, the *Sunday Independent* and the *Sunday Press*, were broadsheets which attempted, not always successfully, to stretch their appeal to cover both the popular and quality ends of the market.

The *Sunday World* was launched on 25 March 1973. Its founders were two businessmen, Hugh McLoughlin and Gerry McGuinness, partners in the Creation group, which published a number of women's magazines and had a relatively sophisticated colour press. McLoughlin, the son of a Co. Donegal stationmaster who had built a business career in Dublin, had an extraordinarily influential role in the creation of new Irish media. As well as his involvement in the Creation group, and the *Sunday World*, he was behind the publication of the first Dublin free-sheet, the *Dublin Post*, and had been closely involved with the restructuring of the *Irish Farmers' Journal* in 1950 (it had been established originally in 1948, but had limited success in its first two years and sometimes suffered breaks in publication). With Nicholas Leonard, up to then financial editor of the *Irish Times*, he also founded, in September 1960, *Business and Finance*, Ireland's first dedicated financial and business magazine.

The *Sunday World* was a publication which had absorbed many insights from its UK competitors, notably a cheeky willingness to engage in sexual innuendo: its marketing slogan was 'We Go All The Way'. It was also in many ways distinctively Irish. It promised, and indeed occasionally delivered, tough and fearless journalism: its first editorial noted: 'In this newspaper, common objects like spades will be known as spades ... They are used to dig with and we intend to dig.' It realised that coverage of television was popular (the existing newspapers tended to ignore their electronic rival). It adopted a campaigning mode, including collecting money for deserving causes. It had a problem page, the first of its kind in Ireland. And it specialised in short paragraphs, screaming headlines, and huge by-lines for journalists.

In spite of the fact that it sold initially for 6p – a penny dearer than both its Irish competitors – it was a success virtually from the start. It had an initial capital of only £40,000, on which it was thought it might survive for six weeks, but by December 1973 its sales were at more than 200,000, and by 1975 its annual profit was £100,000.

Insofar as it had a political line, it was soft-focus Fianna Fail. This party was, after all, the political party which had the greatest following among the urban working classes and among small farmers. Its appeal, however, was not confined to these groups, and it rapidly acquired a circulation which was not only geographically widespread – it was as popular in rural as in urban areas – but whose sociological profile spanned all social classes, making it uniquely attractive to advertisers. It also made substantial inroads into Northern Ireland, where the *Sunday News* had had the field to itself since 1965. It did so by changing a substantial number of pages for its Northern Ireland edition, by maintaining a relatively even-handed approach to news stories emanating from within that divided community. This enabled it to establish a readership which, although to a lesser extent than that of the *Belfast Telegraph*, spread across the sectarian divide. Its southern origins did not, however, go unnoticed: in May 1984 its Northern editor, Jim Campbell, was the victim of an unsuccessful assassination attempt by Loyalists; though seriously wounded, he returned to his desk some months later. In 1988, when the *World's* circulation was at its highest, some 96,000 of its total sale of 355,000 copies were in Northern Ireland.

By then, however, it had changed ownership. In 1977, the fortunes of the Creation group were wavering, as the magazine market suffered, like others, from the long-running economic crisis. McGuinness and McLoughlin toyed with the idea of enhancing their revenues by publishing a tabloid evening paper – the *Evening Herald* and *Evening Press* were both broadsheets. In January 1978 O'Reilly and the Independent board, partly in response to this threat but also because they sensed a unique opportunity, made a successful offer of £1.1 million for McLoughlin's 54% share-holding. This was followed, in April 1983, by the purchase of McGuinness's share-holding for almost £3 million.

The purchase by the Independent group of the *Sunday World* had one other significant consequence for Irish media generally. This was because the *Sunday World* was a major share-holder, as was the *Irish Farmers' Journal*, in a distribution company called Newspread, which had been established in the mid-1970s specifically to distribute the two newspapers. O'Reilly and his board moved shortly afterwards to take control of this company also, overriding the objections of the *Farmers' Journal* with the persuasive argument that if it did not agree to sell the Independent its 40% share-holding in the distribution company, the Independent organisation would distribute the *Sunday World* itself: this would have faced the *Journal* with a massive distribution bill. Newspread is one of only two major print media distribution companies in the country: the other is owned by the Dublin firm, Easons.

By 1984, the contribution of the *Sunday World* to Independent group profits was already approaching £1 million, even after allowing for interest on the borrowings taken out to acquire the paper. Occasionally denounced from pulpits, it softened its campaigning stance as it was hit by increasingly expensive libel actions (in the latter part of the 1980s its lawyers' costs were averaging over £500,000 a year) but maintained a robustly laddish approach to its journalistic agenda. When its editor, Colin McLelland, was summoned before the Oireachtas Committee on Women's Rights in 1985 to answer allegations of sexism, he refused, and sent the committee a letter noting:

> My own view is that there is a considerable difference between men and women. They look different, for a start, and I firmly believe that a tractor adorned by a girl in a bikini is infinitely more pleasing to the human eye than the same tractor adorned by a man in Y-fronts. To me, that's the way that God planned it.
>
> (IT: 18 July 1985)

Others attempted to follow in McLoughlin's tracks, but with less success. Tony Fitzpatrick, who was a former Dublin correspondent for the British Sunday newspaper, *The People*, and who had subsequently occupied a number of senior editorial positions on the *Sunday World*, persuaded a number of investors to finance a new Sunday newspaper, the *Sunday Journal*, which would be aimed at the farming community, and would compete with the *Farmers' Journal*, which published on Thursdays. This development was significant in that it involved the first major investment from non-Irish sources in an Irish national newspaper: a number of the investors, including the British financier Robert Holmes à'Court, were based in the Isle of Man.

Taking on the *Irish Farmers' Journal* seemed like a high-risk enterprise. The *Farmers' Journal* was selling some 84,000 copies a week, and seemed well entrenched. Nonetheless – aided in part by tensions within the National Farmers' Association – the new newspaper did comparatively well, at least in terms of its circulation, which rose soon after its publication on 2 March 1980 to a weekly figure of some 72,000 copies. All this, however, was at a cost, and the investors, alarmed at the rate at which the initial capital was being consumed, tried unsuccessfully to remove Fitzpatrick. Fitzpatrick then turned the tables on them by persuading a native Irish entrepreneur, Joe Moore, to buy into the paper as the original investors departed. Moore, a craggy and despotic businessman who had pioneered low-cost motor insurance in Ireland and had founded the Private Motorists Protection Association, assumed control with great enthusiasm, but with little clear idea of what newspaper readers or advertisers wanted. The *Sunday Journal* went into rapid decline, with an increasing proportion of its decreasing number of pages being devoted to motoring matters, until it expired on 20 June 1982 with a circulation of some 20,000.

Emboldened by his success with the *Sunday World*, the entrepreneur Hugh McLoughlin decided on yet another foray into newspaper publishing and, in 1980, went into partnership with the former editor-proprietor of *Hibernia*, John Mulcahy, and a major printing group, Smurfits, to set up a printing operation and to produce a quality Irish Sunday newspaper, aiming at a perceived gap in Irish journalism. The *Sunday World* was a tabloid; the *Sunday Independent* and *Sunday Press* were established middle-market papers; and the circulation in Ireland of British Sunday newspapers such as the *Observer* and *Sunday Times*, though small, had indicated that there was another market here which might also be tapped.

The *Sunday Tribune*, accordingly, was launched in October 1980, with an energetic and talented ex-*Irish Times* journalist, Conor Brady, as its editor. Initially at least it seemed as if this had been yet another canny gamble. Its 1981 audited circulation was 110,000, certainly enough to make the enterprise viable; and its readership was over 400,000. In May 1981, however, there was a restructuring of the companies involved, in which McLoughlin ceded his part-ownership of the printing operation to Smurfits, and Smurfits in turn ceded to him their share of the ownership of the *Sunday Tribune*. Printing and publishing were now two entirely separate operations, a development which was to have considerable significance for the future.

Initially, the *Sunday Tribune* went from strength to strength. It developed a particular expertise in political reporting, and, at a time when Fianna Fail, the country's largest political party, was undergoing an almost permanent leadership crisis. The *Tribune's* political correspondent, Geraldine Kennedy, was a young woman who had come into national journalism from her local paper in Waterford, but who quickly established a major reputation for herself as the author of a number of political exclusives – so much so that attempts were made, by senior figures within Fianna Fail, to identify her sources of information within the cabinet. Kennedy's appointment not only attracted the attention of political elites, but was an initiative which ruffled the somewhat placid waters of political journalism generally. She was the first of a number of female political reporters whose different work routines and unwillingness to accept unquestioningly the unwritten rules of the – up until then – exclusively male club of political correspondents introduced valuable elements of unpredictability into political coverage generally. Her activities, and those of another talented and independently minded journalist on the *Irish Independent*, Bruce Arnold, were focused on, among other thing, a leadership crisis which was developing within Fianna Fail. That party's new leader (since 1979), was C.J. Haughey, one of the two ministers who had been dismissed from the cabinet in

1970 and subsequently arraigned on a charge of importing arms illegally – a charge of which he had been acquitted. His rise to power in the party subsequently, however, had been bitterly opposed by some of his colleagues, and a number of unsuccessful attempts were made to unseat him.

It emerged in 1983 that while Haughey had been head of government, the telephones of both Kennedy and Arnold had been illegally tapped in an attempt to find out where they were getting information damaging to Haughey's interests. Both sued the state for compensation, and won. Arnold's case was especially interesting in that he was not an Irish citizen: the rights which he successfully claimed had been infringed were, the courts decided, his by virtue of the fact that he was a denizen of the state. Equally, his wife was entitled to damages because her personal privacy had been infringed by the illegal wire-tap. And both the Arnold and the Kennedy cases established the important precedent that the constitutional right to privacy extended to the telephone (Arnold 1984: 2). Kennedy was later (1987) to go into politics directly, as a deputy for the Progressive Democrat party, but lost her seat at the following election and returned to journalism.

The modest but genuine success of the *Sunday Tribune* was about to be seriously undermined by yet another gamble – this time, one which did not come off. McLoughlin had identified what he saw as yet another gap in the market – a gap which could be filled by an Irish tabloid paper. The success of the UK tabloids in Ireland – their sales accounted for a huge majority of the quarter of Irish daily newspaper sales which were attributable to imports – suggested strongly that an Irish tabloid could, if it got the formula right, be a runaway success. Accordingly, after a three-month planning period, the tabloid *Daily News* was launched on 7 October 1982.

The new paper was effectively a subsidiary of the *Sunday Tribune*, which was to be paid some £40,000 a week for printing the new paper – money which the *Tribune* would, in turn, owe to the printing company now controlled by Smurfits. The effect of this operation, however, was to expose the fatal undercapitalisation of the whole enterprise. First of all, Newspread – now controlled, it will be remembered, by the rival Independent group – withdrew from a proposed distribution arrangement, forcing McLoughlin to set up his own system at a considerable cost. Then Smurfits, who now controlled the printing operation, insisted on being paid for their contract on a daily basis. The initial enthusiasm at the *Daily News* was rapidly transmuted into panic, the layout became more and more improvised, and the stories more and more flimsy. It eventually collapsed after only fifteen issues, and its fifty editorial staff were given notice. If McLoughlin had hoped that it would repeat the success of the *Sunday World* (and possibly even attract the interest of the Independent group, as the *Sunday World's* success had done), he had seriously miscalculated. More significantly, the collapse of the *Daily News* helped to drag down the *Sunday Tribune*, as that newspaper went into liquidation in October 1982. Not all the *Tribune* losses were attributable to the *Daily News* experiment: the *Tribune* had launched a very expensive colour supplement which was also a major drain on its resources. But it was certainly the case that, without the haemorrhage of the *Daily News*, the *Tribune* would have had a greater chance of survival.

Unlike the *Daily News*, the *Sunday Tribune* still represented an attractive proposition for potential publishers. Its title was acquired from the liquidator for a nominal sum in November 1982 by a company called St Stephen's Green Publications: two of its principal share-holders were a journalist, Vincent Browne, editor of the current affairs magazine *Magill*, and Tony Ryan, a businessman who was, at this stage, in the process of making a fortune (much of which he was later to lose) in an airline leasing company called Guinness Peat Aviation. The paper was re-launched on 17 April 1983 with Browne as editor and with a staff which had been almost halved to a total of thirty-two.

Although under Browne's editorship the paper rapidly acquired a reputation for news exclusives and outspoken comment on public issues, his somewhat erratic management style, and poor staff relations, began to create problems. In 1984 Ryan put his share-holding up for sale, and it was acquired by other businessmen who were not as in tune with Browne and his objectives as Ryan initially had been. Editorial expenditure was reduced and when, in 1985, the Revenue Commissioners secured a judgment against the paper for a £115,000 tax debt (basically in respect of PAYE contributions from staff), the future of the paper again looked bleak. By April 1986, however, the share-holders had decided to re-finance the company and, in October of the same year, the *Sunday Tribune* was reorganised into two companies, one of which, it was hoped, would supplement the organisation's revenues by publishing a series of supplements designed to cash in on the growing market, particularly in Dublin, for free local newspapers. It was a brave new dawn, but it was to plunge the paper into even deeper financial difficulties.

The see-saw fortunes of these relatively new titles bore witness to the fact that, despite the difficult economic situation, entrepreneurial optimism was not in short supply. The more permanent success that eluded all but a few, however, was more marked in the magazine field. Here, as well as *Business and Finance*, which successfully tapped into a niche market, a number of current affairs magazines appeared to exploit the growing public interest in politics, as well as the commercial potential of colour advertising, as yet unavailable to the newspapers. The most successful of these, *Magill* (1977) outlasted all its competitors, and for a considerable time managed to finance its unique blend of investigative reporting and powerfully original writing by virtually cornering the market in high-gloss colour advertising. Its founder and sometime editor, Vincent Browne, who had cut his journalistic teeth on the *Irish Press*, displayed a rare verve which – although it sometimes ended by alienating many of the talented young journalists he attracted to his magazine – also ensured that it remained a powerful and influential voice.

Apart from the fortunes of the individual titles, newspapers in the Republic experienced, during this period, a number of structural and professional problems. Structurally, newspaper managements had begun to pay increasing attention to government–press relationships, not in the area of censorship, but in the areas of government support for industry. One international study (Picard 1983: 16), which looked at government intervention in the economics of newspaper publishing across sixteen advanced Western democratic countries, came to the conclusion that in six of these (headed by Sweden) such intervention was so heavy that it limited or altered competitive situations or the existing structure of the industry. Concentrating on a range of interventions which included tax advantages, government advertising, telecommunications subsidies, subsidies for research and training costs, and aspects of regulation, the study found that Ireland, with a weighted score of 7.4 (as against Sweden's 19.2) came second-lowest in the list, ahead only of Switzerland. At the same time, Picard noted that 'no allegations that state assistance or regulations have resulted in less freedom or expression have been raised'.

These and related matters had been of increasing concern to the Dublin Newspaper Managers' Committee (DNMC), an organisation which had existed for about half a century, and in which the main national newspapers establishment cooperated on industrial relations matters. By the early 1980s, however, the loss of advertising to television, and a perceptible reduction in newspaper circulations generally, led to joint action by members of the committee to promote newspaper advertising. This was in itself a novelty: the national newspaper managements were traditionally suspicious of, or even hostile to each other in areas other than the necessary coordination of industrial relations policies. The new spirit of cooperation, however, led to the formation in 1985 of a new organisation, National Newspapers of Ireland (NNI), which replaced the DNMC, but had a far wider range of functions, not least those of representing the industry and lobbying for its objectives. It has traditionally been concerned about four major issues: VAT on newspapers, particularly in the light of intensive competition from foreign titles; the defamation laws; taxation other than VAT; and press regulation generally. Its first major success was in 1984–5, when it succeeded in persuading the government to reduce the rate of VAT on newspapers from 23% to 10%: the current rate, at 12.5%, is still one of the highest in Europe. Subsequent campaigns to reform the defamation laws have met with less success to date – in June 2000, one newspaper, the *Irish Times*, announced that it was increasing its financial provision for libel costs and damages in that year to £1.4 million from the previous year's £1 million (*IT*: 2 June 2000) – but it has won two other major commercial victories. The first was in the 1992–3 financial year, when it backed a court case being taken by a small provincial newspaper, the *Sligo Champion*, on the question of the taxation of newspaper profits. This eventually resulted in a High Court victory against the Revenue Commissioners, who up to then had insisted either that newspaper publishing was not a manufacturing industry or that, if it was, the only revenue which could be regarded as coming from manufacturing industry was that representing the cover price. The significance of the decision lay in the fact that manufacturing industry was taxed at 10%, whereas corporation profits tax generally was 40%. The court victory ensured that all newspaper profits, whether generated from advertisement sales or from cover price (which the courts accepted was an uneconomic price) would henceforth be subject to tax at the lower rate. The second was in 1994, when the NNI successfully prevented Cablelink, the principal supplier of cable TV services in Dublin, from subsidising the cost of providing its subscribers with satellite services by slotting in local advertising. Membership of NNI includes all the national newspaper titles (including the *Farmers' Journal*), but its management committee is composed only of proprietors, each of whom has one seat regardless of the number of titles published by their organisation.

The establishment of the NNI was an initiative undertaken against a background of apparently waning interest in newspapers generally as a source of information and commentary on current affairs. One survey (MRBI 1983: 14–15) noted that only 17% of those who expressed an interest in current affairs chose newspapers as their prime source of information, as against 53% who chose television and 20% who chose radio. The 17% who chose newspapers were very noticeably middle class, and were to be found principally in the 25–64 age group. The same study identified three main areas in which media generally were said to have a major source of influence on people's thinking: aid to the Third World, the nuclear threat, and Northern Ireland. On other issues (marriage and family life, abortion, divorce and general issues) media ranked substantially below the family and Church, and ahead only of politicians.

The relationship between the politicians themselves and the media was also evolving during this period, and three developments in particular marked this process. The first occurred in 1973, when the first non-Fianna Fail government in sixteen years came to power. That government substantially reorganised the over-bureaucratised structure of the Government Information Bureau (it later became the Government Information Service, GIS), appointing as its new head a talented young television producer, Muiris Mac Conghail, who had been in charge of the controversial 1969 RTE television *exposé* of money-lending in Dublin. Under Mac Conghail, the media management of government became much more professional and efficient. It also, in time, became much more political. One of the consequences of this is that people who were appointed to the GIS were eventually appointed only as temporary civil servants and – like their counterparts in the United States – to resign on a change of government. Another was that, in multi-party governments, each party forming the government appointed its own person to the government press office. When relationships between the parties were strained (as was the case between Fianna Fail and the Labour Party when they were in government together in 1992–4) the different government press officers could be seen, publicly, pulling in diametrically opposite directions.

The second major development in this area occurred in 1976, when the conflict in Northern Ireland was showing every sign of beginning to spill over into the Republic. Deaths from paramilitary or security force activity in the North were occurring at the rate of one a day; there were large parades in Dublin in support of the Provisional IRA; and, in July, the British Ambassador to the Republic, Christopher Ewart-Biggs, was killed by an IRA bomb near his home in Co. Dublin. Cabinet ministers were under severe pressure, both politically and personally, members of their families received frequent telephone threats and their personal security was increased to extraordinary levels.

This process culminated, in the summer of 1976, in the drafting of new security legislation to curb, as far as possible, IRA activity and support in the Republic. This included a draft section 3 which read:

> Any person who expressly or by implication, directly or through another person or persons, or by advertisement, propaganda or any other means, incites or invites another person (or persons generally) to join an unlawful organisation or take part in, support, or assist its activities, shall be guilty of an offence and shall be liable on conviction on indictment to imprisonment for a term not exceeding ten years.

The thinking behind this draft legislation became dramatically clear later, in September, when Dr Conor Cruise O'Brien, the Minister for Posts and Telegraphs since 1973, unguardedly entered the fray. A former diplomat and university professor who had become a member of parliament in 1969, O'Brien was an opponent of censorship, and had vigorously criticised the previous government's decision to dismiss the previous RTE Authority; but he was also sceptical about journalists' attitudes towards Republicanism. Now he volunteered the view, in an interview with the *Washington Post*'s Bernard Nossiter, that he would not be averse to prosecuting the editor of the *Irish Press*, Tim Pat Coogan, for frequently publishing readers' letters which in his view offered aid and comfort to the IRA campaign. Not long afterwards, he added fuel to the flames by confessing that, for him personally, 'any coverage of Sinn Fein activity is too much' (Akenson 1994: 422–3).

Politicians of all parties – including his own – reacted angrily. So did trade unions, not least the NUJ. The offending section was modified so that newspaper coverage would be excluded from its provisions: it was the price of saving the rest of the legislation.

The third development prefigured a growing interest on the part of the media in the private lives of political leaders. In the 1970s and early 1980s, the politician–media relationship was marked – as it still is to a substantial extent – by a degree of media reticence uncommon in the United Kingdom. Whereas in other European countries, politicians' private lives have generally been regarded as of little or no consequence for the media, unless definable questions of public policy are involved, media in Ireland, North and South, have felt themselves uneasily pulled between competition from the UK tabloid media (which until the advent of the Press Complaints Commission regarded politicians' sexual indiscretions in particular as grist to their mill) and a native conservatism. In October 1979, however, the president of Ireland, Dr Patrick J. Hillery, took the extraordinary step of inviting senior Irish journalists to his office to counter rumours that he was about to resign his presidency for personal reasons: the subtext was the suggestion that his marriage was breaking up and that he was intimately involved with another woman. As one historian – at the time a journalist dealing with the story – later observed:

> Confusion reigned in Dublin newsrooms as editors wrestled with what was on and what was off the record. A strong tradition in Irish journalistic life was being undermined: the private life of a President was not the subject of journalistic comment.
>
> (Keogh 1994: 342)

Rumours that this was the case had been circulating in Irish and British media circles for several months, but, as the president was technically above politics, and in any case never held press conferences, a formal denial was out of the question. Hillery himself, an amiable, highly intelligent former cabinet minister, believed that the rumours had been started to discredit him, as a way of dissuading him from re-entering national politics at a crucial juncture in the history of his party, Fianna Fail (*IT*: 5 August 1981). Although he had no intention of re-entering national politics, he decided that the rumours had to be quashed, and invited journalists to a briefing at which he explained the situation to them. Although it was ostensibly off the record, accounts of this extraordinary event, varying only in the amount of detail each contained and sourced unmistakably to the president himself, all appeared in the media on the following day, and the rumours were never heard of again.

Later politicians, in a media context in which UK competition was noticeably more intense, were not to be so fortunate. Emmett Stagg, a junior government minister in the 1992–4 Labour–Fianna Fail administration, who had been seen by police in an area of the city frequented by gay men, became the subject of enormous media attention when this fact was leaked to the media (by whom was never established). After tip-toeing around it for a number of weeks, the media eventually broke the story: Stagg confronted the issue directly in an RTE television interview, and retained his position. More recently, the private life of Bertie Ahern, a senior member of Fianna Fail who became Taoiseach in 1997, also became a media issue. It was well known that he had separated from his wife of many years and was now living with another partner, but the media generally left the subject alone until a cryptic reference was made to it by Albert Reynolds, when Reynolds was defending his leadership of Fianna Fail against a challenge from Ahern.

Within the NUJ itself, ethical and professional issues, which had not generally been the subject of much discussion, suddenly achieved prominence in the early 1980s with the emergence of deep divisions on the question of abortion. The problem had been incubating for some time: in 1975 the NUJ Annual Delegate Meeting (ADM) had pledged to agitate and organise to achieve the aims of a document called the Working Women's Charter, which included a policy for free and readily available abortion. The following year the ADM instructed the union's National Executive Council (NEC) to give active support to a pro-abortion policy. By 1979 ADM delegates were criticising the

NEC for apparent foot-dragging on the issue, and the agenda for the 1980 ADM, which was held in April in Portrush, Co. Derry, featured a number of similar resolutions.

Three Irish NUJ members working in RTE threatened to resign from the union if these resolutions were passed and, when the motion was passed, did so, despite a plea from the (Irish) president of the union, who pointed out that the NUJ had already accepted that it had no right to legislate on individual views on the matter. They then joined the Institute of Journalists, still technically in existence although to all intents and purposes moribund. They were followed by a number of journalists working for provincial newspapers, and the Irish Institute of Journalists was formally reincarnated at a meeting in Limerick on 25 July. On the same day, the NUJ held a consultative conference on abortion in Dublin, attended by twenty-three women and fifty men (including one priest), which passed a resolution advising the NEC that union policy arising out of British legislation on abortion should not be extended to the Republic. A motion which, while accepting that the union did not need to involve itself in active campaigning on the issue, endorsed the right of women to choose abortion, was defeated by almost five to one. The controversy was defused, and the threatened major split in the Irish NUJ organisation never materialised. There was, however, some ill-feeling: when one provincial journalist, Billy Quirke, left the NUJ to join the Institute he was 'blacked' under the terms of his paper's closed shop. He took the NUJ to court and secured payment of damages in an out-of-court settlement.

One of the by-products of these events was a growing feeling on the part of Irish NUJ members that their area of organisational and policy autonomy should be extended. This was eventually given practical expression, after a lengthy internal union debate, in 1993, when the Irish Area Council was replaced by an Irish Executive Council, with greater local autonomy over a wide range of issues. Another, less welcome, outcome was that, when abortion became a live issue in Irish politics in 1981–2, with the emergence of groups campaigning for and against the insertion of anti-abortion clauses in the Irish Constitution, journalists' attitudes, and NUJ policy, again came under the spotlight. The NUJ ADM in 1981 passed a resolution supporting the Irish Women's Right to Choose Campaign, and instructing the NEC to support liberalisation of legislation wherever the union had members. The Irish Area Council of the union distanced itself from this stance, but this aspect of NUJ policy, particularly during the national constitutional referendum on the abortion issue in September 1983, led to accusations by some promoters and supporters of the amendment that NUJ members involved in reporting the controversy were biased (O'Sullivan 1984).

Broadcasting: new controversies

The evolution of broadcasting in the Republic during the period covered by this chapter was marked by a new Broadcasting Act, the first for a dozen years; by intensified controversies about the role of broadcasting in the Northern Ireland conflict (an issue which also affected Northern Ireland broadcasters, although in slightly different ways); by the organic growth of pirate radio, which had up to now manifested itself only in a sporadic or limited way; and by arguments and decisions about the provision of programming choice in television.

The Minister for Posts and Telegraphs, Conor Cruise O'Brien, had two major items on his agenda. One was the question of providing programme choice: in many areas of the country, television viewers could receive only RTE, whereas in the east and North, viewers had access to multi-channel facilities due to the overspill from the BBC and ITV. The second was the question of the responsibilities of RTE vis-à-vis the Northern conflict.

The previous government had already begun to address the matter by setting up, in 1971, ten years after the passage of the original broadcasting act, a Broadcasting Review Committee. In February 1973, just before the change of government, that committee issued an interim report, rejecting suggestions that greater programme choice could be achieved by re-broadcasting either a BBC or an ITV service across the country, and recommending that a second RTE-controlled channel should be established which would carry, in addition to domestic programming, a wide range of BBC, ITV and other foreign programmes. O'Brien's preference, however, was for a different solution: the re-broadcasting of the BBC service throughout the Republic, coupled with the extension of RTE broadcasts to cover Northern Ireland.

The context in which these alternatives were being canvassed was significant. The 1973 RTE annual report (1973: 7) indicated that 77% of the households in the state, or a total of 542,000 homes, had television sets. But only 530,000 of them had licences, and only 27,000 of them were in colour. The licence fee, at £7.50 (increased to £9.00 in October 1973) compared unfavourably with Sweden (£19) and Germany (£13): this helped to explain the fact that licence fees accounted only for 41% of RTE revenue, compared with 80% in Finland and 73% in the Netherlands. Even these statistics, however, paled into insignificance beside the fact that the national station was attempting to provide a quality broadcasting service in the shadow of two of the best broadcasting networks in the world – the BBC and ITV – whose overspill, without any language barrier, created a virtually unique type of competition, and established difficult benchmarks for the indigenous service to meet.

A national debate ensued, culminating in 1975 with a survey which, when it was published in October, showed that a clear majority of respondents in both single and multi-channel areas favoured the RTE2 option over the re-broadcasting of BBC1. O'Brien accepted these results, and gave permission to the Authority to proceed on this basis although, for financial reasons, the service was not to be inaugurated until 1978. Virtually simultaneously, strategic thinking within RTE was taking the reality of competition with increasing seriousness, for RTE, despite enjoying a monopoly within the state, did not have monopoly access to its own audience. RTE programmers, in the light of this, decided early in 1977 to devise a programming policy – both in terms of a production schedule and a transmission schedule – which would enable the national station to concentrate its resources to best effect in the prime-time slot from 8 to 10 p.m. each evening (later extended to cover the period from 7.30 p.m. to 10.30 p.m.). This policy, in the words of one of its architects, 'was devised both in terms of our competitive role on the one hand and public service obligations on the other' (Mac Conghail 1979: 10). In one form or another, it has been the backbone of programming policy ever since.

Another significant change had already taken place: in 1974, the limit on the number of households which could be connected to a single high-specification television aerial, which had been set at ten in 1961, increased under political pressure to cater for a large working-class housing estate built on the outskirts of Dublin in 1966, and increased to 500 in 1970, was abolished. The quid pro quo for RTE was that aerial contractors would pay a percentage of gross rental income to RTE as compensation for the national stations' presumed loss of advertising income (NAI: Communications: TV 6027). Over the following twenty years, a process of rationalisation took place, in the course of which RTE was to acquire ownership of Cablelink, a company which controlled the major part of the cable system, and which it eventually sold in two tranches in the late 1990s for more than £200 million.

These organisational and strategic choices, however, were to a considerable extent overshadowed by the arguments surrounding the new government's broadcasting bill, which was introduced in 1975 but which did not become law until a year later. O'Brien, whose suspicions about journalists in the print media have already been noted, was no less concerned and about the attitudes of journalists in RTE, for which he had, of course, more direct responsibility (Horgan and Meehan 1987: 3).

Because of O'Brien's known attitudes towards the IRA, frequently repeated and considerably hardened in the years since he left office, the received wisdom about the 1976 Act is that it represented an unacceptable and unwelcome extension of the censorship imposed on the broadcast media by the previous government. Viewed more closely, however, and taken in conjunction with the fresh set of directives issued by O'Brien in relation to reporting political violence in Northern Ireland, it emerges as in some respects a less restrictive, if not exactly liberalising, measure. It is still an authoritarian response to a complex series of political and journalistic problems, and this can be clearly seen in relation to the situation in Northern Ireland itself, where broadcasters continued to work without statutory restrictions on their professional activity until 1988. This did not mean, of course, that they were unfettered: the system of internal checks and balances introduced by the BBC, and UTV's caution in relation to engaging with the problems at a serious level, gave rise to considerable, if intermittent controversy. But the contrast between the broadcasting dispensations in the two parts of the island was a very public illustration of the harsher regime obtaining for broadcasters in the Republic.

The 1976 Act was based in part on the 1974 final report from the Broadcasting Review Committee, in that it provided a statutory description of the purpose and objectives of the broadcasting service and supported the concept of public service broadcasting. It bore a passing – and in all probability not coincidental – resemblance to the British Broadcasting Act of 1973, in its requirement that the Authority should not broadcast anything which 'might reasonably be regarded as likely to promote, or incite to crime or as tending to undermine the authority of the State' (Fisher 1978: 45). It rejected, however, the committee's recommendation for the establishment of a Broadcasting Commission to supervise the whole broadcasting operation – an idea that was to resurface in various forms before finally being implemented as government policy in 1999.

In a number of areas the 1976 Act represented a relaxation of the tight-fitting garment created by the 1960 Act. It maintained the requirement for objectivity and impartiality in matters of current controversy, for example, but made it clear that balance could be achieved over a number of programmes rather than within the boundaries of each presentation. This was a common-sense solution which was already on the way to being adopted in practice. It contained a number of exhortations, such as those referring to the Authority's duty to 'be mindful of the need for understanding and peace within the whole island of Ireland' and to foster awareness and understanding of 'the values and traditions of countries other than the State, including in particular those of such countries which are members of the European Economic Community' (Fisher 1978: 43). The latter injunction, of course, also included Britain.

In other sections, the Act, while retaining the right of the minister to dismiss the Authority, laid down that he could not do so without first having secured majority approval in both houses of parliament for his decision; it created a mechanism whereby a ministerial directive could be rejected by either house of parliament; and it allowed the Authority to depart from the general obligation of impartiality if it wanted to express its own opinion on matters of controversy connected with broadcasting policy. It established a Broadcasting Complaints Commission (although the methodologies of the commission were, and remain, so Byzantine that few disgruntled viewers have the stamina to carry their complaints to a conclusion); it instituted a system under which the standards of advertising would also be scrutinised; and it instructed the Authority to avoid unreasonable invasions of personal privacy by programme-makers. It did not, as has been seen, make any provision for a second channel: this was dealt with separately by the minister.

It retained, as might be expected, the power of the minister to issue directives to the Authority. Even before the passage of the Act, however, O'Brien had issued – in 1974 – his own directive, considerably more detailed than those which had been issued by his predecessors in Fianna Fail. The detail it contained was evidence of the mounting frustration at RTE, where the Authority's repeated requests to the government for clarification of the original directive had been met by the unhelpful assertion that it (i.e. the directive) spoke for itself. O'Brien's version, drafted in the light of numerous representations from RTE, went further in terms of providing detail. It not only specified the organisations whose members were to be banned from the airwaves, but inserted an open-ended provision ensuring that organisations proscribed by the British government would also be automatically included in the list of undesirables.

The basic principle, of course, remained intact: a level of direct and effective government editorial control of broadcasting which, despite intermittent protests by the NUJ and others, was to remain in place for almost another two decades. The Irish headquarters of the union in Dublin organised a questionnaire for its members in 1977 which evoked the comment, from one of them, that:

> The ultra-cautious atmosphere which Section 31 and the guidelines have fostered in newsroom and programme sections has meant that enquiries into controversial areas have not been encouraged … there is now a general anxiety about tackling stories which might embarrass the government on the issue of security.
>
> (Curtis 1984: 194)

The situation was complicated by the fact that, within RTE, not all editorial personnel were of one mind on the issue, and there were strong anti-IRA sentiments, especially in the programmes (i.e. current affairs) division, as opposed to the newsroom, where there would have been more sympathy for the Republican cause in general, although not for the specific violence of the IRA. This reflected the division of opinion within the population generally: a 1979 survey by the Economic and Social Research Institute found that, while 41% of the population of the Republic sympathised with the IRA's motives (a proportion closely resembling the 38–43% who generally supported the Fianna Fail party at elections), some 21% actually supported their activities (Davis and Sinnott 1979: 99).

The detailed clarification in the 1974 and subsequent directives of what the government actually had in mind prompted a revision of the guidelines issued by RTE to its staff, but was also to spawn further anomalies. In 1980, for example, RTE carried an interview with a member of the Irish Republican Socialist Party (IRSP), the political wing of a paramilitary organisation known as the Irish National Liberation Army (INLA): the INLA had been proscribed by the British legislation, but the IRSP had not – whereas the IRA and its political wing, Sinn Fein, were proscribed by both governments (Joint Committee on State Sponsored Bodies [JCSSB] 1981: 66). In 1981, RTE had to secure a special exemption from the government in order to be able to show two episodes of the documentary series, *The Troubles*, because it contained interviews with people who were members of proscribed organisations (it was a RTE/BBC co-production, which underlined the absurdity of the situation). RTE, for its part, interpreted the directives with considerable rigidity, excluding from the airwaves people who happened to be members of Sinn Fein, although their proposed participation in a programme was for reasons quite unrelated to their political role. On the other hand, a new situation arose in relation to a general election in February 1982, when Sinn Fein, by then a registered political party in the Republic, approached RTE to discuss the question of whether the party would be entitled to party political broadcasts during the election campaign. The Authority's problem was that its role in providing time for these broadcasts was to some extent in conflict with the government's directive, at least insofar as Sinn Fein was concerned. However, it decided that democratic considerations should prevail, and announced that Sinn Fein would be facilitated in the same way as other parties. A major controversy ensued: the government issued a fresh directive, prohibiting such Sinn Fein broadcasts; and Sinn Fein appealed to the courts on the issue, but without success.

As the newspapers were not bound by any of the restrictions which applied to RTE, it would be inaccurate to say that the public was deprived of all the information it needed. The consequences of the broadcasting ban however, were pervasive and long term. Although the immediate effect was to force broadcasters into a number of strategems to make sure that viewers and listeners were not kept entirely in the dark (MacDermott 1995: 70–80), the overall picture available to the public from the electronic media was necessarily an inadequate one. Long term, the consequences included a yawning gap in the electronic media archive for more than twenty of the most politically significant years in twentieth-century Ireland, and a consistent tendency (in which, as it happened, the broadcast media were not alone) to under-estimate the strength of Sinn Fein at election times. The existence of a blind spot is nowhere more tellingly illustrated than in McLoone and MacMahon's *Television and Irish Society* (1984), a study of twenty-one years of Irish television, whose otherwise cogently presented and well-researched essays managed to ignore Northern Ireland and the Section 31 directives completely.

Television was increasingly becoming a battleground for other interests as well. Irish-language groups, although to some extent mollified by the earlier establishment of Raidio na Gaeltachta, remained conscious of the relatively greater attraction of television as a popular medium and maintained pressure on the Authority to increase programming in this area. The most popular Irish-language current affairs programme in 1973, *Féach*, attracted an audience of 635,000, a considerable figure by any standards. In this area, inevitably, targets were more frequently set than achieved, although in 1976 television programming in Irish amounted to 10% of total domestic programme output. This was a relatively high figure: Irish-language programming, as a proportion of total output, and even of domestic production, suffered thereafter both from the extension of broadcasting hours and the introduction of RTE2 in 1978. Women, too, added their voices to the clamour for more balanced representation: RTE set up an internal working party on the issue in 1979, a year in which its yearbook indicated, for example, that in the news division, all twenty-four programme editors and presenters were men, and all but two of the seventy-two production assistants were women. This – and the fact that women were conspicuous by their absence from agricultural programmes – were among the issues raised at Dail committee hearings (JCSSB 1981: 85–93). There was also concern about perceived lapses from moral standards: groups such as the Knights of St Columbanus and the St Thomas More Society complained about the inadequacy of the complaints procedure established under the 1976 Act (JCSSB 1981: 94–9, 104–9). Similarly, the Irish Family League alleged that RTE was '99 per cent weighted in favour of contraceptives, divorce, abortion, homosexuality etc.' It also made a number of more specific criticisms, including one about a programme showing the ' full frontal' delivery of a baby, and a *Late Late Show* on which a woman had examined herself for breast cancer, an episode which it described as 'indecent' (JCSSB 1981: 111–13).

While RTE was defending itself against criticisms of this kind, however, more serious problems of a structural nature were emerging. This was the challenge to its monopoly embodied in the emergence and rapid growth of pirate radio stations, and the resulting legal quagmire which defied the sporadic and somewhat half-hearted government attempts to regulate it until the late 1980s. Until the early 1960s, pirate broadcasting had been short term and generally political in character. The Department of Justice maintained files on illegal broadcasts by Republican activists in the 1940s and 1950s (NAI: Justice: S 164/40; S 16/57) but these broadcasts were generally ephemeral and related largely to events in Northern Ireland. In January 1959, at the height of the 1956–62 IRA campaign against Northern Ireland police and military installations, a broadcast from a pirate radio station describing itself as 'Irish Freedom Radio' was heard in Monaghan, on which an unidentified male speaker criticised the introduction of internment without trial by the Northern Ireland authorities (*IT*: 20 January 1959).

Such experiments were short-lived, not least because they generally attracted the keen attention of the security forces. The emergence of pirate radio devoted to popular music, on the other hand, posed an entirely different set of problems and political imperatives. Irish government policy in this area was circumscribed for many years by two separate factors. One was the antiquity of the legislation (effectively the Wireless Telegraphy Act of 1926) and the inadequacy of the penalties it prescribed. Successful prosecutions demanded proof that the accused possessed a radio transmitter; pirate radio operators, by removing a small component even as the police raid on their premises began, could successfully plead that their equipment was incapable of transmitting anything. The second was the popularity of the pirates: neither the UK nor the Irish government, having failed to move swiftly against pirate radio in the early years, was in a position to close down the stations without incurring serious popular displeasure. Stations like Radio Caroline (established in March 1964 by an Irishman, as it happened) created a new problem for both administrations, and led to a coordination of legislative action in a largely unsuccessful attempt to meet this new challenge (NAI: Taoiseach: S 17618/95; 97/6/169).

Initially, it seemed as if the governments were winning the war against the pirates: Caroline was put off the air in 1967, but reappeared in 1972. In Ireland, the pirates were on a much smaller scale, and initially attracted little attention from the authorities: one of the earliest stations, known variously as 'The Colleen Home Service', 'Radio Laxey' and the 'Ballymun Home Service', operated intermittently from a North Dublin housing estate from 1944 onwards, mutating into 'Radio Galaxy' and 'Radio na Saoirse' ('Freedom Radio') in the 1960s and 1970s (Mulryan 1988: 22–3). Fom the mid-1960s to the mid-1970s, however, pirate radio became a much more noticeable phenomenon, and attracted a considerable amount of police attention. The first successful prosecution of a Dublin pirate station, Radio Melinda, in December 1972, attracted widespread publicity, not least because of the derisory penalties imposed. By the late 1970s, there were approximately twenty-five pirate stations operating from various locations, generally in the larger urban areas, attracting an audience of young people tired of traditional radio, and annoyed at the heavy-handed attempts at suppression.

RTE, which had been concerned about the loss of advertising to these stations as well as by the implied threat to its monopoly, moved to defend its position, albeit somewhat lethargically. Its first community radio experiment, Radio Liberties, was broadcast from a mobile studio in a working-class area of Dublin in 1975; similar experiments were carried out in Waterford, Limerick and a number of rural communities in that year and in 1976. It had a decentralised service operating from a studio in Cork, but of a very limited kind.

By 1978, RTE's response had moved up a gear. It was a two-pronged strategy. One prong was the launch of Radio 2, a pop music station which, the station hoped, would wean the listening public away from the pirates (and give the government a window of opportunity for moving decisively against them). Radio 2 came on the air in a rush at the end of May 1979, and almost immediately captured 56% of the audience aged between 15 and 20 (Mulryan 1988: 61). This figure, although hailed as a success by RTE, was also capable of a less flattering interpretation: a new station backed by all RTE's resources had managed to attract only just over half of the potential audience. From now on, up to and after the ultimate legalisation of commercial radio, the battle for audience share was a relentless one.

The second was a detailed set of proposals for a national community radio service, approved by the RTE Authority at its meeting on 14 December 1979 and submitted to the Minister for Posts and Telegraphs early the following year. These proposals expressed the Authority's anxiety with some clarity:

> Any loss of advertising revenue to RTE would have serious effects on RTE's ability to serve the whole Irish community. Commercial radio is viable only in large cities but can, nevertheless, cream off a very important part of broadcasting income. This would seriously undermine RTE's capacity to provide services in other parts of the country and to be truly public in character.
>
> (Radio Pobal na Tire 1980: 3)

These proposals argued that balanced local radio could not be self-supporting in communities of fewer than 100,000–150,000 people, but suggested that, with appropriate infrastructure, a local radio could be created which would allow access on a regular (although unquantified) basis to every community of about 3,000 people. The initial phase of the service, they maintained, could be provided with a minimal 3% increase in the licence fee.

These proposals provided RTE, its trade unions and some politicians with a standard around which to rally, but they were rapidly overtaken by events, and undermined by government inaction. Two government measures were drafted and introduced in 1980 and 1981 to take the pirates off the air and establish a mechanism for overseeing the development of legitimate commercial radio, but they lapsed with the onset of the 1981 general election. This failure coincided with the arrival of Radio Sunshine and, later, Radio Nova. These, described by the historian of this phase of Irish radio, Peter Mulryan, as the 'super-pirates' (1988: 84) were high-powered stations operating openly in defiance of the law, sometimes even carrying advertising from state bodies, paying taxes to the government, and flourishing in a legal and political vacuum. That vacuum was created in part by a lengthy period of political instability, which saw three general elections in eighteen months. In the run-up to the second of these, in February 1982, the country's largest political party, Fianna Fail, took the unprecedented step of advertising its support for pirate stations in the national print media. Pirate radio responded in kind by assisting the party to set up its own radio station at party headquarters (Mulryan 1988: 93). Fianna Fail won the election, but had done nothing to legalise the pirates before they lost office in the second election of that year, in November. In the run-up to that election, the NUJ had retaliated, threatening not to interview on RTE any politician who broadcast on any of the pirate radio stations.

The new government comprised of parties opposed to Fianna Fail took office determined to do something about commercial radio, but even as pressure to regularise the situation increased (apparently also from Britain, where the Irish super-pirate broadcasts could be heard with increasing clarity), the government found itself hamstrung by internal disagreement on the issue. Labour, the junior coalition partner, was steadfastly behind the RTE plan; Fine Gael, the majority partner, was broadly in favour of legalising and regulating what could not be abolished, so that the government could move decisively against the more disreputable stations and in this way tidy up the airwaves. RTE's annual report for 1983 did not mince its words: the present situation was 'anarchic', with over seventy illegal operators, and the Authority was not only disappointed by the absence of a government response to its local radio proposals, but was hampered by 'the indecision regarding local radio' (RTE 1984: 8).

Misjudging the moment, however – and in particular under-estimating the government's ability to sort out its differences – the authorities launched a new and particularly fierce set of raids against the pirates. But these stations now had huge audiences, and the raids triggered a series of demonstrations which served notice on the government that the political costs of suppressing them were incalculable. In an attempt to buy time, and in the vain hope that it might engineer a politically acceptable response, it appointed an Interim Radio Commission in 1985 to study the questions involved. By the time that the government lost office in 1987, the problem was no closer to a solution and the pirates, despite the best efforts of the authorities to close them down, and repeated moves by RTE to block their signals, were virtually mainstream media.

Northern Ireland: a new polarisation

Even before the mid-1970s, the conflict in Northern Ireland had brought about as acute a degree of social and community polarisation as had existed since the 1920s. The 1968–70 period, when it looked for a time as if the Northern Ireland Civil Rights Association would provide common ground for both nationalists and Unionists who wanted to bring about political reform without necessarily changing the constitutional status quo, was only a memory. The re-emergence of the Irish Republican Army, the more sporadic but equally lethal activities of loyalist paramilitary groups, and the increasingly controversial role of the British Army, created a bunker mentality which reinforced traditional loyalties, especially in the print media. In 1973, a political initiative by the British and Irish and Northern Ireland governments known as the Sunningdale agreement (after the Home Counties location where the talks took place) attempted to provide a new basis for stability, but succeeded only in making things worse. It was followed by a politically motivated strike in 1974 in which Loyalist paramilitary forces operated to paralyse the Northern Ireland economy and, immediately afterwards, by the definitive imposition of direct rule from Westminster. If editorial polarisation had not been accentuated by the politics of the situation, the economics of what was happening would have encouraged it in any case. The Northern Ireland economy was in severe difficulties: part of the IRA policy was to wreck the industrial base of the province insofar as this could be achieved by paramilitary methods, and bomb attacks on British and foreign-owned business contributed to a situation in which advertising, in common with many other elements of economic activity like tourism, was severely affected.

There were few exceptions. The *Belfast Telegraph* continued to draw readership and to some extent advertising from both communities, but this was probably as much a result of its monopoly position as for any other reason: its politics remained resolutely Unionist. The Northern Ireland edition of the *Sunday World*, for all that it was well known to be effectively a Dublin paper, maintained its position by de-emphasising politics and sticking to its tabloid last. The major anomaly was the *Sunday News* which, although it was a product of the Unionist Century group, publishers of the *Newsletter*, managed not only to combine Protestants and Catholics on its workforce, but to establish a measurable appeal in both communities. It was founded to exploit a gap in the market – effectively there was no Northern Ireland Sunday newspaper of any description – and from the start its canny choice of columnists and its news agenda ensured that, unlike its stable-mate the *Newsletter*, it had a broadly based readership after its launch on 14 March 1965.

> In the early 1970s, with riots, gunfire, 'action' up and down Belfast city, the paper had editions for the upper, mid and lower Falls [the Nationalist area], the upper, mid and lower Shankill [the Loyalist heartland] … And research done on the readership constantly showed the breakdown spot on to Northern Ireland's Protestant/Catholic 60/40 split.
>
> (Barclay 1993)

The launch of *Sunday Life* in 1988 by the *Belfast Telegraph*, however, brought considerable competitive resources to bear on the ailing *Newsletter* company, and the *Sunday News* eventually expired in March 1993.

Some newspapers were the intermittent objects of the violence. Already, on 15 July 1971, a printing plant which had just been built by the Mirror group outside Belfast, and which had the capacity to accelerate the growth in the circulation of UK papers in the Republic as well as in the North (until then most UK papers arrived via an expensive nightly flight from UK airports), had been so seriously damaged by an IRA bomb that the company withdrew and abandoned its plans to print in Ireland. The *Belfast Telegraph*'s Unionism, rather than its cross-community appeal, was responsible for a bomb attack on the paper's premises in February 1973, and a second in September 1976. Both attacks, presumably by the IRA, evoked a blitz spirit among the paper's work-force. A 4-page 'penny marvel' was produced on printing presses owned by a local newspaper just outside Belfast, and sold some 75,000 copies a day until normal production was resumed (Brodie 1995: 180–2).

Two years later, the paper was nearly closed again – this time by less lethal, but equally forceful, industrial action. The dispute was not of the *Telegraph*'s making, but originated in a conflict between the NUJ and provincial newspaper managements across Britain. The strike, which began in December 1978, lasted for seven weeks and four days, during which time the *Telegraph* continued to appear, most of the journalistic work being done by its editor, Roy Lilley. The striking *Telegraph* journalists decided to produce a rival newspaper, and did so between 11 and 17 January 1979, when they produced three issues of an 8-page paper entitled *Belfast Times* (Brodie 1995: 191). A 14.5% pay increase ended the strike.

A 1984 survey showed that the *Telegraph* was being read by 40% of the adult population of Northern Ireland; the figure would undoubtedly have been higher but for the polarisation of opinion which was weakening its appeal to nationalist readers. Under Thomson's stewardship, however, it continued to invest for a future it no doubt hoped would arrive sooner rather than later: in April 1985 it commissioned its first colour presses.

The same year saw political developments which some hoped would finally reduce, if not eliminate, violence in Northern Ireland. This was the 1985 Hillsborough Agreement between the British government led by Mrs Thatcher and the Irish government led by Dr Garret FitzGerald. Although crafted with more care than its 1973 predecessor, it generated similar suspicion and antagonism on the wilder shores of both Unionism and nationalism, suspicion which the *Telegraph* shared to a degree. 'The price of nationalist consent to participation in Northern Ireland, if this it is', it editorialised the following day, 'has been fixed at an unrealistically high level' (16 November 1975).

Its contemporary, if not exactly its rival, the *Irish News*, saw things in a predictably different light. Hillsborough, it said, was 'a brave and commendable attempt to begin the healing process' (16 November 1975). But by then the *Irish News* itself had already begun a process of change. In 1982, it had acquired a new editor in Martin O'Brien, a 27-year-old university graduate who had served his apprenticeship on the *Belfast Telegraph*. Even as the conflict worsened, O'Brien came to the conclusion that his newspaper would have to take a stand, however limited, against the glorification of political violence by some elements within the nationalist community, or at least against his paper's apparent endorsement of, or connivance at it. He did this by putting an end to the type of death notice normally inserted in the *Irish News* on behalf of members of the IRA who had been killed in the conflict by members of the security forces. Traditionally, *Irish News* death notices for such men (and women) had recorded their rank within the IRA, had stated that they had died on active service and had frequently incorporated strongly expressed ultra-nationalist sentiments. Death notices for IRA members were still accepted, but shorn of the ideological and military terminology in which they had previously been couched. It was a controversial decision, all the more so because it was to some extent unexpected, but O'Brien did not back down. Two years later, he was to leave for a position with the BBC, but the changes he had inaugurated had taken root, even as the paper's ownership was changing. In 1983, half-way through his period as editor, the two members of the McSparran family who were the principal controllers of the newspaper died in an accident, and the paper came into the hands of another Northern Catholic business family, the Fitzpatricks.

The print media were to some extent isolated from the intensity of the conflict by the fact that their partisan coloration was, by and large, unmistakable. The electronic media were in a different position: established and regulated by the state, and with the statutory obligation to maintain impartiality, they themselves became a battleground over which the competing forces – not only nationalists and Unionists, but government and security forces – vied for control or, at least, for influence. In the Republic, the successive directives issued by governments under the Broadcasting Acts had created a sort of eerie silence, in that the voices of some of the principal protagonists had been stilled; in Northern Ireland, on the other hand, the absence of such a clear policy created a no-man's-land for broadcasters in which skirmishing was the order of the day. Whatever the broadcasters did, they were closely watched.

Roman Catholics and Protestants alike are avid news-watchers. They could never be accused of indifference to the image of themselves that appears almost nightly on their television screens. Often, I believe, they switch channels keenly in pursuit of it. They share especially in television's immediacy – being often the witnesses of an event itself and shortly afterwards of television's account of it ... In sectarian conflict, it is not uncommon for each side to regard the camera as the instrument of the other's propaganda and to react to it accordingly.

(Bell 1973: 371)

The guidelines which had been established by the BBC and by ITV in 1971 remained the operative ground rules for the reporting of the conflict, but they did not succeed in averting controversy. They were, in addition, supplemented, although not directly, by two pieces of Westminster legislation. The first, the 1973 Broadcasting Act, forbade any incitement to crime or disorder, and this provision was explicitly cited in a decision by the IBA to ban a programme in 1977 which featured an account of a speech in Dublin by a member of Sinn Fein, even though the recording of his actual words had been excised (Curtis 1984: 155). The second was the 1976 Prevention of Terrorism Act. Although it was suggested during its passage through parliament that it should be amended specifically to prohibit broadcasters from aiding or abetting terrorists, no amendments of this nature were made, on the understanding that such would not be necessary. In the view of a commentator with a relatively benign view of the activities of the BBC management during this period, the effect of this particular piece of legislation was:

almost certainly equivalent to the directive which the Fianna Fail government issued to the Irish broadcasting service, Radio Telefis Eireann, forbidding the service to broadcast interviews with subversives or film of their activities.

(Cathcart 1984: 240)

When this comment was written, no interviews with paramilitaries and almost no film of their activities had been transmitted by the BBC since 1981. This sanitised coverage had implications for elections, too: the 1982 elections to the Northern Ireland Assembly, a short-lived body designed to take the place of the old Stormont parliament, saw the election of Gerry Adams to one of the Belfast seats with almost 10,000 votes, but this aspect of the election was severely distorted by the ambient atmosphere affecting broadcasters generally.

Nor had the situation been much more open prior to that, since the overall tension between broadcasters and government had been heightened by an incident in Carrickmore, Co. Tyrone, in 1979, when a BBC unit had filmed IRA men mounting an illegal roadblock. This had led directly to a tightening of the 1971 guidelines in both broadcasting organisations, but it was, in a sense, only the culmination of a series of incidents which had occurred sporadically throughout the 1970s, which had made such an intensification of the problems for broadcasters inevitable, and which had – for some of them, at least – led to a modification of their view that they were being allowed to do a reasonable job in difficult circumstances.

It is difficult to isolate the more significant incidents in this period, but any list involving ITV would of necessity include a number of interviews carried out by the British journalist, Mary Holland, with Republican leaders for that network in 1973 and 1974. In the case of her 1984 interview, the tension was heightened by the fact that, four days after it was broadcast, the Birmingham IRA bombings, in which nineteen people died, took place. This led some political commentators to argue that there was a direct link between the interview and the explosions (Curtis 1984: 160). The IBA was also involved in controversies surrounding the publication of a report by Amnesty International in June 1978. A planned programme on this report was banned by the IBA, an action which the reporter involved, Peter Taylor, described bluntly as 'political censorship' (Curtis 1984: 62). Similar difficulties attended the broadcasting of some programmes in a series on *The Troubles* in 1981. The role of the domestic contractor in all of this was the subject of a veiled, and somewhat tortured contemporary remark by UTV's chairman, R.B. Henderson, who commented:

On many occasions, particularly in the last decade or so, I had some difficult decisions to take on programmes made by 'visiting firemen' on Northern Ireland. We were mindful of their effect not only in Northern Ireland and upon our viewers but also upon national views and even international ones. It was important to Ulster as well as to Independent Television that this should be balanced and accurate ... Not for one moment would I pretend that all the programmes made by ourselves or by anybody else fell into this category, but I like to think that for the most part they were well in touch ... although it can be argued, and with an arguable degree of incontrovertibility – that television fuelled flames and entrenched prejudices.

(Henderson 1984: 43–4)

If the difficulties experienced by the IBA in relation to the Northern Ireland conflict seemed to be related primarily to current affairs coverage in the general sense, those at the BBC extended much more deeply into the news area, which always had a greater potential for conflict, but which had been much more cautiously handled by both ITV's national network and by its Northern Ireland franchisee, UTV. This surfaced dramatically in May 1974, during the Ulster Workers' Council (UWC) national strike which succeeded in bringing down the power-sharing executive in Northern Ireland created as the outcome of the Sunningdale agreement. The UWC had prepared plans for a pirate radio station of their own, but never went ahead with it because, in the words of one UWC leader, the BBC 'were prepared to be fed any information. They fell into their own trap that "the public must get the news"' (Cathcart 1984: 231).

This did not prevent the BBC from being accused by the Northern Ireland secretary in 1976 of providing 'a daily platform' to the IRA (Cathcart 1984: 234), and hostilities deepened the following year when a programme by the veteran broadcaster Keith Kyle for the *Tonight* team which raised serious questions about the British government's commitment to ending the inhuman and degrading treatment of persons in police custody which had been identified in 1971, and which had subsequently been condemned by the European Court of Human Rights at Strasbourg. Three years after this programme, which featured the experiences, while in police custody, of Bernard O'Connor, a Fermanagh schoolteacher with no political connections, O'Connor was awarded substantial damages in a civil action against the Royal Ulster Constabulary (Kyle 1970: 116).

Worse was to come when, with the IRA hunger strikes of 1980 and 1981, the BBC found itself in a crossfire more intense than any it had yet experienced. Northern Ireland nationalists were incensed by what they saw as pro-government reporting; Unionist leaders – one of whom described a *Panorama* programme in September 1981 as 'a propaganda coup for the IRA' (Cathcart 1984; 245), saw the whole question from a diametrically opposed perspective.

On its way to achieving a stance which might, in the eyes of its defenders, be described as offending everyone more or less equally, the BBC had nonetheless suffered some casualties. Martin Bell, who in 1972, had defended his employers against charges of censorship, still maintained in 1979 that 1969 had been the only occasion on which the BBC had engaged in unacceptable self-censorship. This limitation of unacceptable self-censorship to the 1969 period was endorsed by Keith Kyle (1970: 116), but other critics, such as Hall (1973), Curtis (1984) and, to a lesser extent, Butler (1995), have not been so forgiving. Harshest of all was Raymond Williams, who commented:

> The BBC has in general, and especially in recent months, a less than honourable record on the reporting of events in Northern Ireland. The point has been reached … when some views are excluded because they are prima facie abhorrent – the charter of censors anywhere in the world.
>
> (Williams 1973: 15)

The situation was to change yet again in the late 1980s, when further, this time statutory, restrictions were introduced on the broadcast media, but the Northern arena had by then become the scene for increasingly sophisticated attempts at news management by all involved. The introduction of direct rule in 1974 and the extension of the activities of the Northern Ireland Office in the years that followed led to an intensification of media management techniques. The involvement of the British Army, which had its own press operations (which included disinformation activities), supplemented the already well-developed RUC press office. In 1990 the Northern Ireland Information Service spent £7.2 million in the North for a population of 1.5 million, on top of the considerable sums expended in media management by the police and army

(Feeney 1997: 44). Sinn Fein, too, developed an increasingly agile and focused press relations strategy during this period. Academic criticism tended to concentrate on perceived lapses from standards by broadcasters and other British media, notably the tabloid newspapers, and there were relatively few studies such as that by Clutterbuck (1981) to argue the opposite case. The critics of broadcasting orthodoxy on both sides argued that, by affecting a neutral stance, it was flinching from the necessary task of analysing societal conflict at a significantly deep level – as an attempt by terrorists to subvert the British state, or as the understandable expression of a defensible anti-colonialism, depending on one's point of view. At either end of the spectrum, there were critics who were so *parti pris* in the argument that they tended to see conspiracy theories where there was, in many cases, nothing more sinister (although not, for that reason, particularly excusable) than a combination of political timorousness, bureaucratic muddle and strong Establishment sensibilities.

The smoke from the battleground of news and current affairs appeared to smother creativity in other fields also. At a conference in London in 1980, dramatists and critics complained that Northern Ireland had become off-limits as a subject for television drama, and that only nineteen television plays had been produced in twelve years on the themes of that conflict (McLoone 1996: 80). It was certainly notable that, even before the conflict erupted in 1968, the few television dramas which actually dealt with such topics had generally been centrally produced by the networks, rather than by the – admittedly small – regional centres in Belfast (Sam Thompson's *Over the Bridge* and *Cemented with Love*, Granada 1961 and BBC 1965 respectively; Alun Owen's *Progress to the Park*, BBC 1965; and John D. Stewart's *Boatman, Do Not Tarry*, UTV 1968).

6 Coming to terms, 1985–95

The fluidity and volatility which characterised Irish media from the end of the 1970s into the mid-1980s was maintained and even intensified in the decade which followed. In the electronic media, the already qualified monopoly of the state was further fragmented as the airwaves were opened up to commercial interests in a profoundly significant restructuring of the legislative and regulatory framework. In print, a process of rationalisation began to take place on both the national and regional level; new titles appeared to target niche markets as part of a move away from generalist media; and Irish media, both print and electronic, became the object of increasing interest on the part of non-national entrepreneurs and companies. In the process, the sharp line that could have been drawn traditionally between indigenous and non-Irish media became blurred, raising new issues of ownership, control and content.

The establishment of National Newspapers of Ireland (NNI) in 1985, as already noted, was motivated initially by a need to win back advertising for the newspapers from the electronic media. The organisation evolved, however, into an energetic advocate for issues of significance to newspaper managements generally, notably those of taxation and defamation. Taxation – and in particular the high rate of value added tax – was seen by the NNI as especially significant in the circulation war being waged between indigenous Irish titles and the UK imports.

It was a war in which, initially, it was difficult to discern the relative strength of the combatants. Already in 1984 the Industrial Development Authority (IDA), the state agency charged with promoting industrial development generally, had declined to allocate special aid to the newspaper industry, arguing that import growth was not a major problem. In the preceding decade, the IDA argued, imports had increased only from 17% to 22% of the total market (Horgan 1993b: 36). The newspaper industry, using Central Statistics Office (CSO) figures, charged that the imports had in fact increased to 27%. These assessments were clouded by the fact that most figures for UK imports were, until the mid-1990s, no more than industry estimates, and CSO figures for newspaper imports took no account of unsold or damaged papers.

Whichever figure is chosen, it was at least incontestable that there had been an increase. A 1976 study had suggested that imports were running at about

15% of the total market, and that import penetration was 20% in the daily morning market, and 30% in the Sunday market. Irish readers, the report suggested, bought British newspapers as well as, or instead of, Irish papers because the UK papers 'actually fill a gap in the newspaper publishing spectrum which Irish publishers have been reluctant to fill'. And they appealed to the 'younger and the less inhibited sections of the community' (M.H. Consultants 1978: 12).

It added:

> The view was expressed by more than one publisher that there was scope for only three Dublin dailies: one at the top of the market (the *Irish Times*), one in the middle (where there are currently two, the *Independent* and the *Press*) and one at the lower end of the market (where there are currently no Irish papers).
>
> (M.H. Consultants 1978: 12)

This analysis was to be borne out, with an eerie accuracy, in the period under review, but in ways in which the authors of that prescient report could barely have predicted. The *Irish Times*, which Douglas Gageby had returned to edit for the second time in 1986, had again recorded substantial circulation gains between then and the early 1990s, but was still well behind the *Irish Independent*. The *Irish Press*, however, was faltering. In 1981 it had reached 104,000, its highest circulation since 1966. But that year was characterised, as noted in the previous chapter, by high political excitement centred on the leadership of the Fianna Fail party. From then on, its circulation began a remorseless slide, assisted by a strike in 1985 which kept it off the streets for twelve weeks. By 1988 its circulation had fallen to just under 66,000, and not even the cross-subsidisation from the still successful *Evening Press* and *Sunday Press* could act as a life-line for ever. The circulation of the *Evening Press*, in fact, declined by more than 20,000 copies to fewer than 99,000 between 1987 and 1989. It was not alone: changing commuting habits and competition from other media, including afternoon television, were responsible for a persistent decline in the circulation of both Dublin evening papers throughout the 1980s and early 1990s, despite the fact that they had no direct UK newspaper competitor.

The Independent group's role in the market place was coming in for increasing scrutiny. One international study (Sanchez-Taberno 1993: 101) noted that in 1990 it controlled 51% of the market, the second highest figure for any country studied, after Austria (where Mediaprint controlled 54.4%). In Ireland, the same report noted, the market share of the two largest groups, the Independent and Press, was 75%, a figure not exceeded by any other country (Austria was next with 68%, Switzerland lowest with 21%). The larger group, although outwardly successful, also had problems, particularly from the UK tabloids which were nibbling away at the circulation base of its popular morning daily.

Both the Independent and the Press group now moved to shore up their positions, with strategies that were superficially similar but which had dramatically different outcomes. The mechanism chosen in both cases was co-financing with a foreign source of capital. The venture by the Independent group was, after a shaky start, to produce extraordinarily beneficial results; that of the Press group was to end in catastrophe, and the closure of all the group's newspapers in 1995.

Even before its financial reorganisation, the *Irish Press* had moved to meet the tabloid threat in its own way. In an attempt at diversification, it acquired *Southside*, one of the oldest and most successful suburban free-sheets; but the market for free-sheets was dwindling and *Southside* was closed down in 1987. In the same year, Tim Pat Coogan, who had edited the *Irish Press* for almost two decades, was eased out; a new editor, Hugh Lambert, was installed, and UK consultants were employed to oversee the daily paper's transformation from tabloid into broadsheet, which took place early in 1988. This was another disaster. The new format did not work well – it looked like an attempt to squeeze broadsheet content down into tabloid pages, rather than a fundamental re-design and a new approach to content – and was dramatically unpopular with the paper's traditional readership: between 1987 and 1988 half-yearly circulation slumped by 10,000 copies to just under 67,000. Desperately short of capital, the management, which had been controlled since 1982 by the young Eamon de Valera (grandson of the founder), initiated negotiations on re-financing in December 1988 with a US newspaper magnate named Ralph Ingersoll, who had inherited a substantial network of newspapers from his father and was reputedly worth $200 million. These negotiations, when they concluded in November 1989, produced a commitment by Ingersoll to invest £5 million in the company, and the creation of a complicated network of companies, in some of which Ingersoll and de Valera shared control, with 50% each, and in others of which – notably the company owning the titles – de Valera retained personal control. In May 1990 a reorganisation plan was agreed with the workforce.

Over at the Independent group, however, matters were moving more swiftly. For some time, its management had been in negotiations with United Newspapers in London, publishers not only of the broadsheet *Daily Express* but of the tabloid *Daily Star*. The latter paper sold some 47,000 copies in the Republic. These negotiations resulted in the creation of a jointly owned company – 50% on each side – to publish an Irish edition of the *Star*, printed on the colour presses owned by the *Sunday World*, now part of the Independent group. The new *Star*, which was published for the first time on 29 February 1988, was at the cutting edge of newspaper technology in Ireland, in that its print generation was entirely computer-based, and involved a high-speed computer link to the Express group in London. Whole pages could be – and were – transmitted electronically to Ireland, where they were blended with domestically generated material to produce a new hybrid paper. Initially, however, the experiment did not seem to be a marked success. The formula adopted for the paper was closely aligned with that of the UK imports, in that it printed relatively little Irish-generated news and features, and it lost money.

After a re-design in 1990, the amount of Irish coverage increased dramatically and the circulation figures responded accordingly. It was also assisted commercially by the strength of the Independent group in the advertising market: for some time after its launch, the *Star* did not even publish an advertising rate card, but was sold as part of a discounted package including a number of other Independent titles, thus giving it access to advertising which, on its own, it might have found much more difficult to acquire. By 1992 its circulation was up to 85,000, which helped to engineer a substantial re-balancing of the circulation figures for Irish newspapers generally, as it was now classified as an Irish paper, whereas its predecessor, the *Daily Star*, had been classified as a UK import.

Its editorial differences with the UK *Daily Star* were marked by type of content as well as quantity. It tended to use scandal unconnected with sex as a circulation-builder more frequently than the UK paper; its astrology and agony columns were different; its section for female readers was entitled 'Star Woman', compared with the UK paper's 'Star Girl'; and additional clothing – generally a bikini top – was judiciously added to its cartoon character Katie to obviate the possibility of protests from Irish readers. These changes, however, were probably less important in the long run than the pagination: one 1996 sample showed the *Star*, with 38 out of its 48 pages characterised by Irish content, substantially ahead of its tabloid rivals the *Irish Mirror* (11/36) and the *Irish Sun* (7/36). It began, even, to make inroads into Northern Ireland, not least because of its substantial coverage of Irish sports; it also employed Ireland's first female sports editor. Its Northern Ireland circulation is in itself an anomaly, as part of the understanding between the Independent and Express Newspapers was that Northern Ireland would remain part of the UK *Daily Star*'s circulation territory: today, some Northern Ireland newsagents display both newspapers side by side.

The technology available to the *Star* and the *Sunday World* was in sharp contrast to that available to its parent organisation for the production of its three other titles. Not only were its rotary presses old, and causing maintenance problems with increasing frequency, but they could not print colour as part of the normal printing operation, so that colour advertisements or photographs had to be pre-printed, with a necessarily long lead time. The *Irish Independent* managed to get a colour photograph of the Irish cyclist, Stephen Roche, on to its front page the day after he won the Tour de France in 1987; but keen-eyed observers noticed that it was a photograph taken earlier in the race.

Partly for this reason, and partly because the multinational media proprietors, Rupert Murdoch and Conrad Black, were rumoured to be planning printing facilities on the island, the rumour was floated in 1990 by Independent Newspapers that there was a possibility of a new consortium which would finance a purpose-built printing press to print not only the Independent titles, but the *Irish Times* and the *Cork Examiner*. This overture, if overture it was, evoked little interest from the other two managements, each of which had already re-equipped, and saw no need to help a rival solve its technological problems.

The need to re-finance its physical plant did not, as it happened, deter the Independent from further expansion, although the expansion which now took place was substantially different in kind from the various ventures in which it had become involved since Dr O'Reilly moved into effective control of the company in 1973. These ventures included diversified communications and media interests in Ireland, the UK, France, Mexico and Australia (where it owned a transit advertising company and a 14.95% share in Australian Provincial Newspapers). Simultaneously, it was building up a share-holding in the UK Mirror group, which was in financial disarray following the unexpected death of its controlling share-holder, Robert Maxwell, and in the UK Independent group, publishers of the *Independent* and *Independent on Sunday*. It had created a new company, Independent Wireless Cable Ltd, to spearhead its involvement in the television signal distribution business. This company was a subsidiary of its other vehicle, Princes Holdings, and bid successfully for a number of franchises in the television distribution MMDS network when they were allocated by the Minister for Communications, Mr Ray Burke, in 1989. Independent Wireless Cable later acquired further MMDS franchise holdings from some of the original franchisees. The development of the MMDS system, designed for areas where cable relay systems are too costly, and which has substantial potential for telephony as well as television, was, however, delayed by technological and political factors, and was very slow to materialise. It was to resurface dramatically as a political issue involving the Independent group in 1997.

Another significant development forecast for 1990 actually failed to materialise. This was the projected purchase of some 20% of the Independent group by the *Washington Post*, where Dr O'Reilly, the Independent's chairman, was a board member. This acquisition, had it taken place, would have been the largest incursion into the domestic Irish media market of any foreign interest, and would have triggered alarm bells in many quarters. It did not materialise; but it was not the last time that rumours connecting the Independent group and major foreign interests were in circulation (Truetzschler 1991a: 2).

Instead of opting for inward investment, the Independent now again turned its attention outwards. The object of its attentions at this point, in November 1990, was the *Sunday Tribune*. Although the *Tribune* had been making a steady, if modest profit since its re-capitalisation in 1986, its last year of profit was in 1989/90, when it made £245,000. Shortly afterwards, a downturn in the advertising market and related economic factors indicated that a bleak future was in store. Approaches were made to both the *Irish Times* and Ralph Ingersoll, but 'to little effect' (Competition Authority 1992: 5.6). The alternative – a gamble by any standards – was the launch, in May 1990, of the *Dublin Tribune*, a multi-edition free-sheet (it had no fewer than nine different editions) aimed at generating advertising revenue from all the major segments of the Dublin conurbation. Editorially ambitious, it outran its budgets in spectacular style, bringing the whole enterprise to the verge of collapse. The profit of £245,000 became, in a year, a loss of £2.3 million. This, and the fact that a large parcel of

Tribune shares were known to be on the market, was the context in which the Independent acquired a 29.9% share-holding in the paper, at a cost of £805,000. This transaction took place without the knowledge of the *Tribune* board or its editor, Vincent Browne, who stated that 'at first glance, at least, it seems to threaten the independence of the newspaper and the company' (*ST*: 18 November 1990). The Independent group's rationale appears to have been two-fold: apprehension that the share-holding on offer might become available to the *Irish Times*, which did not publish a Sunday title; and apprehension that the collapse of the *Tribune* would open the 'quality' Sunday market in Ireland up to the predations of, in particular, the *Sunday Times*, with equally deleterious consequences for the *Sunday Independent*. The Independent board's description of the purchase of *Tribune* shares as an investment (Competition Authority 1992: 5.16) was, at the least, difficult to reconcile with the Tribune's financial performance. On the face of it, it appears to have been primarily a defensive strategy.

The *Irish Press* was going from bad to worse. It had re-launched its evening paper as a two-section publication in 1988, but the change succeeded only in alienating readers, and circulation slumped again. In the same year its chief rival, the *Irish Independent*, launched an expensive bonus promotional game for readers called Fortuna, which 'almost wiped out' the *Press*, but which was stopped after the *Press* took court action against it (Competition Authority 1995: 4.40). In 1990, more significantly, relationships between the de Valera directors and the Ingersoll directors began to sour. There were disagreements over appointments to key positions. One executive was dismissed by the Ingersoll side of the management, only to be re-hired almost immediately by the de Valera side. Privately – it emerged later – Ingersoll was already looking for new investors.

In May 1993 the two sides of the company went to court as they were by now totally unable to resolve their differences. Shortly afterwards, the de Valera side initiated brief and fruitless negotiations with the Daily Mirror group in an attempt to source replacement capital. The court case, which it had been thought would last for six weeks, dragged on until December, helping to consume, in the process, much of what capital was left to the business. The court accepted the contention of the de Valera management team that Ingersoll had behaved improperly but, as part of its judgment, required Ingersoll to sell his shares in the jointly owned companies back to the de Valera side, which of course involved a further drain on the company's resources.

The Irish Press group was by now plainly in a desperate state, and predators, or suitors, began to circle. Although its circulation was plummeting, it was not destitute: it owned valuable property in the centre of Dublin, and a substantial share-holding in the Press Association. It needed investment and – possibly – a new management team if it was to be re-launched and survive.

In the autumn of 1994 the first substantial offer materialised. This was from a consortium formed by the Daily Telegraph group in London, owned by the Canadian Conrad Black, and a new Irish Sunday paper, the *Sunday Business Post* (see Chapter 6). This consortium, in which the *Post* would have had a 51% share-holding, valued the Irish Press group operation at £4.5 million. It offered an interest-free loan to the Irish Press group of £2 million for 100 days, to be followed up by an investment programme offering up to £20 million over the following four years. When it became clear that the replacement of the Irish Press group management team was a distinct possibility, the proposal was rejected just before Christmas. A factor in the rejection was undoubtedly an approach in November by Independent Newspapers, which indicated that the company was prepared to give the Irish Press group a £2 million loan in return for a 24.9% share-holding, secured on the titles published by the group. No management changes were envisaged.

After the latter proposal had been accepted by the Irish Press group management, the government asked the Competition Authority to examine the extension of the Independent group's role in the Irish newspaper market and report on issues of possible dominance and the implications of these for competition. The Authority heard evidence from a wide range of interested parties, and came to the unambiguous conclusion that that the transaction represented 'an abuse of a dominant position by Independent Newspapers ... and ... an anti-competitive agreement' (1995: 8.62). It recommended that the minister should take a court action under the Competition Act 'seeking an injunction and or declaration prohibiting these arrangements' (1995: 8.64). As the minister, Richard Bruton, considered his options, the situation deteriorated rapidly. Colm Rapple, a respected *Irish Press* financial journalist, was dismissed by the company after he had published – in the *Irish Times* – an article on his own newspaper's finances. The NUJ retaliated by holding mandatory meetings of the Irish Press group journalists, effectively (if indirectly) halting production of the titles on 25 May 1995. The journalists produced a desktop newspaper, the *Irish X-Press*, at various dates between May and July, which helped to raise money for benevolent purposes and gave the dispute a continuing high profile, but the titles never reappeared and the subsidiary companies in the group eventually went into liquidation, leaving the de Valera interests with some liquidity, based largely on the Press Association share-holding, and the titles.

In the meantime, the Independent group, taking stock of its position in relation to the *Sunday Tribune*, realised that it was locked into a difficult situation. It had two nominees on the board, but the company's financial performance had not been turned around and, at the beginning of 1992 the free-sheets, which had by then lost over £2 million, were given a warning that if they did not become profitable after thirteen weeks, they would close. Accumulated debts were mounting, and profitability seemed as unattainable as ever. The *Sunday Tribune* itself continued to make headlines. Among other notable exclusive stories, its reporter Veronica Guerin secured an exclusive interview with the Catholic bishop, Dr Eamonn Casey, who had left the country after news broke that he had fathered a child and had misappropriated diocesan funds. This achieved huge sales for the paper over a period of some weeks; but the additional revenue was to a considerable extent offset by heavy promotional costs.

The Independent group now moved to assume control of an operation which it was supporting financially, and which was haemorrhaging funds, by proposing to increase its share-holding to 53.09%. The mechanism for this was a rights issue, which would have generated another £1.9 million for the *Tribune*, and which was formally notified to the Minister for Enterprise and Employment – as required by law – on 22 January 1992. This proposal was the outcome of lengthy negotiations by board members, notably the editor, Vincent Browne, and included an undertaking by the Independent group to protect the editorial independence of the *Tribune* by endorsing an editorial charter. It was referred to the Competition Authority in February 1992, and was made the object of the first enquiry carried out by that Authority under the 1991 Competition Act.

The Authority's report, made to the minister the following month, recommended against the proposal on the grounds that 'the proposed merger would be likely to prevent or restrict competition and to restrain trade in the market for Irish Sunday newspapers ... and that it would be likely to operate against the common good' (Competition Authority 1992: 6.17). A minority report by one member of the Authority (Competition Authority 1992: 91–5) argued that the benefits to the *Tribune* would outweigh the dangers, and that there were legal remedies available to many of the objectors (who included the *Irish Times*, the *Irish Press* and the *Sunday Business Post*) if, subsequently, the Independent group abused its dominant position in the marketplace to their detriment.

The Independent group now had to take some hard decisions. It had previously told the Authority that:

> if the rights issue did not proceed, the Tribune would shortly go into liquidation. The Independent, having lost its investment of around £1m, would then have no further involvement in the company.
>
> (Competition Authority 1992: 5.3)

For undisclosed reasons, it now decided that it had no option but to keep the *Tribune* afloat. Its cost/benefit calculations would have included at least the following factors: the threat to the *Sunday Independent* from a newly aggressive *Sunday Times*, which was increasing its Irish editorial and marketing budgets; the danger of leaving a gap in the 'quality' end of the Irish Sunday market which the newly established, but hungry, *Sunday Business Post* would be only too eager to fill; the risk of exposing the Independent group to further accusations that it now held almost total control of the indigenous Sunday newspaper market in Ireland, and possibly even to action under the Competition Act on this score; and the public relations debacle which would have ensued for Independent Newspapers.

These factors evidently weighed more heavily with the Independent board than the ongoing costs of subsidising the *Tribune*. These were now so high that, effectively, regular cash transactions by way of loan from the Independent group were, from then on, the sole reason why the *Tribune* remained on the streets. The Independent group now had effective control of the *Tribune* through this mechanism, despite the rejection of its takeover strategy by the Competition Authority. This was most clearly demonstrated in 1994 when the board of the *Sunday Tribune* terminated Browne's appointment as editor at two hours notice. Browne went on to become a columnist for the *Irish Times* and developed a new career in broadcasting. He was succeeded, first, by Peter Murtagh, a former *Irish Times* journalist who had spent nine years with the *Guardian* in London, and then by Matt Cooper, a financial journalist from the staff of the *Irish Independent*. Under Cooper's editorship, the paper's finances improved slowly, but – although it was making money intermittently on an issue-by-issue basis towards the end of the 1990s – its accumulated debt to the Independent group by 2000 was of the order of £12 million.

This alone underlined the fact that what had occurred was, and remained, a messy solution. The Independent group was now precluded from translating the *Tribune's* indebtedness into equity. Equally, that indebtedness, and its 29.9% equity, operated as a major deterrent to any potential investor, Irish or foreign, who might otherwise have been interested in taking over the *Tribune* as a going concern. Existing Irish media groups, in particular, would not find it easy to make a foray into the Sunday newspaper market on terms which immediately refunded a large sum of money to the most powerful competitor in the market-place. Finally, this continuing subsidy of the *Tribune* undermined the logic of one of the campaigns being waged by the Independent group and other NNI members against UK imports: a campaign against below-cost and promotional selling. Effectively, there was now no definition of below-cost selling which could be deployed in this campaign which did not also catch, *a fortiori*, the *Sunday Tribune*.

Despite the fact that the Independent group did not technically own the *Sunday Tribune*, its position in the Irish Sunday market was now quite extraordinarily powerful. It directly owned the two largest-selling papers, the *Sunday Independent* and the *Sunday World*, which between them had a circulation at the end of 1991 of 477,500 (excluding the *Sunday World* circulation in Northern Ireland). Each of these papers, on its own, was outselling the *Sunday Press's* 200,500; and the *Sunday Business Post*, at 28,300, was still a minnow. If one counted the *Sunday Tribune*, the Independent group's share of the indigenous Irish Sunday market was 71.2%. But UK papers – notably the *News of the World*, the *Sunday Mirror* and the *Sunday People*, with a combined Irish circulation of almost 300,000, still accounted for 32% of the total Irish market, a factor repeatedly adduced by the Independent group to buttress its claim that, taking the market as a whole, its position was not a dominant one.

The existence of the *Sunday Business Post*, at the other end of the scale from the giant Independent group, was an anomaly in itself, but one which – after a number of vicissitudes and some good luck – was to prove that tenacity, vision and an appropriate publishing formula, could still generate significant new opportunities in journalism and publishing in Ireland. It was the brainchild of four journalists and became, effectively, the first modern newspaper to be launched in Ireland by journalists rather than by businessmen. They were Damien Kiberd of the *Irish Press*, Frank FitzGibbon of the monthly *Irish Business*, Aileen O'Toole, then editor of *Business and Finance* and James Morrissey of the *Irish Independent*. In 1989, when they brought their plans to fruition, no Irish newspaper, daily or Sunday, had a separate business and finance section. Their plans for a weekly financial broadsheet did not exclude a weekday publication, but they eventually settled on Sunday – despite the fact that this was where the competition from UK imports was fiercest – because this was the day of the week on which, traditionally, most newspapers were purchased.

Two Irish stockbroking companies and an Irish regional newspaper – the *Kilkenny People* – became investors in the project, and the new paper was to be printed in Kilkenny. But the financing arrangements fell apart twenty days before the first issue was due to appear, and the founders were left with a staff, computers and no funds. A French investor, Jean-Jacques Servan-Schreiber of Groupe Expansion, who had heard of the project and expressed an interest, stepped into the gap at short notice and took a 50% share-holding. The launch, on 26 November 1989, was chaotic, as the original printing arrangements with the *Kilkenny People* had collapsed: the first three issues of the paper were printed by three different companies, before it eventually settled down with Drogheda Web Offset, in which company it later took a 25% stake. By the end of its first year of publication, against expectations, its circulation was 26,000, considerably ahead of its target figure of 17,000.

It was in the process of articulating a formula which would prove increasingly popular with the business community. It saved considerably on editorial costs by taking a firm decision not to emulate other Sunday newspapers' extensive coverage of sport (although it did carry articles on financial and business aspects of sport). Politically, it resembled the ailing *Sunday Press* more than the *Sunday Independent* or *Sunday Tribune*, in that it hewed to a broad nationalist agenda. But it garnered circulation not only from its extensive coverage of business (often hard-hitting business stories nestling uncomfortably beside soft-centred advertorial), but from a succession of journalistic exclusives generated by adventurous, often young and female, journalists. These included Veronica Guerin, who began what was to be a spectacular career with the *Post* as a freelance in 1990, and specialised in writing about fraud and white-collar crime, and Emily O'Reilly, still (in 2000) its political correspondent. Its design, by Stephen Ryan, won it newspaper design awards in Britain and awards from the Society of Newspaper Design in each of the three years 1991–3. By 1995 its circulation had increased to 33,000.

The *Sunday Business Post*'s teething problems, however, remained substantial. In June 1991 FitzGibbon left, after costs had begun to escalate: the original plan for a 24-page paper had given way to a 68-page paper with a staff of sixty. In 1992 Morrissey left, but in the same year Barbara Nugent joined the company from the *Sunday Tribune*: she was to prove a valuable asset to the *Post*, indicating the measure of her loss to the *Tribune*. At this time, tentative moves to establish a bridgehead, and even a possible merger, between the two publications, foundered, not least because of the strained relationship between Nugent and her former employer. In 1993, there were two further significant developments. The first was the move to Belfast, where the *Post* was now to be printed by the *Belfast Telegraph*. This had cost savings and technology advantages, although it necessitated an earlier deadline – initially Friday afternoon – which meant that news which broke on Saturday could not be covered in the paper on sale the following day. In the long run, it was a problem which did not affect the *Post*'s readership and circulation to any significant degree. The second was the departure of Schreiber, who reduced his company's stake in the company to 10%, being replaced by a German entrepreneur, Norman Rentrop. Even more critically, Schreiber wrote off his investment debt to the *Post*, now standing at more than £2.5 million, which effectively re-launched the paper on a considerably more secure financial footing than previously. By early 1995, the Joint National Readership Research (JNNR: March 1995) figures showed that the *Post*'s readership had increased by 14% to 105,000, and that it had the highest proportion of social class AB readers of any national newspaper: 49.5%, as against 25% for the *Sunday Tribune* and 16% for the *Sunday Independent*, its direct Sunday competitors, and 40.9% for the *Irish Times*. This had important and enduring consequences for advertising, as well as for circulation, which was now at 33,000.

The *Irish Times*'s circulation was also showing a steady increase during this period, and despite the fact that the economic boom, as such, did not really develop a full head of steam until 1995. A new colour press, which arrived in 1986, allowed the paper to have colour in editorial and in advertising to increase the size of the paper. In 1986, it was carrying an average of 108 columns per day; by 1996 that had grown to nearly 220. The average size of the paper in 1986 was 18 pages daily; fifteen years later, it was in excess of 50 pages.

There were a number of other, related editorial developments, notably increased sectionalisation, aimed at particular groups. Sports was on Monday from 1994 onwards, Working & Living (later to be renamed Education & Living) on Tuesdays. The property section on Thursday (1990) and the business section on Friday (1993) also boosted sales on those days. An additional sports section was added in 1996.

The paper also invested in staff. At a time when editorial numbers at the Independent group were more or less constant at around 250 journalists for the three titles, the *Irish Times*, which had about 190 editorial staff in 1986 for its two titles (plus the *Irish Field*), had expanded ten years later to a figure, including full-time contract staff, of about 280. There was a conscious shift to go further into specialisation: science, legal affairs, environment, health, social affairs, media and food. It also developed a number of overseas offices. In 1986, its furthest-flung office was Brussels. Ten years later it had Moscow, Washington, Beijing, Paris, Rome and Bonn and a lot of new stringers. Then in

1996 it started expanding its regional coverage with the opening of offices in Galway and Tullamore.

Part of this was due to the *Irish Times*'s unusual corporate structure. It was making comfortable profits, but had no share-holders, and therefore did not have to pay dividends. This left more finance available for expansion, particularly on the editorial side. On the other hand, it had – for the same reason – no way of raising additional capital for new equipment and presses, short of borrowing, so had to maintain large liquid balance-sheet to finance such operations.

The Independent group was, by virtue of its size, even more profitable. If its investments in the *Irish Press* and the *Sunday Tribune* had been defensive (and expensive) moves disguised, or perceived by its opponents, as ruthless expansionism, the group was simultaneously engaged in a wide-ranging series of moves outside Ireland which were in the process of turning it into a substantial international media conglomerate. Its chairman, Dr A.J.F. O'Reilly, whose eye for business opportunities and skill at financial engineering had made him into one of the wealthiest – and most controversial – Irish entrepreneurs (O'Toole 1996: 63), oversaw an expansion of the company which exceeded all previous initiatives by a substantial margin.

Between 1990 and 1995 the group broadened its media portfolio in a remarkable series of manoeuvres and acquisitions. In 1991 it was unsuccessful in a bid for the Fairfax publishing empire in Australia, despite having successfully engaged the goodwill of the then Australian Prime Minister, Bob Hawke; this led to a long and costly lawsuit. Virtually the only other defeat suffered by the group was in an attempt to launch a scratch-card system in the UK in the early 1990s, which lost an estimated £7 million. These expensive ventures apart, however, its acquisitions added considerably to its asset base, on occasion producing windfall profits, as in 1992, when its raid on *Daily Mirror* shares (it acquired £8 million worth) was seen off by UK investors and the Independent group was refused a seat on the Mirror group board: it withdrew from the battle, selling its share-holding (whose value had been pushed up by the battle for control) for a paper profit of £3 million.

Throughout 1993, the group extended its ownership of Australian local and regional titles, and formed a network of local radio stations in that country. Its most active year, however, was probably 1994. In January, following its rebuff by the Mirror group, it moved on Newspaper Publishing. This company, which published the London *Independent* and *Independent on Sunday*, had originally been founded by a group of European broadsheets and journalists, with the intention of providing a challenging alternative to the London *Times* and even to the *Guardian*. The titles, however, were not doing well, and as original investors withdrew, the Independent group moved in, acquiring a 43% share for a total investment of some £9 million. Here, too, it was met with considerable hostility: the Mirror group, which now controlled a 46% share-holding, initially refusing to offer the Independent group a board seat: 'We won't invite anyone to dinner if they kick down the front door.' The Mirror group eventually ceded control to O'Reilly, although the titles continue to lose money.

In February 1994, O'Reilly's group bought a 31% stake in the South African Argus group, later increasing that stake to 60%. Almost simultaneously, it acquired for £4.8 million Capital Newspapers – a UK chain of local newspapers published largely in the Greater London area. In 1995 it bought into the Morton newspaper group in New Zealand, and also acquired the New Zealand Radio Network, giving it access to 41% of New Zealand's radio advertising. It also owned an outdoor advertising company in France, an 11% share in a profitable Portuguese newspaper, ten provincial Irish titles, a controlling interest in Newspread, one of Ireland's two newspaper and magazine distribution companies, and a 24.9% share-holding in Drogheda Web Offset Press, printers of the *Sunday Tribune*. By 1995 it was printing, globally, 12 million papers every week.

It was also engaged in defensive strategies on several fronts. Its quick response to the dangers posed by the weakening *Sunday Tribune* and Irish Press group have already been noted. It had another battle to fight in 1993, when Drogheda Web Offset went into receivership, largely because it had lost the *Sunday Business Post* printing contract to the *Belfast Telegraph*. News International expressed an interest in acquiring the company, which would have been an ideal base for printing the Irish editions of its daily and Sunday newspapers, but stipulated that the receiver should first of all secure agreement from the workforce on manning practices (Flynn 1983: 17).

The receiver failed to get agreement on the changes sought by News International – largely, industry sources suggested at the time, because the Independent group management had indicated to their own printers, who were members of the same union, that they would be looking for similar concessions to any won by the receiver on behalf of News International. A similar scenario manifested itself the following year, when the future of the Irish Press group was suddenly thrown into the balance. A takeover of the Press group by a UK interest would undoubtedly have cost the Independent group dearly in a keener battle for advertising and circulation revenue: in the event, O'Reilly secured acceptance of his defensive strategy by publicly warning the workforce in January 1994: 'Employers and unions have a stark choice. They can have brutal rationalisation *à la* Wapping, or they can have an equitable solution to an Irish problem.'

The acceptance by the Press management of his offer of support, as has been noted, postponed rather than prevented the closure of the titles: plainly, having found itself in a cleft stick vis-à-vis the *Sunday Tribune*, which it was still supporting with periodic injections of loan working capital, the Independent management was not going to repeat the experiment. The Press titles closed, in a context in which there was increasing concern about the diminution of media diversity and the towering presence of the Independent group in the Irish newspaper market, particularly its indigenous sector. The Minister for Enterprise and Employment, Richard Bruton, now declined the invitation issued by the Competition Authority to take action against the Independent group and, instead, established a Commission on the Newspaper Industry, under the former Chief Justice, Thomas Finlay, to examine all the issues concerned.

The confusion and hype generated by the battle between the Irish newspapers themselves, and between them and the UK imports, operated to conceal the fact that newspaper sales generally were falling. In other words, the intensity of the competition between papers generally was being exacerbated by the fact that the cake was getting smaller. Some sectors, however, were more immune than others to the vagaries of the market, but for widely differing reasons. Although more than a quarter of weekly magazines were imported from the UK (and in the important sector of women's magazines more than half were imported), indigenous ventures like *Women's Way* were holding their own, supplemented by magazines targeted at younger sectors of the market such as *Image* and *U*. The magazine *IT* (inheritor of the mantle of the nineteenth-century, and originally very staid, *Irish Tatler and Sketch*), is part of a group of small consumer magazines which was acquired by Robert Maxwell's interests prior to 1991 (Truetzschler 1991a: 2). The *RTE Guide*, which had moved into profit after struggling to make ends meet during the 1970s, was proving a valuable addition to the national broadcasting station's cash flow. Other niche publications like the *Irish Field* and the *Irish Medical Times* were sufficiently embedded in the local topography to be able to resist outside competition (although the *Irish Medical Times* was sold to the UK Haymarket group, and remained in UK ownership for part of the 1990s before being re-sold into Irish hands).

The current affairs magazine, *Magill*, continued to prosper, although it had a high turnover of editors under its volatile proprietor, Vincent Browne (also for much of this time editor of the *Sunday Tribune*). But the success of two other publications deserves to be noted, in part because they were organic developments from previous media, in part because, as case histories, they could hardly be more different.

One of them, launched on 6 January 1982, was the *Phoenix*, a fortnightly magazine owned by John Mulcahy, whose career in journalism as proprietor and editor, had included twelve years as editor of the now defunct *Hibernia*, and six months as editor of the *Sunday Tribune* in its first incarnation. Modelled to some extent on the British publication *Private Eye*, and even to some extent resembling the former *Hibernia* in its provision of high-grade business and company news stories, the *Phoenix* carried a mix of information, scandal and gossip which saw it exceed 20,000 sales per issue by the autumn of 1992, and its regular pagination increase from 24 to 48. Its articles were anonymous – a contrast, in itself, from the high-profile by-lines which were at this time becoming the staple of Dublin journalism – and, despite an annual bill for libel settlements and costs of between £50,000 and £100,000, it has never succumbed to a really expensive defamation action. One businessman who claimed he had been libelled by Mulcahy took the unusual step of publishing, in another magazine, a series of allegations about the *Phoenix*'s style of journalism (*IT*: 26 January 1966).

The intense legal care devoted to the pre-publication process of the *Phoenix* magazine at least helped to ensure that it was handled by orthodox wholesalers and appeared on news-stands. Other publications did not so appear, either by choice or because the two distribution companies regarded them as too great a legal risk. One of these, arguably one of the most popular political periodicals, was *An Phoblacht* ('The Republic'), the organ of the Sinn Fein party. *An Phoblacht* was unique, not least in that it survived for many years, in one form or another, while newspapers and periodicals published by other parties appeared briefly, and disappeared leaving little trace of their existence. Fianna Fail had *Gléas* from 1952 until the mid-1960s. It was succeeded by *Iris Fianna Fail* between 1974 and the mid-1980s, and which, in its current incarnation, is the *FF Newsletter*. Fine Gael published *The Democrat* in the 1960s (NLI ILB 05.n.2), partly under the editorship of Vincent Browne. Its current, sporadic newsletter is *Forum Fine Gael*. The Labour Party has *Labour Forum*, which also appears sporadically. One party, the Socialist Labour Party, which existed between 1978 and 1983, published briefly no fewer than three publications – an internal newsletter, a periodical for the wider public and a theoretical journal – but this level of commitment was itself more theoretical than actual. *Militant*, the organ of the entryist Militant Tendency within the Labour Party from 1977 to about 1990, had similarities with *An Phoblacht* in that producing and selling it was an integral part of that group's political activity.

An Phoblacht was itself the product of a merger. Up to 1979, the party had published two journals: one in the North of Ireland, called *Republican News*; the other in the Republic, called *An Phoblacht*. As the Northern conflict intensified, the circulation of *Republican News* grew steadily: one of its contributors between 1975 and 1977 (including the period when he was in prison) was Gerry Adams. By 1978, when its circulation was approaching 30,000, it was the target of frequent harassment by the security forces, and its offices on the Falls Road in Belfast were frequently raided.

By the end of that year, however, an internal power struggle within the Republican movement was having a visible effect on that movement's publications and, on 27 January 1979, the two publications merged into a new magazine with the title *An Phoblacht/Republican News* (*AP/RN*). The change seems to have reflected a power shift away from the orthodox nationalism of Southern Republicans and towards a more socially radical version of the same ideology which had for some time been emerging in its Belfast leadership (Hickie 1994: 34). An editorial in the last pre-merger issue of the *Republican News* noted that the merger had been agreed:

> to improve on both our reporting and analysis of the news in the North and of popular economic and social struggles in the South ... the absolute necessity of one single united paper providing a clear line of republican leadership ... [and] the need to overcome any partitionist thinking which results from the British enforced division of this country and of the Irish people.
>
> (*RN*: 20 January 1979)

But the new paper did more than simply provide a bulletin board for the Republican movement and its ideas. In contrast with the lacklustre and politically vacuous tone of the press of the political parties generally, it performed a hugely important function in alerting a wide readership to issues and events which media lack of interest or (in the case of radio and television) censorship had kept below the political horizon. It was avidly read by politicians, senior public servants and administrators in Dublin, Belfast and London concerned with ongoing attempts to resolve the Northern Ireland crisis. Miniaturised versions were smuggled into Northern Ireland prisons – notably the Maze, outside Belfast – to keep Republican prisoners abreast of political developments outside, and some prisoners (including Gerry Adams, as already noted) smuggled their contributions out for printing.

Its role within Sinn Fein itself was also substantial. It not only offered its readership a consistent and internally coherent ongoing analysis of events in Northern Ireland, but its sales operation was closely tied into the organisational structure of the party itself. Monthly party meetings were timed to coincide with the publication of the paper, and at the conclusion of the meetings party members sold it in public houses. This distribution system, organised almost on military lines, not only obviated most of the costs associated with normal wholesaling, but helped to create an *esprit de corps* which – especially during the hunger strike crises of 1981 – made the party as a whole particularly efficient in getting its message across. It produced, in addition, a circulation of approximately 25,000 copies per issue, and the absence of distribution costs in the normal sense of the word (it did not need wholesalers or retailers) probably made it a profitable venture into the bargain.

The broadcasting ban under the Section 31 directives, which helped to ensure the continuing viability of AP/RN, continued to dog RTE's footsteps until almost the end of this period. Although there were intermittent protests by journalists and others, its existence was accepted by and large almost as a fact of life. There was no 'peace process' as such in existence, although occasional secret contacts would take place between nationalists and the British authorities. The relentless continuation of the IRA campaign, and some of its excesses – particularly the frequent shootings of unarmed part-time policemen in Northern Ireland – eroded much of the sympathy for its political objectives which had long been a feature of politics in the Republic. In these circumstances no political party thought it worthwhile, or wise, to move a parliamentary resolution to scrap the directive when it was renewed in January of each year, whatever individual parliamentarians (some of them members of the NUJ) might have thought about it. Not even the most publicised incident evoked more than a transitory protest. This was in March 1988 when an RTE reporter, Jenny McGeever, was covering the journey from Dublin Airport to Northern Ireland of the funeral cortège containing the bodies of three IRA members who had been shot by SAS men while on a mission in Gibraltar. Ms McGeever was first suspended, and then dismissed by RTE after a disciplinary hearing: a Sinn Fein voice had been heard in an interview she recorded in

Dundalk in the course of the day. The NUJ subsequently took a case against Section 31 censorship to the European Court of Human Rights in Strasbourg, but despite its lack of success the case uncovered RTE documentation which cast the Section 31 directives and their operation in an even more unflattering light.

Although the Section 31 directives were, and continued to be, a major irritant and an obstacle to serious journalism, RTE was more preoccupied throughout this period with the anticipated formal end of its broadcasting monopoly (which the pirate radio stations had already ended informally), and the consequences of this for its finances and for public service broadcasting generally. In May 1985 the Minister for Communications, Jim Mitchell, appointed consultants to carry out a management study of RTE. This study, which was completed in September, did not deal with programming issues, but indicated that RTE's finances were in poor shape: as the RTE Chairman, Jim Culliton, pointed out, it revealed that under existing circumstances the station could not even 'meet its statutory financial obligations' (*IT*: 20 September 1985). Radio came best out of the study: it was attracting the second-highest share of a national advertising pool in Europe. Overall, however, the financial situation was such that cost control – including shedding 320 of the 2,239 workforce in the next three years – was essential. The report provoked major management changes, and a sense of urgency on the part of a younger team which immediately had a huge impact both on programming quality and advertising – but principally in television rather than in radio. Home-produced programming increased by 20% in the autumn 1986 schedules; many Irish programmes were at or near the top of the TAM viewer ratings; by late 1987, the station had doubled its profits; and by 1988, in spite of the fact that staff numbers had been cut by almost 200, RTE's share of multi-channel viewers had increased by some 14% (Mulryan 1988: 137–8).

Radio, however, remained a problem. If RTE looked to the Interim Radio Commission ('CORA', from its initials in Irish), which was established by Mitchell in the same year, it was to be disappointed. The commission, which met regularly until 1987, never published a final report, but commissioned a number of consultancies which, though their findings erred on the side of caution, indicated that legal commercial radio was a viable proposition. Even if the commission had managed to produce a final report with firm recommendations, it would not have got any further than the Dail, where the stand-off between the two political parties in government on this issue continued and, if anything, became even more bad-tempered.

In the circumstances, RTE moved as best it could to plug the gaps in its defences, hampered not only by its acute lack of finance, especially on the capital side, but by government indecision. It had already, on 5 November 1984, launched FM3, a classical music service which shared a wavelength with Raidio na Gaeltachta, each service taking part of the day. In mid-1987, Radio 2 went to 24-hour broadcasting, but it seemed almost a forlorn hope: it had fewer listeners than Radio 1, and fewer than two of the strongest pirate stations, Sunshine and Q102. In the period since 1980/81, its audience share had nosedived from 43% to 25%. Outside Dublin, some pirate stations were causing embarrassment of a different kind, this time to the government, as they deliberately targeted Northern Ireland listeners and advertisers. By 1986, according to one estimate, pirate stations in counties Donegal and Louth were claiming some 14% of the Belfast listeners, compared with the commercial station, Downtown Radio, which was at 17% and Radio Ulster (the BBC station) at 35% (Mulryan 1988: 135).

This was the context in which, in February 1987, the government finally fell apart, a general election was held, and Fianna Fail – which had promised commercial radio its support as long ago as 1981 – was returned to power. It was a single-party government but, on this issue, the largest opposition party, Fine Gael, was also in favour of rejecting the position advanced jointly by RTE and the Labour Party, and opening up the airwaves fully to commercial competition. In November of the same year, the new Minister for Communications, Ray Burke, published the texts of two bills: one of them, the Broadcasting and Wireless Telegraphy Bill, was to put an end to the pirates; the other, the Sound Broadcasting Bill, was to establish commercial stations on a legal footing for the first time. Fine Gael voted with the government on the two measures, guaranteeing them overwhelming majorities when they passed into law the following year.

The legislation envisaged a relatively tightly regulated commercial sector, with stations being required to observe the directives under Section 31 as well as provisions on fairness and impartiality culled from the 1976 Act, and to provide a minimum quotient of 20% for news and current affairs. It envisaged a two-tier system, with a number of orthodox commercial stations supplemented by a network of small, community stations operating largely on a voluntary basis. The latter provision was particularly welcomed by the National Association of Community Broadcasters, an organisation which was already in existence, which had strong local (including Church) support in many areas, and which published a booklet to make clear the important distinctions between the stations operated by its members and the mainstream pirate stations then popular (1988). Finally, the new structure was to be under the control of a new body – the Independent Radio and Television Commission (IRTC) – which had the power to award licences.

Local and regional newspapers were not prevented from joining with each other in applying for broadcasting licences in their area, although the legislation made it clear that this should not occur if it created a monopoly in any area covered by a licence, and any newspaper involvement in a radio licence should, in any case, be limited to a maximum of 25%. Other interests were subject to the same limitation: national newspapers, other radio stations, non-nationals and religious denominations.

Finally, it made provision for a new commercial television service, the franchise for which was awarded to an Irish consortium, the Windmill Lane Consortium, although it was to be quite a few years, and a number of controversies later before this particular service materialised. These controversies included a decision by the government in 1990 to award the contract for tele-vising the Dail and Seanad to Windmill rather than to RTE (although RTE's pitch for the rights was lacklustre); a decision by the IRTC in 1991 to revoke the franchise because it believed that the new TV network did not have suffi-cient financial backing (a decision which Windmill managed to overturn on judicial review); and continual difficulties about funding which were ended only when a Canadian company came in as a major investor, thus adding to the increasing level of foreign investment in Irish media companies.

Pirate radio reacted in different ways to the impending legislation. Some stations went off air, in order to provide a sort of *cordon sanitaire* between their previously illegal existence and the award – or so they hoped – of an orthodox licence to broadcast. Others amended their schedules to reduce the amount of music broadcast and to offer a news and current affairs service – at first skimpy – with which to enhance their claims to legitimacy.

There were thirteen applications for the two Dublin licences and seventy-two for the provincial ones. After a series of public hearings which concentrated on the economic viability of the proposed stations (Truetzschler 1991b: 27), the IRTC awarded two licences for Dublin, and twenty-four for provincial areas. Later, a franchise for a national commercial station was awarded to a consortium called Century Radio. The first of the new stations to go on air was the Dublin-based Capital Radio (later renamed FM104), which began broadcasting on 20 July 1989 from temporary accommodation on top of the St Stephen's Green shopping centre. The first provincial station was MWR FM in Co. Mayo, which began broadcasting on 24 July.

Probably the greatest interest, however, surrounded Century, the first station to be licensed as a direct competitor for RTE on a national basis. Initially, there seem to have been no plans for a national competitor for RTE radio, and this development appears to have been a personal initiative by the Minister for Communications, Ray Burke. The launch of the station on 4 September 1989, however, was dogged by problems. It failed to attract high-profile presenters away from the national radio station, and became engaged in a lengthy wrangle with RTE over the cost of using the national station's transmission links, which eventually had to be resolved by arbitration. Although it attempted to supple-ment its income by providing a national news service for the smaller local stations, this did not succeed in offsetting costs to any significant extent, and its financial situation rapidly became extremely difficult. At this point the minister, Mr Burke, intervened dramatically with a new package in which he proposed that RTE's second radio service should become a cultural and educa-tional service (thus leaving the popular music field completely at the disposal of the commercial sector), that up to a quarter of the licence fee should be diverted from RTE to support the public service obligations of the commercial channels, and that RTE's advertising should be capped, thus diverting revenue from that source into the commercial sector.

His proposals aroused considerable controversy, and evoked a threat by the NUJ to refuse to cover a planned European summit which was due to be hosted in Dublin by the Taoiseach, Mr Haughey. After a brief but intense public discussion, the government abandoned the first two proposals but, in its 1990 Broadcasting Act, implemented the third. The permissible amount of advertising was reduced, from 10% to 7.5% of total daily programming time, and the maximum permissible in any one hour was reduced from 7.5 to 5 minutes. It also placed an absolute maximum on RTE advertising revenue, in that it stipulated that this should not exceed the amount received by the station from the licence fee. In effect, this was a double limitation as, given that it controlled the level of the licence fee (and was notoriously slow to increase it), the government could now also control the total revenue of the station. He was later to enforce a solution to an ongoing dispute between Century and RTE about the price to be charged by RTE for Century's access to the RTE transmission network, which Century needed to ensure country-wide reception of its signal. All these matters, which were controversial enough at the time, resurfaced dramatically more than a decade later. In 1999, a judicial tribunal was set up by the Irish government to examine questions of political corruption; by the end of 2000, while its deliberations were far from complete, it had established that Mr Burke had received a political donation of £30,000 from one of the directors of Century, Mr Oliver Barry, and that Mr Burke had intervened personally, and decisively, in favour of Century, in a lengthy dispute between Century and RTE about the amount that Century would be charged by RTE for the right to use RTE's physical transmission network. It was also established that Century directors had intervened directly with the minister in an attempt to get RTE's 2FM pop channel closed down (*IT*: 20 July 2000).

The Burke proposals, although evidently aimed at succouring the ailing Century Radio, were also emblematic of the now deeply embedded antipathy of certain elements within Fianna Fail towards the national broadcaster. This antipathy, which had its origins in the contested decade of the 1960s, and to some extent in the policies which gave rise to the Section 31 directives, was by now an open secret. Whatever their motivation, however, these measures were not enough to achieve their objective. The station had already gone again to the market for capital, raising a £1.5 million loan from the London commercial station, Capital Radio London, in 1990, as part of a deal in which the British station effectively assumed total management responsibility, but Century finally succumbed to mounting losses (about £7 million in 26 months) and closed down on 19 November 1991, when it had achieved a 6% share of the national audience.

Elsewhere, however, stations were not closing down. A national organisation of commercial radio stations, the Association of Independent Radio Stations (AIRS) had been established in 1990 to act as a lobby group, and continued to do so effectively. Twenty-two of the original twenty-five stations were still broadcasting in 1992, although revenue projections were being stretched to the limit, according to Denis O'Brien, an entrepreneur who was to build his own local radio station in Dublin, 98FM, into a major media empire. O'Brien commented in 1992 that only two of the new stations were making a profit, while the majority were still striving to break even (O'Brien 1992: 55). 'The local stations', he added, 'are ... demonstrating that broadcasting, without state aid or influence, can be both non-elitist and of good quality.'

The advertising cap had not only failed to save Century: it had diverted advertising revenue out of the state, to Ulster Television. This was because the cap meant that RTE increased its price for advertising time, to make up for having to reduce the time available for advertising, to the point at which numbers of Irish advertisers found that RTE was no longer cost-effective, and took their custom across the border. UTV, which is in the extraordinary situation of being the only ITV franchisee which has a larger audience outside its franchise area (i.e. in the Republic of Ireland) than inside it (i.e. in Northern Ireland) is thought to have benefited to the extent of some £3 million in the second half of 1990 as a direct result of this legislative change. RTE, for its part, had to engage in further staff cuts and programming economies of about 10% across the board (Truetzschler 1991b: 33). This hidden competition – hidden in that technically Ireland had no domestic commercial television, although the competitive pressures from BBC and UTV were in fact intense – also had an effect on serious programming: one 1992 study showed that the percentage of total amount of time devoted to serious programmes on RTE, at 39%, was lower than in a number of other countries (Belgium, Netherlands, France, Norway, for instance) whose public broadcasting services had direct domestic commercial rivals (Kelly 1992a: 84). By 1993, in spite of the fact that there had been no increase in the licence fee for six and a half years, home-produced material had reached a level of 45% of all transmissions, and RTE was winning, against increasingly stiff opposition, more than 50% of the audience in the 70% of homes which had access to multi-channel viewing (i.e. a choice between Irish-based and non-Irish-based channels) (Finn 1993: 75).

The climate of cutbacks which was affecting RTE during this period also had an effect – and a highly deleterious one, as it was to prove – on its involvement in another radio project, Atlantic 252. This was an extraordinary development, based on an approach which had been made to RTE by Radio Luxembourg as long ago as 1981. Luxembourg's initiative related to permission which Ireland had received in 1975 for a long-wave frequency – a right which it had never exercised. This eventually led to the establishment of Radio Atlantic 252, physically based in Tara, Co. Meath, but carefully concealing its actual location from the British audiences to which it was largely directed (phone-in numbers given on air are generally UK freephone numbers). It was an extraordinary turnaround from the 1960s, when Ireland was resolutely setting its face against broadcasting commercial radio to the UK because the British authorities might object: it was now participating actively in a project directly aimed at tapping the UK market – one, moreover, which was quite unhindered by statutory restrictions of any kind. The station broadcasts a diet of non-stop pop music, its playlist drawn from currently best-selling music (Kenny 1998b).

The problem for RTE was that the complex financial arrangements under which it went into business with the other sponsor, now the Luxembourg multinational CLT, exposed it to substantial losses during the start-up period. Panicking somewhat in 1992, it sold two-thirds of its majority share-holding to help it balance its books, and was later to sell its remaining 20%, again under pressure of financial stringency. By this time, however, Atlantic 252 was in the process of becoming extraordinarily successful: by 1994, it had reached an audience of 4.9 million in Britain, higher than Radio 5 Live, as commercial radio in Britain overtook the BBC for the first time since the establishment of the commercial sector twenty-one years before (Foley 1994). RTE was not to share in the fruits of success.

One contemporary verdict on these developments suggested that they showed that:

> Ireland has no explicit or coherent national broadcasting policy. Developments in broadcasting tend to proceed with little or no public debate and to be in line with the interests of the members of the various elites in Irish society. The wider social and cultural implications for Irish society of changes in broadcasting are rarely debated – in fact decisions are made and justified in line with economic and commercial criteria.
>
> (Truetzschler 1991b: 33)

The evidence adduced above suggests that this was a rather narrow verdict. The lineaments of a policy could in fact be discerned principally in the 1988 and 1990 legislation – legislation which plainly envisaged the emergence of a strong private sector as a countervailing influence to the untrustworthy and overly critical (from the point of view of the largest political party in the state) public service agenda of RTE, and one which would, in the process, provide business opportunities for financiers favourable to that party: the initial investors in Century were very closely associated with Fianna Fail. The fact that the second of these policy objectives failed to materialise, and that the first was never really discernible as non-RTE journalists inevitably followed their own agendas, was not evidence that the policy did not exist, rather that it had simply been misguided or unsuccessful.

That policy was itself a contested one, as was shown when a new government took office in 1992. This government was composed, unusually, of the Labour Party, which had traditionally favoured a public service broadcasting agenda, and Fianna Fail, which had opposed it. This amalgam of opposing viewpoints produced one initial result favourable to public service broadcasting – the removal, in the 1993 Broadcasting Act, of the 'cap' on RTE's advertising revenues which had been created by Fianna Fail when previously in government. That government collapsed in 1994 for reasons unconnected with broadcasting, and was replaced by a new coalition of which Labour was still a member, but which excluded Fianna Fail.

The longest-lasting element of broadcasting policy, irrespective of party, had been the various directives issued under the original Section 31 of the 1960 Act. These remained in force until January 1994, when Michael D. Higgins, the

Labour Minister for Arts, Culture and the Gaeltacht (whose brief also included the policy elements of broadcasting) secured the government's agreement for a proposal not to renew the ban on the organisations named in the directives. From this time onwards, therefore, RTE was free to interview across a much wider political spectrum than hitherto, as were the BBC and ITV, whose restrictions were similarly relaxed, no doubt as a result of coordination between Dublin and London. There were to be no dramatic developments, as the RTE guidelines were further revised to deal with the new situation: but an appearance on the *Late Late Show* by Gerry Adams, president of Sinn Fein, marked the watershed in a significant, and predictably controversial fashion, as he was subjected to uncharacteristic coolness from his host, and to sustained criticism from four panellists. The ending of the ban had been widely touted as a confidence-building measure in support of the peace process, and was so to prove when, on 31 August 1994, the IRA announced its cease-fire.

Northern Ireland: conflict and self-examination

In Northern Ireland, newspaper changes were slight. At the *Newsletter*, continuing financial losses led to job cuts in April 1991 – some 20% of the workforce were made redundant in 1985. In a portent of what was to come, however, a Scottish media company, Scottish Media Holdings, bought into the profitable Morton local newspaper group, establishing a bridgehead which was to have substantial consequences for the pattern of media ownership on both sides of the border. It also acquired a substantial share-holding in UTV. The *Irish News* acquired a new editor in 1990, an English journalist named Nick Garbutt, who brought a new sense of openness to what was still in some respects a rather traditional paper. Ironically, in view of this, the paper was the subject in 1993 of a successful complaint by its political editor – a Protestant – that he had been discriminated against on religious grounds (*SBP*: 12 September 1993).

Structural changes in broadcasting were relatively minor during this period. Commercial radio had arrived on 17 March 1976 when Downtown Radio went on air: it was the seventeenth local commercial station in the UK to go on air. Initially, however, it was confined to the greater Belfast area, partly because of the difficult topography of Northern Ireland. In 1986–7, it extended its reach into the western and north-western areas of Northern Ireland, and in 1990 split its wavelengths: Downtown remained on medium wave, while a new service, CoolFM, targeted the younger urban audience, and is currently broadcasting (again because of topographical factors) on no fewer than seven different frequencies across the province. In 1996 the station was taken over by Scottish Radio Holdings, and has a cumulative weekly audience of 587,000. There are two smaller commercial stations, City Beat, in Belfast, and Q102, based in Derry. The BBC's only local opt-out, Radio Foyle, went on air in Derry on 11 September 1979.

The policy battles, on the other hand, continued to generate considerable attention and were increasingly involving the central authorities of both networks. One of the two major controversies in this period was the BBC documentary *At the Edge of the Union*, shown in 1985, whose depiction of the Sinn Fein leader Martin McGuinness as someone leading a fundamentally ordinary and non-threatening lifestyle provoked (despite the insertion of a thirteen-year-old film clip depicting the results of IRA violence in Belfast) a major controversy (Butler 1992: 39). An equally critical clash came in 1988, when Thames Television prepared a documentary for its *This Week* slot on the death of the three IRA members in Gibraltar, referred to above. The British Foreign Secretary objected strongly to the proposal to screen the documentary, which was nonetheless broadcast on 29 April, touching off a major controversy involving television executives at all levels and the British prime minister, Mrs Thatcher.

Almost immediately the British Home Secretary used his powers under the 1981 Broadcasting Act and in the BBC's Licence and Agreement of the same year to ban all direct interviews with members of Sinn Fein and a number of specified paramilitary organisations, both Republican and Loyalist. The situation in Britain and Northern Ireland now paralleled, almost exactly, that which had obtained in the Republic since 1972. Two years later, the 1990 Broadcasting Act replaced the Independent Broadcasting Authority, which had done its best to defend the programme, with an Independent Television Commission, which took a much more mercenary approach to the whole question of franchising (Fleck 1995: 10). Under the new dispensation Thames lost its contract to Carlton, which distinguished itself later in the 1990s by broadcasting a number of documentaries which were shown to have been based in part on falsified or highly unreliable material.

One of the consequences of this was what has been described as the turn towards the drama-documentary.

As the ability to make factual programmes decreased journalists turned to dramatisations, which offer increased space for dramatic licence and make it easier to represent events without requiring informants to appear on television.

(Miller 1994: 275)

The same author suggests (1994: 276) that the overall performance of the media can best be described as contradictory. The media, for example, may have helped (evidently at different times and in different ways) both in creating the climate of opinion which enveloped and probably influenced the wrongful conviction of the defendants who were charged with the 1974 Guildford and Birmingham bombings, and their subsequent release after it had been shown that their convictions were unsafe and unsatisfactory. The legal process which ended their imprisonment was initiated, at least in part, as a result of a series of documentaries made by Granada and Yorkshire Television between 1984 and 1987, as well as another by Granada in 1990, which went so far as to name the actual culprits.

In the course of this process, the simplistic arguments of the early 1970s about censorship had given way to conflict and self-examination on the part of many broadcasters and administrators. But there was little in common between the often over-simplified analyses which saw each contested incident as yet another example of Saxon perfidy, and those which took the constitutional high ground in proclaiming that people who engaged in or supported armed insurrections against the Crown thereby forfeited all their civil rights, especially the right to appear on national television. The complex questions about the role of the media in a civil society where the predominant mode was conflict rather than consensus were touched on only intermittently, and it is difficult in the end not to sympathise with David Butler's verdict:

> In general, coverage of Northern Ireland displays a depressing dependence on second-hand motifs, visual and thematic, which mars all but the most painstaking and imaginative representations. And this is also the root of the problem for broadcasters, the makers of fiction and documentary films and academic analysis alike: how does one go about representing 'culture and identity in Northern Ireland' in ways which avoid depoliticizing their seamier aspects while at the same time not falling into the trap of reliance on cliché?
>
> (Butler 1995: 44)

7   Local, national, global, 1995–2000

The last decade of the century, and in particular its last six years, saw an acceleration of the trends which had already become evident in media over the 1980s. As the economy improved dramatically from 1995 onwards, media profits improved, media companies changed hands with increasing frequency as the tempo of rationalisation increased, new titles appeared and globalisation began to make its presence felt. Broadcasting was in flux: the new commercial radio stations were taking audience share from the only possible source available – RTE's audience – and the launch of a national commercial television competitor for the public service station, although delayed by what appeared to be interminable wrangles and financial difficulties, finally materialised.

The increasing degree of control being exercised by multinational media companies, particularly those involved in satellite-based broadcasting, over the material formerly available on a free-to-air basis to terrestrial stations, provoked a flurry of controversy, as well as national and multinational attempts at regulation. These factors, in turn, prompted a renewed focus on the perceived vulnerability, in the new era, of the public service broadcasting (PSB) component of the national media of a small country with an open economy, such as the Republic, and, paradoxically and unexpectedly, saw a forging of new relationships between some media in both parts of the island. In addition, these developments were to be accompanied by technological changes which focused attention on media distribution and relay systems, developments which, if they did not entirely displace the old arguments, meant that they had to be considered in a radically altered context.

Seen from the perspective of 1995, little of this was at first apparent. The Irish Press group had collapsed in the summer of that year. The role of the Independent group in its demise was the subject of much speculation, as was the now enhanced position of that group, particularly in the indigenous media sector. In the relatively few newspapers now left outside the Independent group's direct or indirect sphere of influence, concern was being expressed about the reduction in the number of media outlets involved in the closure of the Press group. Simultaneously (and not entirely consistently) all the print media, through their organisation, National Newspapers of Ireland (NNI), were putting pressure on the government to take action against the overspill of the

British print media into Ireland. The paradoxes inherent in this situation were neatly exemplified in the decision of the *Cork Examiner* – a member of the NNI – to take on a large and lucrative printing contract for sections of the Irish edition of the UK *Sunday Times*, which was of course in direct competition with a number of papers published by other members of the NNI.

The government's response was to set up a commission – the Commission on the Newspaper Industry – which was established in September 1995 by the Minister for Enterprise and Employment, Richard Bruton, with a former Chief Justice, Mr Tom Finlay, as its chair. If this was intended to buy time for the government, it did not buy much: the commission, despite its unwieldy size (it had twenty-one members representing directly almost every conceivable interest with the exception of the print unions) reported on its twelve wide-ranging terms of reference in less than a year, on 24 June 1996.

Its deliberations addressed a number of core concerns, all of them to some degree interrelated: the perceived danger of a threat to diversity of opinion caused by the demise of the Press group and the increasing role of the Independent group; the dangers posed by the overspill of UK titles; the competitiveness of the industry generally; and legal and taxation issues.

It was immediately faced by problems of definition. If the *Sunday Business Post*, which was largely owned by non-Irish interests and which was printed outside the Free State, was an indigenous Irish newspaper, what about the *Irish Mirror*, which had Irish editorial offices and was printed inside the Free State. The commission eventually adopted a somewhat cumbersome formula, which finessed the question of the border, to get around this problem. The indigenous newspaper industry, it noted, was 'one located in Ireland, staffed predominantly by Irish residents; directed to the people of Ireland and mainly dealing with Irish affairs national and local'.

It went on:

It consists of daily, Sunday and weekly newspapers which:–

(i)   in their editorial and advertising content were directed to the Irish market either nationally or locally;

(ii) are published in Ireland and in the main controlled by Irish interests;

(iii) are written by journalists and editors, the great majority of whom are ordinarily resident in Ireland and

(iv) in most instances are printed and distributed by persons working in Ireland.

(Commission on the Newspaper Industry 1996: 23)

This formulation did not entirely conceal the reality, which was that the island of Ireland and its neighbouring island increasingly shared an information ecology in which black and white distinctions were becoming more and more difficult to make. In some cases, indeed, it operated to benefit freedom of information generally. Just as, in 1932, the existence (and circulation in the Republic) of Northern Ireland newspapers had operated to foil the government's attempt to censor the domestic press on the controversy involving the governor-general, the occasional interest of UK media in Irish affairs sometimes served to highlight issues which the national media had ignored. The classic example of this was Yorkshire Television's documentary exposé of problems in the Irish beef industry, which in January 1995 led to the (unsuccessful) prosecution of an Irish journalist involved, Susan O'Keeffe, for refusing to reveal her sources of information, and eventually to a judicial inquiry which cost more than £20 million and uncovered at least some of the major scandals in the industry.

The commission's report (Commission on the Newspaper Industry 1996) adopted the industry agenda almost entirely in a limited number of areas. On taxation, for instance, it supported without reservation the industry's plea for a reduction of the rate of VAT on newspapers (although it recommended a zero rate in ignorance of the fact that this was not permissible under EU regulations). It also adopted, and to some extent refined, the findings of the 1994 Law Reform Commission report on defamation, suggesting a number of measures which would have the dual effect of making it possible for genuinely aggrieved people to obtain low-cost remedies from the media, while at the same time protecting newspapers, radio and television to some extent against opportunist claimants. It responded in an even-handed way to allegations that the media were guilty of too-frequent invasions of privacy, by accepting that while privacy was important, there were always circumstances in which the public interest demanded that it be given a lower priority. It suggested changes in capital acquisitions tax (CAT) which would shield smaller media companies, particularly those owned by family interests rather than by publicly quoted companies, from exposure to potentially crippling taxation on the deaths of major shareholders. This recommendation would have been of particular interest to the *Cork Examiner*, which was precisely such a company, as well as to a number of family-owned regional newspapers.

In a number of other areas, however, the commission fell somewhat short of the industry's expectations. While it accepted that the closure of the Press group posed distinct problems for newspapers in Ireland, and that the aggressiveness, low cover price and marketing budgets of the UK papers circulating in Ireland posed equally real problems, it tended to define these problems in slightly different ways, and indeed suggested that some of them were of the industry's own making. The report was, in turn, reviewed by the Competition and Mergers Review Group of the Department of Enterprise, Trade and Employment. When its comments were finally published in June 2000, this group suggested that a number of criteria specifically relating to the newspaper industry might be articulated in competition legislation. It rejected, however, the idea that a specific protection, by way of definition, for 'indigenous' newspapers should be inserted into competition legislation, not least because it might 'amount to a form of discrimination (even if indirect) on grounds of nationality' (Competition and Mergers Review Group 2000: 254). Its approach, in effect, was considerably more low-key than that of the Competition Authority itself (1992, 1995), and it noted:

> While in practice there may be some degree of overlap between some criteria (for example a competition concern with ensuring that there are enough thriving newspapers in the market place will tend to serve the public policy goals of maintaining cultural and political diversity), it still seems appropriate that the Competition Authority's analysis should not be cluttered by public policy considerations which do not sit particularly easily with a micro-economic analysis conducted in terms of concentration, market power and dominance.
>
> (Competition and Mergers Review Group 2000: 258)

Certainly 1995 was a low point in the fortunes of Irish newspapers generally. Their share of the total market had dropped by 7% in the five-year period from 1990, precisely the share by which the UK published titles had increased. They held 69% of this market overall, and only 64% of the hotly contested Sunday market. These figures, however, tended to mask another trend: the fact that newspaper circulations generally were declining: between 1990 and 1995, the total number of papers sold in the Free State had gone down from 2.023 million to 1.878 million, a substantial decrease. In this context, the main problem, as identified by the commission, was not the threat from UK papers as such, but the threat from a generally declining newspaper readership. The commission went even further, in that it identified the high cost base of Irish newspapers as a factor which made them more vulnerable to UK competition (where massive economies of scale of course applied), and hinted strongly that remedial steps in this area were primarily the responsibility of Irish newspapers themselves.

The commission also strongly recommended that, insofar as declining newspaper circulations could be seen to reflect public dissatisfaction with their activities and standards, newspapers could also play a part in rectifying this situation by cooperating on a voluntary basis in the establishment of an industry-wide Ombudsman (the commission rejected the idea of a Press Council as being too unwieldy in a country of Ireland's size) who would also be statutorily protected against any actions for defamation arising out of the performance of his or her duties. This proposal was not universally popular among newspaper management representatives on the commission, but received substantial and, in the event, effective support from the other members.

The central dilemma faced by the commission, and which it was unable satisfactorily to resolve, was that one of the problems with which it was attempting to deal – the diminution in the diversity of Irish print media reflected in the ever-increasing role and power of the Independent group – could be interpreted (and, by the Independent group, was consistently interpreted) as a legitimate, indeed inevitable response to the other problem with which the commission was grappling: the threat from imported titles.

In this context, the Independent group interpreted the Irish newspaper market as meaning the entire market, including imported titles. In this market, they argued with some justification, their presence, although substantial, was not a dominant one within the somewhat technical definition of that term in competition legislation. They also argued – and on the face of it this was not unreasonable either – that one of the best defences against foreign predators was national support for policies designed to encourage the growth and development of strong indigenous newspaper interests (such as the Independent group). They should not, they argued, be penalised for success, especially if the outcome of such a policy would be a weakening of the capacity of Irish newspapers to counter UK-based competition. And they maintained that diversity of viewpoint could be supplied as readily by diversity of titles as by diversity of ownership.

Their critics preferred to define the indigenous Irish newspaper market as the central location for the argument, and maintained that, within this more restricted arena, the presence and size of the Independent group was now becoming an effective barrier to diversity. That group, at the time the commission's report was written, owned or had substantial interests in seven out of the eleven indigenous morning, evening and Sunday newspapers. Its size could also be interpreted as a potential source of danger: the Independent group, although a multinational with considerable assets, was not necessarily immune, by virtue of that fact alone, from predators – in fact, its success and profitability might, in certain circumstances, make even it an attractive takeover target. Nor could it be protected by national legislation from such a threat, if it ever emerged: Ireland's membership of the European Community precluded such a course of action, at least in relation to initiatives originating in another EC country.

The commission concluded on this issue that there was in the Republic generally 'a sufficient plurality of ownership and of title to maintain an adequate diversity of editorial viewpoint and of cultural content' but it added:

> Considering the indigenous industry separately, the recent disappearance of the Irish Press titles has involved an unwelcome reduction in diversity. Nonetheless the Commission believes that the existing industry and in particular the indigenous sector of it provides a valuable representation of contemporary Irish culture. The Commission would be concerned that any further reduction of titles or increase in concentration of ownership in the indigenous industry could severely curtail the diversity requisite to maintain a vigorous democracy.
>
> (Committee on the Newspaper Industry 1996: 30)

The qualified gloom of the commission's report echoed its times: 1995, when it was written, was by any standards a difficult year for Irish newspapers, as the Irish Press titles collapsed and the threat from UK imports loomed larger. Even in 1995, however, newspaper profits in all the major groups apart from the Irish Press group were healthy and improving; and subsequent events were to indicate that this particular year had, in fact, marked the bottom of the curve in what has always been a cyclical business.

The critical factor was, undoubtedly, the state of the economy rather than any measures taken specifically by, or on behalf of, newspapers themselves. The five-year period 1995–2000 saw an economic upswing in Ireland greater than that of all other EC countries, led to a reduction in national debt, the disappearance of emigration (and the beginnings of immigration) and associated rises in advertising revenue for all major media. Advertising in newspapers which are members of the NNI, which was running at £91.9 million in 1995, almost doubled by 1999 to £181.3 million.

Sales of daily newspapers, over the 1990–9 period, grew by 93,000 overall notwithstanding the loss of 60,000 sales by the *Irish Press* morning paper in 1995, i.e. the total market grew by 55% more than the sales lost through the *Press*'s demise (Barrett 2000: 3). UK titles, it is true, increased by marginally more than indigenous titles, but the bulk of this increase was accounted for by one title – the *Irish Sun*. In the Sunday market, Irish titles actually recovered market share in the period from 1995, with increased sales of 70,000 copies compared to a reduction of 26,000 in imports. These trends were favoured by price stability: Irish daily and Sunday newspapers, which were traditionally (especially the daily papers) more expensive than the UK imports, managed to hold their prices steady for almost all of this period, only increasing them in 2000.

Existing and new titles contributed in different ways to this improved market share on Sundays. The most dramatic performance, in percentage terms, was registered by the *Sunday Business Post*, which rose from 33,000 in 1995 to almost 50,000 at the end of 1999. Along the way, it changed hands: in 1997 both the German investor (who had replaced the original French investor) and the original journalist-owners, were bought out by Trinity Holdings, the UK newspaper group which was then engaged in a massive expansionary programme. The new title was *Ireland on Sunday*, which began life as the *Title* on 28 July 1996. The *Title* was an attempt to launch a Sunday paper which would cover only sport, made by a group of businessmen, some of whom had interests in printing. It was a brave and colourful effort, but a gamble that did not quite come off: after little more than a year, it was merged into a new publication, *Ireland on Sunday*, which appeared for the first time on 21 September 1997: by the end of 1999 it was selling more than 65,000 copies, its editorial a mixture designed to appeal at least in part to the slightly more conservative, more nationalist readers who had been left high and dry by the collapse of the *Sunday Press*.

Its finances, however, were never entirely secure, and it was taken over in June 2000 by Scottish Radio Holdings (SRH), whose presence on the Irish media landscape was becoming a significant one. SRH, whose holdings in Northern Ireland had included substantial shares in both UTV and Downtown Radio, had for some time been in the process of refocusing its activity. In 1998 it sold its 18% shareholding in UTV to CanWest, now the major investor (45%) in the Republic's TV3 station, for some £24 million (*IT*: 24 February 1998). A year later, SRH sold an 18.6% share-holding to Granada, thus giving one of the 'big three' UK ITV companies a major stake in Irish media, North and South. SRH, which in 1998 had already purchased the regional newspaper, the *Leitrim Observer*, added not only *Ireland on Sunday* to its portfolio on this occasion, but two other regional titles, the *Midland Tribune* and the *Tullamore Tribune*, on whose presses *Ireland on Sunday* is printed. By the end of the decade, *Ireland on Sunday* had a circulation which was peaking at around 70,000. Some 17,000 of those sales were in Northern Ireland, and under the new SRH management, plans were being made to print a more fully editionised Northern Ireland edition at the Morton newspapers plant in Portadown, also owned now by SRH.

On the import side, the most spectacular growth was registered by the *Sunday Times*, which opened permanent offices in Dublin in 1996, and which by the end of 1999, had increased its circulation in the Republic from 59,000 (in 1995) to 89,000.

The one black spot was, and remained, the evening newspaper market, where the continuing weakness of all titles tended to undermine the other newspapers' argument that their main difficulty was posed by UK competition. Between 1990 and 1999 sales in this sector declined by some 522,000 a week, a figure which is coincidentally, but interestingly, almost identical to the increase of 513,000 in the sales of UK daily and weekly titles (Barrett 2000: 5). In this context, one of the bravest – or most foolhardy – decisions was that by a group of investors to launch a new evening newspaper, the *Evening News*. It was even more ill-advised to launch it in June 1996, just on the edge of the holiday season, when there is traditionally a dearth of advertising, and to have it printed in Tullamore, 66 miles away from its major potential market in Dublin. A shortage of working capital was compounded by investment decisions which favoured the purchase of expensive technology over marketing: it closed in September of the same year.

Three of the four daily papers were the primary contributors to the resilience in the morning daily market: the *Irish Independent*, the Independent part-owned *Star* and the *Irish Times*, all of which put on substantial circulation during this period. Proportionately, though, the biggest gainer at the upper end of the market was the *Irish Times*, which between 1995 and the end of 1999 added almost 17,000 copies daily, compared with the growth in the *Independent* circulation of some 11,600. At 113,800, it was now 51,000 copies behind the *Irish Independent*, compared with some 57,000 in 1995, when the *Independent* had benefited to a greater extent from the closure of the Press group titles.

Circulation of the newspapers generally was enhanced by the political volatility of the 1990s, and by the development of an even more adversarial relationship between journalists and governments than had been the case hitherto. Three journalists secured substantial financial damages from the government because of the fact that their phones had been tapped over lengthy periods going back as far as the 1970s. Two of them, Bruce Arnold of the *Irish Independent* and Geraldine Kennedy of the *Irish Times* (who at the relevant time had been working for the *Sunday Tribune*) secured agreed damages after the government admitted that their telephones had been tapped (by a previous government) without proper authorisation. Formal authorisation had been secured for the taps placed between 1975 and 1983 on the telephone of the third journalist, Vincent Browne, whose settlement was announced only in July 1995, but the government agreed in this case that there had been no justification for the taps and that they had been used for improper purposes. Another factor was the coming into force of the Freedom of Information Act on 21 April 1996, which gave Irish journalists a new weapon. They used this – with more enthusiasm and to greater effect than their colleagues in other jurisdictions with similar legislation – continually to embarrass both governments and public servants on issues of current controversy.

It was a period during which journalists themselves were also becoming news. The most dramatic example of this was the case of Veronica Guerin, who had begun her journalistic career on the *Sunday Business Post*, and then progressed, via the *Sunday Tribune*, to the *Sunday Independent*, where she specialised in crime reporting. She was threatened on more than one occasion by members of drug gangs about whose activities she was writing regularly, and was the victim of one unsuccessful assassination attempt. Then on 26 June 1996, aged 37, she was shot dead by a gunman on a motorcycle as she sat in her car at a set of traffic lights on the outskirts of Dublin. Her death caused profound shock, but not always for the obvious reasons. Some of her friends alleged that her employers had failed to give her sufficient protection in what was becoming known as a difficult and dangerous calling; the Independent group responded that she had refused all offers of protection, and set up an award in her honour. A Dublin criminal was later sentenced for her killing, but questions remained – about the lengths to which journalists should go in any given set of circumstances, and about the murky half-world in which police and criminals traded information about each other to journalists, and used publicity as a weapon.

An almost equally dramatic series of events surrounded an attempt in 1999 by the British authorities to force Ed Moloney, the Northern editor of the Dublin-based *Sunday Tribune*, to surrender to the security forces notes he had made of an interview with a murder suspect in 1989. An initial court ruling, in September 1999, went against him, but he won a landmark decision on appeal on 27 October. Mr Justice Carswell, in the Court of Appeal (http://indigo.ie/~nujdub/judgment.htm), while declining to accept that Moloney (or any journalist) had a right to withhold sources of information at will, and even though he accepted that Moloney's notes might have been useful to the police, concluded that the police had not produced persuasive evidence that they were essential, and in effect declined to authorise a fishing expedition. His judgment was warmly welcomed by the National Union of Journalists as a significant step towards greater protection for journalists' sources.

Increasing competition between newspapers led to a renewed focus on exclusive stories. They varied in quality: at the tabloid end of the market, the exclusives tended, increasingly, to be more about the private lives of public figures – politicians, musicians and television personalities – than about major social and economic issues. Among the broadsheets, there was a relatively greater interest in the doings – or, more accurately, the misdeeds – of government. The last two years of the decade, in particular, were marked by a plethora of stories about scandals in the planning process, and a whole series of questionable payments by major business interests to leading politicians, which resulted in the establishment of a number of judicial tribunals. The tribunals themselves spawned further investigative journalism, as the slowness with which they wended their way through the voluminous evidence prompted some journalists to reveal significant details in advance.

This in turn prompted a renewed debate about journalistic ethics, although in a different context to that in which it had been advanced at the time of the abortion controversies of the early 1980s. In the privately owned print media, the debate tended to be about the degree to which a public person's private life could become a legitimate matter of public interest. This threw up sharply differing viewpoints, as in the 1999 controversy about the fact that two cabinet ministers had taken holidays in a French villa owned by a major Irish business figure. The Minister for Finance, one of those involved, bluntly told reporters that where he took his holidays was none of their business, which only made them redouble their attention.

Although it is difficult to disentangle cause and effect, the growing public (and not just journalistic) interest in media matters was further evidenced by the introduction of regular media pages in the two leading national newspapers, the *Irish Times* and the *Irish Independent*. Much of this material, particularly in the *Irish Times*, was aimed at schoolchildren: the syllabus in post-primary schools was simultaneously being widened to take in the study of modern media, especially in Ireland, as a key element. Educational institutions themselves were also adapting: by the end of the century, public undergraduate and postgraduate education in journalism was already well established (Dublin City University 1982, University College Galway 1986, Dublin Institute of Technology late 1960s), and was complemented by courses offered in a number of private colleges.

In the area of public service journalism, attention turned more to RTE, and to critiques that it was adopting a liberal consensus to the detriment of its public service, pluralist role. In 1999, it lost an important constitutional action taken by a private citizen who persuaded the Supreme Court that it had unfairly allocated more time, in party political broadcasts preceding the 1996 referendum on divorce, to the pro-divorce argument than to its opponents. RTE argued unavailingly that, since most of the recognised political parties were formally in favour of introducing divorce, they were simply reflecting public opinion. In June 2000, there was another controversy surrounding the appointment, by the government, of a former Supreme Court judge to a position with the European Investment Bank. On that occasion, RTE received formal notification from the judge's legal advisers that they considered the station to be in breach of their legal requirement to be impartial on all matters of public controversy, and demanding – instead of recourse to the Broadcasting Complaints Commission – an impartial enquiry into the whole matter. The historian J.J. Lee, in no sense an enemy of public service broadcasting, suggested in this general context that imported television culture, replicated to some extent in the national station, risked promoting a 'consensus in favour of the principle of an atomised society based on the value of no-fault individualism' (Lee 1997: 18).

These controversies, if anything, helped to contribute to media growth and profitability. The success of the *Irish Times* in colonising its niche and its apparent encroachment on the *Irish Independent*'s middle market dominance, however, masked a problem which continued to restrict its opportunities for growth. This was the fact that although the *Irish Times* could offer advertisers not only colour but a high penetration of the upper socio-economic readership groups, the *Independent* could offer huge numbers of readers across a wider social spectrum, not least by means of discount packages across some or all of the various titles it controlled. This prompted the *Irish Times* management, at various times in the late 1990s, actively to consider the introduction of a Sunday paper, which would give them a greater pool of readers to offer advertisers as well as utilising their relatively under-used printing capacity. A decision on this proposal, however, was repeatedly deferred, and the management instead began to plan a re-design of the high-selling Saturday paper and its magazine section in an attempt to exploit a section of the market in which it was snapping much more closely at the heels of the *Independent*. Coincidentally, management at the *Cork Examiner* had been thinking of launching a Sunday edition also: the Saturday edition of their evening paper, the *Evening Echo*, sold poorly, and it seemed to make more sense to roll it over into a Saturday night/Sunday morning edition. Market research, however, gave them second thoughts: it indicated strongly that readers in the *Examiner*'s circulation area were not necessarily interested in more of the same on a Sunday, but preferred something different. Equally significantly, the financial projections indicated that if it launched a Sunday paper and failed to make a success of it, there would be a financial crisis which might even threaten the success of the daily paper. In the circumstances, the safer option was to continue with its printing contract for part of the Irish edition of the *Sunday Times*.

The *Independent*, meanwhile, was conscious of the competition, and moved simultaneously in two areas to keep it at a distance. The first was its decision to launch, on 15 November 1997, a colour supplement with its Saturday edition. This addition, with part of its editorial material sourced from the *Daily Mail* and a seven-day television programme section, certainly helped to keep the competition at bay (it was announced as a free supplement on the day of first publication; a note elsewhere in the same issue of the paper, however, noted that the cover price had been increased by 5p to cover higher printing costs).

The second was to take action on a long-delayed decision to invest in new printing equipment. This involved a move to a purpose-built £60 million printing plant on the outskirts of Dublin, with excellent motorway access, which was commissioned in the summer of 2000, giving it a hugely improved capacity for colour and more reliable printing generally. The *Irish Times* was also in the process of moving to a new, purpose-built plant in the same part of the city, but at a slower pace. Both newspapers would maintain their centre-city locations for editorial and commercial purposes.

Although the Independent group's profitability was by now legendary, it was still experiencing difficulties in another area – one judged critical to its future growth. This was its investment in new media, specifically its involvement in Independent Wireless Cable, the company which it had originally formed for the purpose of applying for MMDS franchises in the late 1980s, to broadcast television signals and telephony to non-metropolitan areas on micro-wave frequencies. In September 1989 the then Minister for Communications, Ray Burke, announced the award of a number of MMDS franchises. Independent Wireless and Cable received seven, although these were largely in areas where viewers could already pick up UK signals with relative ease; the company also had minority interests in two other companies in Limerick and Cork, which had also received franchises.

Two years later, in a climate of some anxiety caused by the government's inability or unwillingness to deal with the problem caused by the operators of illegal deflector systems, Burke issued a 'letter of comfort' to the Independent group, in which he assured them that once MMDS was available in any franchise region, his department would apply 'the full rigour of the law' to the illegal operators (*IT*: 30 May 1998). This reassured a number of US potential investors, who acquired 50% of Princes Holdings, the Independent holding company of which Independent Wireless and Cable was a subsidiary. The anticipated revenue flow was simply not materialising, despite heavy investment, and accumulated losses by 1997 were of the order of £25 million, despite a subscriber base of 140,000.

This was for a number of reasons. The principal one was that the introduction of the MMDS technology required customers to pay several hundred pounds a year for the necessary equipment. On its own, this might have slowed down take-up of the new system, but there was an additional problem: a number of private individuals and companies were operating unauthorised and technically illegal relay systems, which were channelling UK television services (and some satellite-based services) to subscribers for a fraction of the cost of the MMDS. Although they were illegal, the government could not close them down without incurring severe electoral consequences. But, unless they could be closed down, the MMDS franchises were risky investments. It was, in a sense, the pirate radio scenario all over again. The illegal operations were popular, and they could not be terminated unless something realistic and acceptable was poised to take their place.

The situation was further complicated by a number of legal cases. In one of them, the government failed to persuade the courts that it should be allowed to go ahead with a plan to shut down an unauthorised relay station in Cork. MMDS franchisees were, for their part, threatening legal action to force a declaration that they were entitled to exclusive rights of re-transmission in their franchise areas. The government, caught in the middle, was flailing around looking for a compromise, without much evident prospect of success. Feelings ran high: in the 1994 general election, one disgruntled operator of an unauthorised relay service (all such services were by now looking for government action to regularise their position) was elected, as an independent member of parliament, for one of the Donegal constituencies where this was a major local issue.

Matters reached a head at the climax of the general election campaign in June 1997 when the *Irish Independent*, on the morning before polling day, published a front-page editorial urging its readers to vote for the Fianna Fail/Progressive Democrat opposition. It was unusual enough for this paper to publish a front-page editorial. To publish one urging such a course of action on its readers, on the part of a paper which had been sceptical of Fianna Fail at best for most of its existence, or at least until 1979, was unprecedented. The editorial argued its case on economics and taxation policy alone. Taxpayers, it maintained had suffered enough under the so-called 'Rainbow Coalition' of Fine Gael, Labour and progressive left parties which had held power for the previous three years: now it was 'payback time' (*II*: 5 June 1997).

When the votes were counted, it emerged that Fianna Fail and their allies, the Progressive Democrats had a large enough number of seats to form the next government with the support of a number of independents. The brouhaha about the supposed role of the *Irish Independent* in bringing about this result to some extent obscured the fact that the Fianna Fail vote was the second-lowest in that party's seventy-year history, and that its seat total was due primarily to highly effective vote management under the proportional representation system (which, as it happened, Fianna Fail had twice unsuccessfully tried to abolish). The *Irish Independent* itself received an inordinate number of protesting telephone calls from its readership, and the controversy was re-ignited dramatically within days when the *Irish Times* published extracts from government documents indicating that, at a meeting with government ministers on the MMDS issue before the election, representatives of Princes Holdings had indicated that failure to resolve the MMDS impasse would result in a loss of goodwill towards the government.

The implication of the conjunction of these facts was unmistakable: that the *Irish Independent* had threatened the government that its titles would be used against them politically if the government refused to take the necessary steps to sort out the mess. This interpretation, however, was emphatically rejected by the Independent group, which maintained that there was another, more benign explanation. The meeting and the editorial, they argued, were unconnected. The threat (if this is what it was) at the meeting was made in a different context entirely – the increasing pressure from their co-investors in Princes Holdings to bring a court action against the government to establish their rights and force the closure of the illegal relay stations. Up to that point – the Independent version had it – they had been successful in persuading their foreign investors that the problem could be resolved by negotiations. If negotiation proved fruitless, they would no longer be able to argue convincingly against legal action and the government would, for this reason, have forfeited their goodwill.

There was a flurry of statements and counter-statements. The editor of the *Irish Independent*, Vincent Doyle, threatened to sue the *Irish Times* for defamation, and the sudden drop in temperature in the relationship between the two newspapers, situated on opposite sides of the River Liffey from each other, was palpable. It blew over but, whatever its origins and intentions, the editorial marked a watershed in Irish journalism which few would forget.

Regardless of the MMDS controversy, the Independent group was moving swiftly into new media. It was not the first Irish newspaper to establish a website – that honour went to the *Irish Emigrant*, which was established in 1987 as an entirely net-based newspaper, and which was so successful that – in a reversal of what might have been expected – it found itself producing a hard copy edition for US readers in 1995. Currently (2000), it has paid subscribers in 112 countries, and was presented with the net Visionary Award by the Irish Internet Association in November 1999. The *Irish Times* launched its website in February 1994, purchased a portal site, Ireland.com, in 1998, and was consistently registering usage figures which put it among the leading newspapers in the world. There was even a regional paper which preceded the *Irish Independent*'s venture into cyberspace: the *Clare Champion*, which did so in 1994.

It became clear early in 2000, however, that the website was not the only, and probably not the primary, focus of the Independent group's venture into new media. In January, the company – renamed Independent News and Media plc since the previous year – bought Internet Ireland, a company formed in 1997 to provide internet access to a large number of corporate clients. Three weeks later, on 5 February, the company announced the creation of a new venture called Unison. This initiative associated the Independent directly not only with Internet Ireland, which it now owned, but with thirty-eight regional newspapers. The newspapers would promote Unison – a set-top Internet connector designed to help increase Irish adult internet usage from 17% to 34%, or 800,000 adults, within a year. And Unison would promote the newspapers and the services they offered, in a form of commercial synergy which would be free – at least to the newspapers concerned. Each regional title participating would have 100 free set-top boxes to give away; thereafter, they would cost some £300 apiece. There were other linkages, too: International Network News, a Dublin-based radio news service, was not only providing timed news bulletins for the regional radio stations, but was acting as part of the platform for Unison and, additionally, was involved in creating a link for news from the Republic for UTV's website in Northern Ireland.

This in turn was part of a wider strategy, involving the simultaneous promotion of another company called iTouch, a 60%-owned subsidiary of the Independent's South African operations created with the aim of linking the internet to mobile phone use. It was not long before commentators were seeing, in these moves, a plan by Independent News and Media to succeed in getting itself re-rated on the stock markets as an e-commerce company rather than simply a proprietor of newspapers and radio stations (*SBP*: 16 January 2000). In June 2000, plans were announced to float the company on the London Stock Exchange, where it was expected to raise some £100 million sterling (*IT*: 23 June 2000).

Its move into new media did not mean that the Independent group had taken its eye off terrestrial opportunities. One such had been in the process of emerging since 1998, when the UK-based Mirror group had bought the weakened *Newsletter* in Belfast. This was a strategic purchase, not least because it gave it access to printing facilities in Ireland for its daily and Sunday titles. In 1999, however, the pattern of media ownership in Northern Ireland was again dramatically disturbed when Trinity Holdings, now the owners of the *Belfast Telegraph*, and its associated titles (including *Sunday Life*), made a bid for the Mirror group. This bid succeeded, creating a new media giant to be known as Trinity Mirror; but only at a price. This was the decision by the British government that Trinity would have to sell off the *Belfast Telegraph* if it wanted to finalise the Mirror bid: had it not done so, the new company would have controlled an unacceptably high 67% of the Northern Ireland print media advertising market. The previous year, the *Telegraph* had contributed almost a quarter of the entire Trinity group's profits, making some £21 million on sales of £54 million.

As suitors circled, the Independent said little, but it was hardly entirely unexpected when, on 29 April 2000, details of its £350 million bid for the *Telegraph* were finally revealed. It had already, in anticipation of Unionist objections (which were duly forthcoming, not least from the deputy leader of the Unionist Party, Mr John Taylor, himself the proprietor of a number of Northern Ireland regional papers) indicated that the *Telegraph* would be guaranteed continuation of its editorial independence. A further guarantee would be provided by a new board, headed by Lord Rogan, the Chairman of the Unionist Party itself. Buyer and seller alike believed that the UK Monopolies Commission would not raise any serious obstacle to the purchase, although the possibility that the Northern group might have to divest itself, in turn, of the *Sunday Life*, was an option which was being discussed as the UK government's examination went into its final stages in the summer of 2000. Independent News and Media, keen to erect a Chinese wall against the possibility that it might be accused of exploiting a dominant position in the marketplace, gave undertakings in advance that it would not change employment structures in its Northern titles, would not change the *Telegraph's* editorial policy, and would not introduce cross-border deals with the group's titles in the Republic (*SBP*: 18 June 2000). Coincidentally, both the *Belfast Telegraph* and the *Irish News* were undergoing significant design changes: the *Telegraph* came out in a re-designed format on 9 March 2000, while the *Irish News* came out four days later in 'Euro-format', an intermediate size which is bigger than tabloid but smaller than broadsheet. The *Irish News*, in addition, changed its printing location to the Morton newspapers plant in Portadown owned by SRH, giving it a new potential maximum pagination of 56, as against its former maximum, at its own printing plant, of 28. As part of the promotion of the new format, the paper was being delivered free of charge to some 200,000 homes for a period.

The significance of this consolidation of indigenous Irish newspaper interests was underlined by another development: News International (NI) secured an option in February 2000 on a site for a printing plant outside Drogheda, situated strategically between Dublin and Belfast: it was considering the possibility of establishing a £70 million printing plant which would take over the printing of NI titles from the *Belfast Telegraph* when it expired in 2001, and produce, for the Irish market, a quarter of a million copies of its daily newspapers (the *Irish Sun* and the *Times*) as well as 450,000 copies of the *News of the World* and the *Sunday Times* combined.

The continuing threat from UK-based newspapers appeared as if it might be stalled later in the same year when the Republic's Minister for Health, Micheal Martin, indicated that he planned to introduce a complete ban on cigarette advertising in 2001, some four years before it was due to become mandatory across the EU (*IT*: 20 May 2000). The *Irish Times* had voluntarily adopted such a ban in 1992, the only Irish newspaper to do so. If such a ban were rigidly enforced, it would prevent the sale of UK-based or edited papers, or force them to change or drop all cigarette advertising to comply with Irish legislation (the international magazine *Playboy* had been appearing without advertisements for UK-based abortion clinics since 1996, when it was threatened with seizure for breaches of the censorship laws if it continued to carry them). However, the possible impact of this measure was rapidly qualified by an opinion delivered at the European Court of Justice by one of its advocates general (ironically enough, an Irish lawyer), who argued strongly that the ban was one solely in restraint of trade, and should therefore be void under EU competition legislation (*IT*: 20 June 2000).

The censorship laws (not referred to at all by the Commission on the Newspaper Industry, as it happened) continued to make themselves felt, infrequently and controversially. In 1999, the popular listings magazine *In Dublin* was banned by the Censorship Board after the Board had taken note of its practice of including advertisements for establishments which were in all probability brothels, although they were described as 'massage services'. The magazine succeeded in having the ban temporarily lifted by a higher court on the grounds that it had not been offered an opportunity to reply to the charges, but simultaneously sanitised its advertising pages. Its publisher was subsequently charged with offences under public order legislation relating to the advertising of brothels and prostitution (*IT*: 19 May 2000). The British magazine *Loaded* was removed from shops by its distributors shortly afterwards (*IT*: 22 May 2000).

The new Trinity Mirror conglomerate, as it happened, retained ownership of two other Irish newspapers, titles in the *Derry Journal* group, which it had acquired in 1998 for £18.25 million. This was unmistakable evidence of a trend of growing interest by UK media companies in Irish newspapers and radio stations. Scottish Radio Holdings, as already noted, were by 2000 the owners not only of the regional *Leitrim Observer* (since September 1998) and the national *Ireland on Sunday*, but also of Downtown Radio in Northern Ireland, and were strongly rumoured to be interested in the purchase of further Irish titles.

These moves confirmed a phenomenon that had already become noticeable: moves towards rationalisation and acquisition in the Irish regional newspaper market generally. It was a landscape which had, until the 1990s, remained unchanged for the best part of a century. Originally a Protestant and settler phenomenon, the local or regional newspaper had, by the second half of the nineteenth century, become increasingly a Catholic and nationalist one. Catholic emancipation in 1829 and the failed rebellion of 1848, combined with increasing popular literacy and the emergence of a new Catholic middle class, were all factors which accelerated these developments. In 1855 there were 100 such papers; by the beginning of 1859 there were 130; by the end of 1859 there were 140. By 1870, however, they had shrunk in number to 103 (Stapleton: 1974: 33–4). In 1950, there were 71, and every town with a population of 5,000 or over had its own paper, with four notable exceptions: Dun Laoghaire and Bray, within the Greater Dublin conurbation; Cobh, which was too close to Cork city to support a separate paper, and Killarney, in Co. Kerry, which had boasted a paper of its own in the past and was to do so again in the future. Six cities and towns had no fewer than three or four local newspapers apiece (Haughton 1950: 54). By 1969, however, when a government committee on industrial reorganisation reported on the prospects of the 41 remaining titles in an era of free trade, it was anticipated that many of them were doomed to closure.

Although these predictions were to a large extent unfulfilled, the general situation was stagnant well into the 1980s, when a substantial number of regional papers were owned by private limited companies or family partnerships – some forty different companies, controlling the 87% of regional newspaper circulation (the remainder was controlled by companies within the Independent group) (Horgan 1986: 11). In one 1984 survey (O'Neill 1984: 42) 65% of local editors placed 'supporting local values' at the top of a list of functions exercised by their newspapers.

By 1993, however, their number had risen to fifty-three and, despite gloomy predictions that they would suffer inordinately from the introduction of local commercial radio, in which some regional newspapers had a stake (*IT*: 27 August 1983), they not only survived, but prospered. As this happened, they became increasingly attractive prospects for both domestic as well as foreign predators. The *Cork Examiner*, which had already acquired the *Waterford News and Star* in 1959, moved completely outside its natural hinterland in 1995 with the purchase of the *Western People* in Co. Mayo; in 1996 it extended its ownership in Connaught by acquiring the *Sligo Weekender*, a free-sheet. In 1999 it acquired a weekly paper in Killarney, the *Kingdom*, and was pushing its own daily paper outside Munster, for example by including a weekly Kilkenny supplement in its paper on one morning each week from mid-2000. It had already, in a bid to increase its circulation and its attraction to advertisers, dropped the word 'Cork' from its title in 1996; in 2000 it was to re-launch itself yet again as the *Irish Examiner* and, although each move was accompanied by an increase in circulation, the modest scale of such increases indicated the difficulties of taking on the established national media on their own doorstep, particularly in Dublin. It was also running into problems with newsagents, after initiating a two-tier policy on margins. In common with the *Irish Times* and *Irish Independent*, it paid its existing retailers a gross margin of 23.5%, but decided to pay new retailers at a new 18% rate, provoking claims of anti-competitive practices (*II*: 1 June 2000).

By 2000, also, rationalisation was continuing apace in other areas. The *Leinster Leader* and *Leinster Express* merged in December 1998 and, in early 2000, subsumed the *Dundalk Democrat*, a small and old-fashioned but nonetheless profitable paper (it was, at this stage, the only regional paper still devoting its front page entirely to advertisements). The *Kilkenny People*, owner of one of the most advanced printing presses in the country, was now the owner of the *Tipperary Star* and the Clonmel *Nationalist*; at the end of June, it was itself taken over by the expanding Scottish Radio Holdings group for a consideration of almost £30 million. This latest acquisition made SRH – whose cost-cutting, bottom-line-oriented management style was already becoming a byword in the other Irish enterprises it had acquired – the third-largest regional newspaper group in the country. And these were only the most noticeable developments in an industry which was expanding apace. Its association, the Provincial Newspapers Association of Ireland, which had existed for more than twenty years as an organisation mainly dedicated to handling wage negotiations with the NUJ, had become, by 1999, the National Association of Regional Newspapers (NARN), dedicated to selling advertising space in all its associated titles on a cooperative basis and, incidentally, providing part of the platform for the Independent's Unison initiative.

The growth of the regional newspaper sector during this last decade of the century was all the more remarkable in that it was accompanied by an equally noticeable growth of free-sheets: by 1998 it was estimated (*ST*: 18 October 1998) that whereas NARN's titles sold 600,000 copies a week and were read by 2 million people, advertising in free-sheets, which accounted for some £5 million of the £250 million annual advertising spend in the regional press, was still only half the UK per capita expenditure, and could be expected to increase substantially.

Northern Ireland's forty regional newspapers were more protected against rationalisation and closure than their counterparts in the Republic, although not necessarily against acquisition. The purchase of Derry papers by the Mirror group has already been noted; and Mr John Taylor, the prominent Unionist politician, has over the course of his business career assembled a portfolio of six Northern Ireland regional newspapers. The relatively higher number of regional titles in Northern Ireland, on a per capita basis, can be explained in part by the divided nature of Northern Ireland society: in the city of Derry, for instance, two different papers exist side by side, one catering almost exclusively for nationalist, and the other for unionist readers. This factor also acts to prevent amalgamations that might, under other circumstances, have made economic sense. Nonetheless, some of the overtly nationalist and unionist regional papers in the more rural areas were, towards the end of the century and in the light of the fitful but real achievements of the peace process, beginning to modify the rather narrow political perspectives which had tended to characterise them in the past.

In the urban areas like Derry and Belfast, where social and political tensions were higher, and housing was in any event more dramatically segregated, newspaper readership was more predictable in its characteristics and occasionally spawned strong local initiatives. An interesting example of this was the weekly *Andersonstown News*, which appeared in the West Belfast suburb of that name on 22 November 1972. The context was highly political, in that the conflict between the IRA and the security forces was particularly virulent, and the *Irish News* was increasingly seen, by more militant Republicans, as overly cautious and even, on occasion, unsympathetic to their nationalist agenda. The steady growth of the *Andersonstown News*, with its strongly Republican agenda, continued throughout the period from then until the end of the century: on 17 March 1998 it launched a separate edition for North Belfast, and on 7 February 2000 went bi-weekly. Although it had not, at the time of writing, published any audited circulation figures (the first set was due at the end of 2000), it was claiming a combined circulation of 75,000, and, by extension, promoting itself as the most widely read nationalist newspaper in Northern Ireland. The comparison with the *Irish News* was evidently unfair, given that the latter appeared six times a week rather than twice, and had a circulation of some 50,000, but at the very least the success of the Andersonstown paper indicated the existence of a need which the *Irish News* was not entirely able to meet.

In the course of its growth, the *Andersonstown News* made one, unusual, acquisition. This was another Belfast paper, *Lá* ('Day'). Even in the special circumstances of Northern Ireland, the appearance, and continuing existence, of *Lá* would have been a matter for comment. It appeared for the first time on 13 August 1984, just after the death of a civilian in civil disturbances in Andersonstown, and was a cyclostyled daily newsheet written entirely in Irish and produced from an abandoned flax mill. It might be thought that its choice of language indicated an allegiance to the more extreme elements of Republican ideology, but in fact it maintained, from the outset, that it was not associated with any political movement and, indeed, made consistent and occasionally successful efforts to persuade some Unionists that the Irish language and culture was also a part of their heritage, and one which they could share without betraying their political principles. 'The Irish language movement must be above politics – and so must *Lá*,' declared one of its founders, Eoghan O Neill (*Guardian*: 3 April 1989). Despite a disastrous fire which destroyed most of its printing equipment in 1985, it staggered along on a shoe-string (and with occasional support from the Northern Ireland Office). In 1991 it became a weekly, giving Northern Ireland yet another distinction: it was the only part of the United Kingdom – perhaps the only part of the world – in which there was a weekly publication called 'Day', and a monthly one called 'Fortnight'. It was absorbed by the *Andersonstown News* organisation in April 1999 and, despite fears that its agenda might become more political and less cultural under its new ownership, continues to sell a modest but satisfactory 2,500 copies per issue. It is no less successful in its own way, and proportionately probably more so, than *Foinse*, the Irish-language weekly which replaced the subsidised Irish-language weekly *Anois* in Dublin in October 1996, after the Department of the Gaeltacht, which provides substantial financial backing for publications in Irish, had declined to renew its contract with the Anois publishers. *Foinse*, although it marked a distinct advance on its colourless and sloppily produced predecessor (it seems to have been the first Irish-language publication to include, in its first issue, a wine appreciation column) continues to struggle against public indifference and, perhaps more worryingly, the continual difficulty of finding reporters and sub-editors with sufficient command of the language to enable the production of a fully professional newspaper.

Broadcasting North and South

The simultaneous ending of the broadcasting bans in the Republic and in Northern Ireland in 1994 was absorbed into both BBC and UTV practice with very little fuss. The major change, as far as the viewers and listeners were concerned (particularly viewers) was the ending of the practice which had been adopted by the Northern Ireland electronic media (but not by their counterparts in the Republic) of having actors read, in lip-synch, the words spoken by certain political figures whose faces, but not voices, were allowed on the airwaves. Some of the actors had perfected the accents of their alter egos to such a degree that the only noticeable difference, on television, was the disappearance of the caption which had previously informed viewers that the voice they were hearing was not actually that of the person who appeared to be speaking.

Both BBC NI and UTV had, by the end of 1999, evolved into steady state broadcasters, each of them operating under virtually the same conditions as the BBC and ITV franchisees operated in other UK regions, and with the political controversies which had marked their evolution rapidly fading into the past. ITV's major characteristic remained its profitability. By 1998, its pre-tax profits were up to £12.5 million, a 50.8% increase in the previous year. In the same year, it served notice that it might take legal action against RTE if it attempted to boost its signal into Northern Ireland. This threat was plainly related to its decision, in 1999, to mount an aggressive advertising drive in the Republic: it argued that RTE, which has Irish rights for popular soap operas like *Coronation Street*, would be in breach of copyright if it broadcast across the border this and other programmes for which UTV has rights in Northern Ireland. Cabletel, the US-owned group which is currently cabling many Northern Ireland homes, decided in 1999 not to include RTE on its cable until these legal issues had been resolved. RTE, of course, could make a similar claim about the UTV over-spill signal.

In the meantime, however, UTV was making its own forays south of the border. Charting a path which Independent News and Media were to follow almost immediately in the Republic, it acquired, in the same year, Direct Net Access Ltd, Northern Ireland's leading internet service provider, for £4.25 million. Simultaneously, it disposed of its entire share-holding in Société Européenne des Satellites for a total profit of £13.4 million. Nonetheless, it did its best to put these figures into perspective, arguing that, pro rata, its profits were still below the optimum on a per-household basis, and that, indeed, it would be difficult to push them any higher – an assertion to some extent discounted by its continuing rapid growth in revenues.

Its combination of successful locally produced chat shows with popular presenters, and the access to sports and soap operas guaranteed by the ITV connection, continued to guarantee it massive audiences on both sides of the border. Underlining its evident belief that globalisation begins at home, it noted, in its annual report for 1999, that UTV remained 'committed to our objective of developing our service in the Republic of Ireland within the concept of extending the accessibility of all the indigenous channels in Ireland throughout the whole island' (p. 4). In November 2000, it moved even more energetically into the Republic's media market by offering £28.5 million for County Media, a Cork-based company which owns three local radio stations in that county and which posted a profit in 1999 of some £1.5 million (*IT*: 24 November 2000).

BBC NI, on the other hand, was in a slightly more problematic position as the region's only public service broadcaster, in that the political developments, including the successful re-establishment of the power-sharing executive in June 2000, inevitably created greater expectations on the part of nationalists that their agendas would be given more prominence. This in turn is likely to create greater pressure on cultural institutions like BBC NI which, precisely because they are not susceptible to direct political influence, may be slower to adapt to altered political circumstances.

The BBC's adaptation in this area has been slow. It was reluctant, for example (for reasons which do not need to be guessed at) to take initiatives in relation to Irish-language broadcasting, but has done so. The problem here is that to do any at all is to risk the ire of both communities – of the Unionists, because they feel that it is inherently non-British or in some sense opening yet another unwelcome door to the Republic and its machinations; to the national-ists, because they can be predicted to believe that nothing the BBC does in this area will ever be enough. As things stand, BBC NI produces four hours of radio in Irish per week, and approximately ten hours of television per year, which is almost guaranteed to achieve both these results. The problem also extends into sport: BBC NI has the Northern Ireland broadcasting rights from the Ulster Branch of the Gaelic Athletic Association (GAA), but rarely avails itself of these for live transmission, preferring to broadcast edited highlights in the late evening. There are, of course, two or three related problems here. One is the anticipated reaction of Unionists to airtime being squandered, as they would see it, on such nationalist pursuits. This attitude is accentuated by the resolute refusal of the GAA to open its ranks to members of the security forces – specifically the Royal Ulster Constabulary – on political grounds. And finally there is the general religious objection among sections of the Unionist community, on Sabbatarian grounds, to the playing or broadcast of any sport on Sundays. Rugby football, on the other hand, which is a minority – though growing – sport within the nationalist community, but of considerable interest to Unionists (the sport is, like the GAA, organised on an all-Ireland basis) receives more live coverage. The implications for BBC NI and UTV in this area are implied rather than spelt out in the Belfast Agreement, which, as one nationalist commentator has pointed out, specifically in relation to broadcasting, 'does not just seek a new method of political partnership in the North but sets out the template for a whole new society' (McGurk 2000).

BBC NI, however, is not alone in experiencing problems in connection with Irish-language broadcasting. It has been a contested area also in the Republic for many years, as the controversies preceding and surrounding the establishment of Raidio na Gaeltachta demonstrate. The same has been true, at a possibly even more intense level (because of the greater costs involved) of the establishment of the Republic's Irish-language television service, which went on the air for the first time on 31 October 1996.

The history of this initiative, going back over thirty years, is a story partly of political inertia, partly of an ongoing argument about whether broadcasting in Irish, whether on radio or on television, should be integrated into the national public broadcasting service as seamlessly as possible, or should be given an independent existence and status (with the consequent risk, as many Irish-language enthusiasts saw it, of ghettoisation). The 1965 report of the Commission on the Restoration of the Irish Language (set up in 1958) saw television, which had been established in 1961, as a prime motivator of, and location for, the language revival movement; indeed, it had been so exercised by this prospect that it had issued an interim report in 1959, when the establishment of RTE was under active consideration, focusing in large part on the opportunities presented by the new medium. The early years of RTE saw the emergence of a struggle between those who saw this as one of the station's prime aims (including a number of those who served on the RTE Authority in its early years) and broadcasting executives who were anxious that too great an emphasis on Irish would handicap its attempt to secure a national audience. Tensions ran high on this issue, at one stage provoking the resignation of the first chairman of the

Authority, the broadcaster and businessman Eamonn Andrews (Horgan 1997: 320).

Even among those who favoured the use of the new medium for the revival, there were strong differences of opinion: radicals suggested a low-cost, almost pre-fabricated individual station (Doolan 1969: 221); the official language movement preferred to make inroads, insofar as this was possible, into the programming structure of the existing national station. RTE, for its part, generally opposed the creation of a separate channel, which would undermine its monopoly status, as in its submission to a 1977 government Advisory Committee on Irish-language broadcasting, whose report was never published but which recommended an internal RTE solution. Attempts to set up a pirate television initiative in Irish in 1980 failed, and in 1983 Bord na Gaeilge, the official government body with responsibility for promoting the language revival, voiced the opinion that a service separate from the national broadcaster would be a good idea, tacitly accepting for the first time that the internal RTE option was perhaps not necessarily the best one, and accepting the implicit risk of marginalisation.

The pirate project was not dead, however: it surfaced briefly on 3–5 November 1987 in the Connemara Gaeltacht, when some eighteen hours of live television and video recordings were broadcast, mostly music programming and some debate on issues connected with the Irish language. Bob Quinn, a director, who was one of the authors of *Sit Down and Be Counted* (Doolan et al. 1969) (and to become a member of the RTE Authority itself in the late 1990s), was among those involved in the experiment, which was repeated, equally briefly, in December 1988. These and other initiatives prodded the government into action. A Working Group on Irish Language Broadcasting in 1987 made suggestions similar to those which had been made ten years earlier, but no action was taken. A feasibility study was carried out by consultants in 1988 and published in 1989: it recommended that a new service should cater both for Gaeltacht and non-Gaeltacht audiences, with a special emphasis on children. Again, nothing was done, although it prompted the emergence in 1989 of a new organisation, Feachtas Naisiunta Teilifise ('National Television Campaign') which broadened the demands to include a television service in Irish for the whole country, and not just for the Gaeltacht areas. RTE output in Irish at this time was some 2% of an increasing amount of air-time. In 1991 the Taoiseach, Charles Haughey (who as Minister for the Gaeltacht had promised in 1987 that £500,000 would be spent on a new service, but had not delivered on this commitment), told the annual meeting of his party that an Irish television service would be established in 1992, but this did not happen. In 1992, however, Maire Geoghegan-Quinn, the Minister for the Gaeltacht, appointed a special adviser to take the project further, and she and her successor, Michael D. Higgins (both represented the Galway West constituency, which has a sizeable Gaeltacht population), although members of different governments, were actively involved in bringing it to completion.

Telefis na Gaeilge began broadcasting on 31 October 1996. Its viewing figures were held down by the fact that initially it was not available nationally, and the annual cost of some £20 million was the subject of intermittent but intense controversy, as was the fact that it did not – because it simply could not – broadcast entirely in the Irish language. At different times, it found creative uses for its spectrum allocation, ranging from live broadcasts of the proceedings of controversial parliamentary committees (notably in 1999, when one of these committees was focusing on malpractices in the banking system), to European football matches, to old recordings of GAA matches (on which the original commentary was in Irish in any case), and late-night classic films. Its most successful programmes included a soap opera in Irish, *Ros na Rún*, and (quite unexpectedly) a long-range weather forecast service, provided by a UK company, which attracted some 100,000 viewers nightly. By March 2000, it was attracting a daily audience of 500,000 which, though lower than its target and still a source of criticism for those who believed that the new service was a waste of money, was respectable in the circumstances. It was broadcasting an average of nine hours of programming daily, five of them in Irish. It was produced by a staff of fifty people, the majority of them women, and with an average age of 25, from its studios west of Galway. In the long term, its difficulties appear to mirror those of the radio station, in that it has the problems of balancing the needs of its local, Irish-speaking audience and the national audience, and of appealing to young people in particular (Hourigan 1996: 6).

The question of funding, however, remained a difficult one. A 1991 report by an ad hoc group commissioned by the government had recommended that the cost could be met by increasing RTE's permitted advertising time by half a minute in every broadcast hour. The technically simple method proposed was, however, fraught with political dangers. Plans for TV3, the new national television competitor for RTE, were already in hand; its first projected launch date of 1990 had fallen through, and it was having difficulties with its financial planning; any move to increase RTE's access to advertising revenue would imperil it further.

At the same time, RTE's own finances were deteriorating steadily. Although the cap on the amount it was allowed to earn from advertising had been removed by the government in the Broadcasting Authority (Amendment) Act 1993, and operating profits for 1994 were almost £10 million, this concealed a loss of some £2 million on broadcasting. The overall profit was accounted for largely by ancillary revenues, such as income from the *RTE Guide*, money from the part-sale of Cablelink, and investments in Radio Tara, RTE's vehicle for its involvement in Radio Atlantic 252, and the Riverdance company, set up to market the hugely successful dance company, in which it had a 25% stake. By the following year, the loss on broadcasting had risen to £7 million, and the situation was looking even more bleak.

The government's priorities in relation to broadcasting at this stage, however, were not financial – at least, not yet. What it had in mind was a major restructuring of the electronic media, and its ideas on this subject were contained in a Green Paper published in 1995 (Department of Arts, Culture and the Gaeltacht 1995).

With its stress on the cultural process and the broadcasting context, the Green Paper focused on the 'centrifugal and centripetal pressures' affecting the development of broadcasting in an era of globalisation (Department of Arts, Culture and the Gaeltacht 1995: 131). 'What', it asked, 'is the optimum balance of power we should strive for in the multiple relationships between technologies, regulators, providers and users?' (1995: 143). Building its response to this question on foundations securely anchored in public service broadcasting philosophy and traditions, the Green Paper suggested that there might be a case for 'merging the policy and regulatory functions of the RTE Authority and the IRTC to form one over-arching Authority' (1995: 166). This proposal, which was to be found in embryo form in the report of the Broadcasting Review Committee twenty years earlier, was to be the subject of intense discussion and disagreement for the next seven years. It strongly supported the case for a separate television channel for Irish-language programmes, although it rejected the idea that this should be under a separate statutory authority (Department of Arts, Culture and the Gaeltacht 1995: 207).

All in all, although the document raised a large number of points for discussion, and gave an indication of government thinking on some of these issues, it was insufficiently focused as a framework for legislation and, to some extent, did not have the opportunity to consider the full impact of the new technologies, whose downstream implications were at this stage seen only indistinctly. By 1996, this framework was already being overtaken by the debate about transmission systems and their control, and new legislation was being prepared which in effect accepted that some of the Green Paper ideas were now redundant. Current events were also adding to the pressure for decisions. UTV, which had been part of the re-financed TV3 consortium, withdrew from it in 1996 because it planned to concentrate, instead, on developing its own digital service, which could be made available to many viewers in the Republic without cable or satellite links.

The details of the legislation, which was predicated on a decision in favour of digital terrestrial television (the other options being terrestrial cable and satellite) were finally announced by the minister, Michael D. Higgins, on 18 March 1997 (although they were not as yet embodied in a Bill). The key elements of his proposal were:

- a statutory definition of public service broadcasting;
- the establishment of a Broadcasting Commission that would replace the Independent Radio and Television Commission and take over some broadcasting control functions from a number of government departments;
- the creation of a separate structure for Telefis na Gaeltachta;
- the control of rights to broadcast certain major sporting events; and
- the possibility of allocating start-up grants to news services.

The overriding function of the new commission, the minister announced, would be:

> to endeavour to ensure that the number, categories, structures of, and arrangements for broadcasting best serve the needs of the people of Ireland, bearing in mind our traditions, our language and our cultures and respecting the distinction between the roles and objectives of public service and independent broadcasters.
>
> (*IT*: 19 March 1997)

Public service broadcasting was, and remains, a battlefield. TV3 and the commercial radio stations, together with their counterparts in Europe, continually maintained that RTE's dual funding system – by licence fee and advertising – was unfair. Not only was the licence fee a hidden subsidy to RTE's non-public service programming, the private stations argued, but they too were engaged in substantial public service broadcasting for which they received no subsidy. Commercial radio was required by the IRTC to devote a fixed percentage (20%) of air-time to news and current affairs (although the definition of broadcast material that met this criterion was generally elastic, and monitoring was episodic). TV3 was not bound by such detailed restrictions; although the IRTC insisted that 15% of its programming had to be of Irish origin, the 1988 Broadcasting Act which was effectively its charter only required it to devote 'a reasonable proportion' of its time to news and current affairs.

While the commercial stations argued that equity demanded they be given a share of the licence fee for their news and current affairs, the argument was being moved on to the European plane. Here, Higgins succeeded – in the teeth of powerful opposition, not least from European Commission officials whose views about the value of competition left little room for any Habermasian concept of the public space – in having written into the 1995 Amsterdam Treaty the following protocol defining and defending public service broadcasting.

> The provisions of the Treaty establishing the European Community shall be without prejudice to the competence of the Member States to provide for the funding of public service broadcasting (PSB) insofar as such funding is granted to broadcasting organisations for the fulfilment of the public service remit as conferred, defined and organised by each member State, and insofar as such funding does not affect trading conditions and competition in the Community to an extent which would be contrary to the common interest, while the realisation of the remit of that public service shall be taken into account.
>
> (*Official Journal of the European Community* 40, 10 Nov. 1997: 109)

The definition, focusing as it did on organisations and not, as the private sector would have preferred, on the public service content of broadcasts from all

stations, was vital to the interests of RTE and indeed of other national broadcasters within the Community: it was a definition of public service broadcasting
as the activity of a public service broadcaster – not as a generic activity which
was common to publicly and privately owned broadcasters and which should get
a subsidy from public funds regardless of its point of origin.

This definition, now given statutory expression at European level, was a
valuable bulwark for public service broadcasters. It came up for discussion again
late in 1998, when the Commission's DG IV (directorate in charge of competition policy) circulated a discussion document exploring the criteria on which
public service broadcasting might be recognised. There was a brief debate on
the document at European level, which ended when the document was rejected
by the EU member states. Few people were under any illusions, however, that
the argument was over.

The Amsterdam initiative in favour of public service broadcasting, significant though it may have been, did not solve the financial problems of PSB
stations anywhere, and certainly not in Ireland. These were now, at least insofar
as RTE was concerned, reaching crisis point with the inauguration of Telefis na
Gaeltachta, and the requirement that this new service be subsidised by RTE, to
an extent estimated by RTE itself at some £9 million annually. This was almost
certainly a deliberately conservative over-estimate; but the money still had to
be found somewhere.

Given that the option canvassed earlier – an increase in the proportion of
broadcast time available to RTE for advertising – was politically unacceptable,
there was really only one, almost equally politically unpopular – option left.
This was to raise the licence fee, which was increased from £62, at which figure
it had remained since March 1986, to £70 in September 1996. The fact that it
took a decade for the ceaseless representations from the Authority to government to be heard spoke for itself and – although the possibility of any
connection between this and the voracious appetite of the infant TV3 for funds
was not so much as hinted at – the fact that the £5 million raised by the
increased licence fee was almost exactly equal to the (revised) cost of the
subsidy which RTE was now required to give to the Gaeltacht station was, at
the very least, an extraordinary coincidence.

This had solved the Telefis na Gaeltachta problem; but it did not solve RTE's
problems. These were partly related to the structural model proposed by the
government. If decisions about the future of broadcasting were to be made by a
new, super-Commission on which both public service broadcasters and private
interests would be represented, the fear in RTE was that the public service side
of the table would be consistently out-voted. This would, they anticipated, lead
to a further financial squeeze (the question of the share-out of the licence fee
again), erosion of the standards of public service broadcasting itself and diver-
sion of the broadcasting audience towards the private channels. It meant,
according to RTE's director-general, Bob Collins, that 'more decisions about
what Irish people watched would be made outside Ireland' (*IT*: 19 March 1997).

A change of government in June 1997 gave a breathing space, and the new minister, Sile de Valera (a grand-daughter of the founder of the *Irish Press*) addressed the problem again. As she was considering her options, the RTE Authority unveiled its own proposals, which envisaged groups of channels offering viewers tiered subscription options: the first tier would be RTE1, Network 2 and Telefis na Gaeltachta (re-launched and re-baptised as TG4 in 1999); other channels would contain the current crop of UK services, a 24-hour news channel, a catch-up channel with access to recent programmes and a pay-per-view channel. The following year, the government decisions were published as 'Irish Television Transmission in the New Millennium'. They envisaged a network of up to thirty channels of digital terrestrial television, grouped in multiplexes which would have five channels each. RTE would be allocated one of these, giving it three additional channels (*IT*: 23 July 1998). The bullish atmosphere engendered by the new plan, in which the government effectively took on board many of RTE's proposals, was underlined when the station launched yet another new service on 1 May 1999. This was Lyric FM, a serious music station, successor to a similar service known as FM3 which had shared the Raidio na Gaeltachta wavelength for part of the day before Raidio na Gaeltachta expanded its broadcasting hours. In May 1922, Raidio na Gaeltachta adopted 24-hour broadcasting on the internet.

This series of government decisions also embodied a solution to a problem which had dogged the RTE Authority since 1993. In that year, a Broadcasting Act had stipulated that RTE should set aside a certain proportion of its programming budget for productions from independent companies. Implementation of this proposal was controversial, not least because there was no agreement on which elements of RTE's programming budget were to be included in the total sum subject to the percentage, and which overheads could legitimately be excluded. The minister now proposed, instead of a percentage, a flat sum of £16 million, subject to some indexation, which achieved a measure of stability in the equation satisfactory both to RTE and the independent producers.

There was one critical difference from the 1994 Green Paper plan, in that the RTE Authority would continue to exist as a public service enclave, ring-fenced to some degree from the new super-commission. Structurally, this was an advance, from RTE's point of view, but the question of finance was still up in the air, all the more so as de Valera had announced in June 1998 that she was not prepared to index the licence fee by linking it to inflation (*IT*: 19 June 1998). RTE, in these circumstances, was plainly in need of an ongoing source of finance, and the most obvious source of that finance was its physical transmission network. Under de Valera's proposals, this was to become the property of a new company called Digico, in which RTE would participate with partners from the private sector, who would be able to contribute a large part of the capital investment needed. When she introduced her Broadcasting Bill in 1999, she indicated that RTE would be given a 40% share in Digico, that would guarantee it an income stream into the foreseeable future. This was a modification of the situation obtaining in the UK where, in January 1997, the BBC had sold its transmission network for £220 million as part of its funding plan for digital transmission, but had not retained a role in the enterprise to which the network was sold. By the end of 1999, however, a major controversy had emerged about the value of the transmission network, and the minister appointed a mediator in an attempt to secure agreement on the sharply differing figures suggested by RTE and by consultants. In addition, by early 2000, the minister had changed her mind on the structure of Digico, saying that she now saw no need for RTE to be involved at all (SBP: 12 March 2000). The final resolution of the problem in June saw a decision to award RTE a 28% stake in the company owning the transmission network, but – in a move designed to reassure other interests – RTE would have no share in a separate company which would be established to sell digital services to the consumer (*IT*: 28 June 2000).

RTE's financial projections now began to look distinctly over-optimistic. It needed a strategic partner on the physical side, to help carry the cost of capital investment into the new millennium. Here, however, it was locked into an increasingly bitter conflict of interest with the major media companies, notably multinational ones, anxious to ensure a rapid increase in the number of outlets for the televisual products in which they had invested, and in a climate in which there was a poor prognosis for the agenda of public service broadcasting generally, and in which much of that agenda was being dismissed as anti-competitive, special interest whingeing.

It also needed a strategic partner on the programming side. It could offer such a partner not only access to a benevolent tax regime for programming generated in Ireland, but also access, through an Irish portal, to major potential audiences with strong Irish cultural roots in the United States and elsewhere. It had already substantially improved its transmission facilities in areas covering Northern Ireland, where an estimated 70% of viewers can now receive the RTE television signal. For the time being, however, this prospect had to take second place to the more urgent structural and financial problems, exemplified by decisions in September 1998 to transfer responsibility for afternoon and breakfast television to private contractors. GMITV, the company to which breakfast television was sub-contracted, had Bob Geldof of Planet TV as one of its investors: the company was also allowed to sell the advertising time within its programme slot.

These financial problems were themselves in the process of being exacerbated by the re-launch of national commercial radio and the successful launch of TV3. National commercial radio had been in the doldrums since the collapse of Century in 1991. By late 1995, however, the IRTC had invited new tenders for a replacement station and, in February 1996, the franchise was awarded to a new consortium which included the progenitors of the Riverdance company, the *Irish Farmers' Journal* and the *Cork Examiner*. One of the unsuccessful applicants was a consortium which included the *Irish Times* and Richard Branson's Virgin company (*IT*: 9 February 1996).

The launch of the new station on 17 March 1997 was mired in controversy: its chief executive, Dan Collins, who had been recruited from one of the more successful regional stations, Radio Kerry, was dismissed. The *Irish Farmers' Journal* withdrew its investment because of fears that its status as a charity might be compromised (the *Cork Examiner* had withdrawn in February, citing policy differences with the IRTC). In June, three months after it had gone on air, three-quarters of the national radio audience were saying that they had never heard of it, and there was an ongoing dispute with RTE about the cost of the physical links on which the service was being distributed.

The withdrawal of the *Irish Farmers' Journal*, however, had left the way open for a new investor, Scottish Radio Holdings, which began a process of reinvigorating the management team and re-financing the entire operation. Additional capital of £2 million was raised in November 1997 and, in January 1998, the station was re-launched as Today FM. The turnaround was dramatic. CanWest, a major Canadian media company, was added to the list of investors; Today FM (albeit from a low base) was the only radio station not to lose listeners in the first three months of 1998. In a tribute to its success, RTE lured one of its most popular music presenters, John Kelly, to the state station; another, the current affairs presenter Eamon Dunphy (whose career with the station was temporarily in jeopardy at the time of the re-launch), went from strength to strength, with a daily audience of 144,000 to RTE's equivalent of 200,000. At the end of 1999, the radio audience figures disclosed that, for the first time, RTE's share of the total radio audience (including the regional stations) had fallen below 50% (to 49%). It was ten years since the first legal broadcasts by commercial stations. In February 2000, the station reported an operating profit of £100,000 for 1999, and now had some 7% of the national audience (including a mere 5% of the Dublin audience) (*SBP*: 27 February 2000; *ST*: 27 February 2000). It was, ironically, almost exactly the same figure on which Century had found itself incapable of surviving. One anomaly was that Today FM was not a member of IBI – Independent Broadcasters of Ireland – the successor organisation to AIRS (Association of Independent Radio Stations), which had been set up in 1990 as a lobby group, particularly on issues relating to the licence fee and to digitalisation. Also outside any formal structure were the pirate stations: despite repeated legislative initiatives designed to curb their activities, there were still, in mid-June 2000, at least thirty-two such stations operating in the greater Dublin area, offering a fare that varied from religious broadcasting to black music. Unusually, there are no viable student radio stations as yet: an early experiment, DCU FM, ran from 1995 to 1997, when it ceased broadcasting and its licence lapsed.

The launch of TV3, after a series of tribulations which made those experienced by national commercial radio relatively trivial, took place on 21 September 1998. It made steady, if unspectacular progress, dogged to some extent by technical problems (it was not being carried on the MMDS system, which made it more difficult to access in the 160,000 households where this system was in operation, and it was having arguments with Cablelink about its position in relation to other programmes on the cable 'dial', complaining that, as an Irish station, viewers should be able to access it before imported channels). It was the first station to start breakfast TV (on 20 September 1999), although audience results were initially disappointing, partly for the technical reasons already mentioned. In November 1999, however, it secured rights to an important series of football matches for three years from September 2000, which will undoubtedly increase its audience share: by the end of 1999 it had a share of 8% of its main target audience of 16–44-year-olds across all channels (16% share of the audience for Irish channels). It had also reduced its average monthly losses from £565,000 at start-up to £383,000, and had taken approximately £13 million in advertising revenue, compared to RTE's £121 million. It was also taking a legal initiative about RTE's access to licence fee income, launching a case in the European courts alleging that it was the subject of discrimination on this score (ST: 30 January 2000). Perhaps more significantly, it had secured investment from CanWest Global, the company which already had a 29.9% stake in UTV.

In fact, cross-border activity in the media – particularly electronic media – was already beginning to adopt new modalities, quite apart from questions of ownership and control. In July 2000, RTE began a marketing campaign to recruit viewers in Northern Ireland. The problem, as far as RTE was concerned, was that only 19% of Northern homes have cable, a much smaller proportion than in the Republic. Nonetheless, some 50% of Northern households have adjusted their sets to receive the RTE signal, and RTE aims to expand that to 75% by targeting retailers and others with details of the appropriate tuning procedures (some 64% of homes in the Republic receive UTV, either on cable or directly). In spite of the technical difficulties, RTE has already built up a significant audience in Northern Ireland, even for programmes such as *Coronation Street*, which are screened by both UTV and RTE at the same time. Its reach into Northern Ireland has been enhanced by the fact that the Dublin station is able to schedule some popular syndicated material, such as the shows *Friends* and *The Simpsons*, in advance of the Northern stations (IT: 6 July 2000). TV3, equally anxious to increase its audience, has even argued that facilitating the extension of Republic-based networks into Northern Ireland is a concomitant of the Good Friday Agreement.

The five-year period up to 2000, therefore, saw a number of radical changes in prospect for media in Ireland, not only in broadcasting but also in print. In each sector, a combination of technological change, the pressures of globalisation and rationalisation, and the increasing involvement of non-national and multinational interests in every sector, was reshaping the environment and work practices as never before (Hazelkorn 1996). In the process, new links were emerging between media in Northern Ireland and the Republic, even if the shape of future strategic and other alliances was as yet indistinct. Within the next two years, Ireland will have access to some 200 broadcast channels, some 98% of them originating outside the state. Control over the gateways and relay mechanisms through which these channels are distributed to the Irish population is already, as in other small countries, a matter of considerable concern, and the cultural and political questions raised by these developments will become even more pressing in the years ahead.

Appendix

Table 1 Republic of Ireland newspaper circulation

National newspapers	1990	1991	1992	1993	1994	1995	1996	1997	1998	1999*
Irish Independent	151,927	150,872	149,593	143,769	144,738	153,761	158,713	160,137	162,715	165,365
Irish Times	94,058	93,944	93,409	91,460	93,372	97,089	101,842	107,839	111,486	113,835
Examiner	57,061	56,574	55,565	53,188	52,062	52,932	55,196	56,628	58,536	62,413
Star	53,533	55,980	60,209	66,037	71,048	81,497	86,518	88,528	90,262	91,811
Irish Press	60,461	58,895	51,305	45,392	38,848					
Total mornings	417,040	416,265	410,081	399,846	400,068	385,279	402,269	403,132	422,999	433,424
Evening Herald	98,529	99,362	97,642	93,640	91,998	110,187	115,983	112,546	106,989	105,386
Evening Echo	30,525	29,355	29,134	26,579	25,179	25,432	25,697	26,520	26,973	28,407
Evening Press	95,857	86,112	71,979	63,026	54,061					
Total evenings	224,911	214,829	198,755	183,245	171,238	135,619	141,680	139,066	133,962	133,793
Total dailies	641,951	631,094	608,836	583,091	571,306	520,898	543,949	552,198	556,961	567,217
Sunday Independent	230,344	233,404	247,279	251,900	255,791	333,753	339,501	327,153	309,912	317,193
Sunday Tribune	101,680	90,770	90,438	88,158	79,404	78,825	77,817	86,766	83,314	
Sunday World	328,702	312,727	301,415	276,386	272,214	287,623	296,085	307,162	308,753	309,604
Sunday Business Post	25,853	27,650	29,763	29,982	29,248	32,723	37,430	43,698	47,934	49,035
Sunday Press	207,507	200,899	182,566	172,365	156,522					
Total Sundays	894,100	865,440	851,461	818,791	793,179	732,744	750,833	764,779	753,220	759,146

Source: Audit Bureau of Circulation
Note: * July–September

Table 2   Republic of Ireland, UK newspapers ('000s)

UK Sunday newspapers	1990	1999
News of the World	169	164
Sunday People	71	65
Sunday Mirror	65	44
Sunday Times	31	89
Sunday Express	22	7
Observer	5	4
Mail on Sunday	n/a	10
Independent on Sunday	n/a	7
Total UK Sunday titles	376	398
UK daily newspapers		
Daily Mirror	60	62
Sun	30	103
Daily Express	5	4
Daily Mail	4	6
Daily Telegraph	4	4
Financial Times	3	5
The Times	2	5
Guardian	2	3
Independent	1	2
Total UK daily titles	112	194

Source: Barrett (2000)

Table 3   Northern Ireland newspaper circulation, 1980–99

Northern Ireland newspapers	1980	1990	1999*
Newsletter	55,335	34,338	33,395
Irish News	44,444	43,353	50,353
Total mornings	99,779	77,691	83,748
Belfast Telegraph	149,273	132,817	117,207
Total evenings	149,273	132,817	117,207
Sunday News	n/a	n/a	
Sunday World	n/a	74,430	71,847
Sunday Life	(est. 1988)	56,463	94,768
Total Sundays	n/a	n/a	166,615

Source: Belfast Telegraph
Note: *   July–December

Table 4   Northern Ireland radio weekly reach, September 1999–March 2000

BBC	(000's)
Radio Ulster	400
Radio 1	259
Radio 5 Live	131
Radio 2	91
Radio 4	73
BBC Local*	29
Radio 3	21
Commercial	
Cool FM*	338
Downtown Radio	314
Atlantic 252**	146
City Beat*	138
Classic FM	88
Virgin AM	74
Q102.9*	54
Talk Radio	42

Source: Radio Joint Audience Research (RAJAR)/Downtown (2000)

Notes: *   Partial cover
      * * Republic of Ireland

Table 5   Northern Ireland TV audience (%), July 2000

ITV	Channel 4	Channel 5	BBC1	BBC2	Other
29.5	9.9	4.2	24.7	9.4	22.3

Source: Broadcasters' Audience Research Board Ltd (BARB) (2000)

Table 6 Republic of Ireland TV audience (%)

Year	RTE1	Net-work 2	TG4 (TnaG)	TV3	BBC1	BBC2	UTV/HTV	CH4/S4C	Satellite
1994	36.1	20.8			11.4	4.3	13.4	5.2	9.4
1995	35.3	18.2			11.8	4.7	13.3	6.1	9.8
1996	34.8	18.6	0.3		11.8	4.8	12.6	5.7	11.2
1997	34.3	18.7	0.7		10.4	4.8	10.8	5.6	14.8
1998	33.4	18.2	0.8	1.6	9.9	4.4	10.2	5.5	16
1999	31.9	16.7	1.1	5.8	8.9	3.8	10.2	4.9	16.6
Prime-time shares (18:00–23:30)									
1994	42.6	20.7			10.5	3.8	13.0	4.0	3.8
1995	42.0	17.9			10.6	4.3	13.3	5.2	5.0
1996	42.1	17.7	0.3		10.8	3.9	12.7	4.6	6.5
1997	41.8	17.6	0.8		9.4	4.0	11.2	4.2	11.1
1998	40.1	17.1	1.0	1.8	9.0	3.8	10.7	4.5	12.1
1999	38.3	15.0	1.2	6.2	8.2	3.4	11.3	4.1	12.3

Source: RTE/Nielsen

Table 7 Republic of Ireland radio audience (%; adults; weekday average)

Year/ Station	RTE Radio 1	2FM	Lyric FM*	Today FM**	Any local	Home local	Other local
National radio market share (07:00–15:59)							
1994	37	21			41	36	5
1995	33	22			44	40	5
1996	33	21			46	40	6
1997	33	22			43	39	4
1998	31	20		6	43	38	4
1999	27	20	2	7	45	40	5
National radio reach							
1994	39	28			50	44	9
1995	35	29			51	46	9
1996	35	29			54	48	10
1997	35	30			52	47	8
1998	33	28		11	52	47	8
1999	31	28	4	14	54	50	9

Notes: * May–December 1999;
* * Radio Ireland March 1997 –January 1998

Table 8   Newspapers online

Title	Web address
An Phoblacht / Republican News	http://www.irlnet.com/aprn/index.html
Athlone Observer	http://ireland.iol.ie/littlebug/athobs/
Belfast Telegraph	http://www.belfasttelegraph.co.uk/
Clare Champion	http://www.clarechampion.ie/
Connacht Tribune Newspapers	http://www.iol.ie/ctribune/
Connaught Telegraph	http://www.mayo-ireland.ie/Mayo/News/ConnTel/ConnTel.htm
Derry People and *Donegal News*	http://www.donegalnews.com/
Examiner, The	http://www.examiner.ie/
FluX-On-Line	http://www.ennis.ie/digital newspapers/rice/
Foinse	http://www.foinse.ie/
Galway Advertiser	http://www.galwayadvertiser.ie/
Gay Community News	http://homepage.eircom.net/ nlgf/
Ireland on Sunday	http://www.irelandonsunday.com/
Ireland Today	http://www.ireland-today.ie/
Irish Echo	http://www.irishecho.com/index.cfm
Irish Independent	http://www.independent.ie/
Irish News	http://www.irishnews.com/
Irish Times	http://www.ireland.com
Irish Voice Online	http://www.irishvoice.com/
Irish World	http://www.theirishworld.com/
Kerry's Eye	http://www.iol.ie/kerryseye/
Kerryman, The	http://www.kerryweb.ie/kerryman/default2.htm
Kilkenny People	http://www.kilkennypeople.ie/
Leinster Leader Indexation Project	http://www.kildare.ie/employment/fas/cytpprofiles/leader/1798/1798.htm
Nationalist and Leinster Times	http://www.lowwwe.com/nationalist/index.html
Limerick Leader Online	http://www.limerick-leader.ie/
Limerick Post	http://www.limerickpost.ie/
Marine Times Online	http://indigo.ie/ marine/
Mayo Gazette	http://www.mayogazette.com/
Mayo News, The	http://www.mayonews.ie/
Munster Express	http://www.munster-express.ie/
Northside People	http://www.northsidepeople.ie/
People Newspapers	http://www.peoplenews.ie/
Saoirse	http://ireland.iol.ie/ saoirse/
Skerries News	http://www.cognition.ie/skerries news/
Sunday Business Post	http://www.sbpost.ie/
Sunday Tribune	http://www.tribune.ie/
Limerick Post, The	http://www.limerickpost.ie/
Waterford Today	http://www.waterford-today.ie/
Workers Solidarity	http://www.geocities.com/Athens/2724/worksodx.html

Table 9   Radio and television stations online

Station	Web address
RTE Radio; 2FM Ireland; Lyric FM	http://www.rte.ie/radio/; http://www.2fm.ie/; http://www.lyric.ie/
98 FM	http://www.98fm.ie/
Anna Livia FM	http://slarti.ucd.ie/annalivia/index.html
Clare FM	http://www.clarefm.ie/
Connemara Community Radio	http://www.connemaraaccommodation.com/ccradio/latch.htm
Cork 96 FM	http://www.96fm.ie/
Cork Campus Radio 97.4 FM	http://www.ucc.ie/ccr/
Cork Hospital Radio	http://www.geocities.com/Broadway/1507/c-106.html
Emerald Radio Student Radio	http://www.emeraldradio.com/
Energy 88 FM Dublin	http://listen.to/energyfm
FM 104	http://www.fm104.ie/
Galway Bay FM	http://www.wombat.ie/gbfm/
K FM	http://www.partyradio98fm.8m.com/
Kiss 102	http://www.iol.ie/ scatman/
Limerick 95.7 FM	http://www.95fm.ie/
Midlands Radio 3 – 103.5 & 102.1	http://www.iol.ie/mr3/
Power FM 98.7 Dublin	http://www.powerfm.org/
Radio Caroline Dublin	http://www.dojo.ie/caroline/
Raidio na Gaeltachta	http://www.rnag.ie/
RTE Radio 1	http://www.rte.ie/radio/
South East Radio	http://www.southeastradio.ie/
Today FM	http://www.todayfm.com
St Ita's Hospital Radio	http://www.connect.ie/users/hospital radio/
WLR FM	http://www.wlr.tinet.ie/
XFM	http://www.isis.ie/xfm/
BBC Northern Ireland	http://www.bbc.co.uk/ni/
RTE Television	http://www.rte.ie.tv/
TV3	TBA

Bibliography

Adams, Michael (1968) *Censorship: The Irish Experience*, Alabama: University of Alabama Press.

Akenson, Donal Harman (1994) *Conor: A Biography of Conor Cruise O'Brien*, vol. 1, Montreal: McGill-Queen's University Press.

Alexander, Yonah and O'Day, Alan (eds) (1986) *Ireland's Terrorist Dilemma*, Dordrecht: Martinus Nijhoff.

Arnold, Bruce (1984) *What Kind of Country? Modern Irish Politics 1968–1983*, London: Jonathan Cape.

Barclay, Andy (1993) 'Final death notice for the *Sunday News*', *Irish Times* 25 March.

Barrett, Sean D. (2000) *Competitiveness and Contestability in the Irish Media Sector*, Trinity Economic Paper No. 3, Dublin: Department of Economics, Trinity College.

Bell, J. Bowyer (1969) 'Ireland and the Spanish Civil War, 1936–1939', *Studia Hibernica* 9, 137–63.

Bell, Martin (1973) 'Reporting from Ulster', in Karl Miller (ed.) *A Second Listener Anthology*, London: British Broadcasting Corporation, 370–2.

Blanshard, Paul (1953) *The Irish and Catholic Power: An American Interpretation*, Boston: Beacon Press.

Broadcasting Review Committee (1974) *Report*, Dublin: Stationery Office.

Brodie, Malcolm (1995) *The Tele: A History of the Belfast Telegraph*, Belfast: Blackstaff Press.

Brown, Terence (1981) *Ireland: A Cultural and Social History*, London: Fontana.

Browne, Noel (1986) *Against the Tide*, Dublin: Gill and Macmillan.

Browne, Stephen, S.J. (1937) *The Press in Ireland: A Survey and a Guide*, Dublin: Browne and Nolan; New York: Lemma (reprint 1971).

Bundock, Clement J. (1957) *The National Union of Journalists: A Jubilee History 1907–1957*, Oxford: Oxford University Press.

Butler, David (1995) *The Trouble with Reporting Northern Ireland*, Aldershot: Avebury Press.

Byrne, Gay (1972) *To Whom it Concerns: Ten Years of the Late Late Show*, Dublin: Torc Books.

Campbell, James J. (1961) *Television in Ireland*, Dublin: Gill and Co.

Camerawork (1981) No. 14, *Reporting on Northern Ireland*, London: Half Moon Photography Workshop.

Carr, Bunny (1975) *The Instant Tree*, Dublin: Mercier Press.

Cathcart, Rex (1972) 'TV coverage on Northern Ireland', *Index on Censorship* 1 (1), 15–32.

Cathcart, Rex (1974) 'BBC NI: 50 years old', *The Listener* 2372, 12 September, 322–4.

Cathcart, Rex (1984) *That Most Contrary Region: The BBC in Northern Ireland*, Belfast: Blackstaff Press.

Cathcart, Rex (1986) 'Mass media in twentieth-century Ireland', in *The History of Ireland*, vol. 7, Oxford: Oxford University Press.

Chubb, Basil (1972) 'Media and the state', *Irish Times* 31 August.

Chubb, Basil (1974) *Cabinet Government in Ireland*, Dublin: Institute of Public Administration.

Chubb, Basil (1984) 'The political role of the media in contemporary Ireland', in Brian Farrell (ed.) *Communications and Community in Ireland*, Cork: Mercier Press, 75–86.

Citizens for Better Broadcasting (1978) *Aspects of RTE Television Broadcasting*, Dublin: CBB.

Clarke, Paddy (1986) *'Dublin Calling': 2RN and the Birth of Irish Radio*, Dublin: Radio Telefis Eireann.

Clutterbuck, Richard (1981) *The Media and Political Violence*, London: Macmillan.

Coady, Treasa (1989) *The RTE Book*, Dublin: Town House.

Commission on the Newspaper Industry (1996) *Report: PN 2841*, Dublin: The Stationery Office.

Committee on Industrial Progress (1970) *Report on Paper, Paper Products, Printing and Publishing Industry, Prl 1356*, Dublin: The Stationery Office.

Committee on Irish Language Attitudes (1975) *Report*, Dublin: The Stationery Office.

Competition and Mergers Review Group (2000) *Final Report: PN 8487*, Dublin: Department of Enterprise, Trade and Employment.

Competition Authority (1992) *Report of Investigation of the Proposal whereby Independent Newspapers plc would Increase its Shareholding in the Tribune Group from 29.9% to a possible 53.09%*, Dublin: The Stationery Office.

Competition Authority (1995) *Interim Report of Study on the Newspaper Industry*, Dublin: The Stationery Office.

Conway, Catherine (1997) 'Recipes for success in a woman's world: Irish women's magazines in the 1930s', *Pages* 4 (Dublin: Faculty of Arts, UCD), 31–40.

Conway, Eamonn and Kilcoyne, Colm (eds) (1997) *Twin Pulpits: Church and Media in Modern Ireland*, Dublin: Veritas.

Coogan, Tim Pat (1993a) *De Valera: Long Fellow, Long Shadow*, London: Hutchinson.

Coogan, Tim Pat (1993b) 'Dev and the *Irish Press*: from national crusade to nest-egg?', *Irish Times* 29 September, 11.

Cooney, John (1999) *John Charles McQuaid: Ruler of Catholic Ireland*, Dublin: The O'Brien Press.

Corcoran, Farrel (1996) 'Media, children and RTE', *Irish Communications Review* 6, 83–9.

Cullen, Paul (1991) 'An Irish World Service: the story of Ireland's shortwave broadcasting station', MA in Journalism dissertation, Dublin City University.

Curran, Catherine (1994) 'The Irish Press and populism in Ireland', PhD thesis, School of Communications, Dublin City University.

Curran, James (ed.) (1978) *The British Press: A Manifesto*, London: Macmillan.

Curtis, Liz (1984) *Ireland – The Propaganda War*, London: Pluto.

Dail Eireann (1924) *First, Second and Third Interim Reports and Final Report of the Special Committee to Consider the Wireless Broadcasting together with Proceedings of the Committees, Minutes of Evidence and Appendices*, Dublin: Stationery Office.

Darby, John (1983) *Dressed to Kill: Cartoonists and the Northern Ireland Conflict*, Belfast: Appletree Press.

D'Arcy, Margaretta (1996) *Galway's Pirate Women: A Global Trawl*, Galway: Women's Pirate Press.

Davis, E.E. and Sinnott, R. (1979) *Attitudes in the Republic of Ireland Relevant to the Northern Ireland Problem*, vol. 1, ESRI paper No. 97, Dublin: Economic and Social Research Institute.

Department of Arts, Culture and the Gaeltacht (1995) *Active or Passive? Broadcasting in the Future Tense: Green Paper on Broadcasting*, Dublin: The Stationery Office.

Department of Communications (1990) *MMDS: The Dawn of a New Era in Television Reception*, Dublin: Stationery Office.

Devane, R.S., S.J. (1927a) *Evil Literature: Some Suggestions*, Dublin: Browne and Nolan.

Devane, R.S., S.J. (1927b) 'Suggested tariffs on imported newspapers and magazines', *Studies* 16, December, 545–63.

Devane, R.S., S.J. (1950) *The Imported Press: A National Menace – Some Remedies*, Dublin: Duffy and Co.

Devenport, Mark (2000) *Flash Frames: Twelve Years Reporting Belfast*, Belfast: Blackstaff Press.

De Vere White, Terence (1967) 'Social life in Ireland 1927–37', in Francis MacManus (ed.) *The Years of the Great Test 1926–39*, Cork: Mercier Press.

Devereux, Eoin (1998) *Devils and Angels: Television, Ideology and the Coverage of Poverty*, Luton: University of Luton Press.

Doolan, Lelia et al. (eds) (1969) *Sit Down and be Counted: The Cultural Evolution of a Television Station*, Dublin: Wellington Press.

Dunne, John J. (1988) *Headlines and Haloes*, Dublin: The Catholic Press.

Earls, Maurice (1984) 'The Late Late Show – controversy and context', in Martin MacLoone and John MacMahon (eds) *Television and Irish Society: 21 Years of Irish Television*, Dublin: RTE/IFI, 107–23.

Elliott, Philip (1976) *Reporting Northern Ireland: A Study of News in Britain, Ulster and the Irish Republic*, University of Leicester: Centre for Mass Communications Research.

Elliott, Philip (1978) 'All the world's a stage: or what's wrong with the national press', in James Curran (ed.) *The British Press: A Manifesto*, London: Macmillan, 141–70.

Elliott, Philip (1983) *Televising Terrorism*, London: Comedia.

Evelegh, Robin (1978) *Peace-keeping in a Democratic Society: The Lessons of Northern Ireland*, London: C. Hurst.

Fahy, Tony (n.d., 1984?) *The Role of the Media in Irish Society*, Dublin: Media Association of Ireland.

Fahy, Tony (1985) *Research in Broadcasting*, Dublin: Radio Telefis Eireann.

Fahy, Tony (1991) 'Audience research in RTE', *Irish Communications Review* 2, 1–8.

Fallon, Brian (1998) *The Age of Innocence: Irish Culture 1930–1960*, Dublin: Gill and Macmillan.

Fanning, Ronan (1983) *The Four-leafed Shamrock: Electoral Politics and the National Imagination in Independent Ireland*, Dublin: National University of Ireland.

Farrell, Brian (ed.) (1984) *Communications and Community in Ireland*, Cork: Mercier Press.

Farrell, David (1991) *Public Broadcasting in a New State: The Debate over the Foundation of Irish Radio, 1922–26*, Manchester Papers in Politics 7/91, Manchester: Victoria University.

Fay, Liam (1997) *Keeping the Faith*, Dublin: Hot Press.

Feeney, Brian (1997) 'The peace process: who defines the news – the media or the government press offices?', in Damien Kiberd (ed.) *Media in Ireland: The Search for Diversity*, Dublin: Open Air, 41–59.

Feeney, Peter (1985) *The Television Treatment of the Subject of Unemployment*, Dublin: Radio Telefis Eireann.

Finn, Vincent (1993) 'Thirty years a'growing: the past, the present and the future of Irish broadcasting', *Irish Communications Review* 3, 73–8.

Fisher, Desmond (1978) *Broadcasting in Ireland*, London: Routledge and Kegan Paul.

Fisher, Desmond (1985) *A Policy for the Information Age*, Dublin: Radio Telefis Eireann.

Fisk, Robert (1975) *The Point of No Return: The Strike which Broke the British in Ulster*, London: Times Books/Deutsch.

Fisk, Robert (1983) *In Time of War*, London: Deutsch.

Fleck, Tony (1995) 'Thatcher, the IBA and *Death on the Rock*', *Irish Communications Review* 5, 1–11.

Fleming, Lionel (1965) *Head or Harp*, London: Barrie and Rockliff.

Flynn, Gerard (1983) 'Newspapers in crisis', *Business and Finance* 23 September, 14–17.

Foley, Michael (1994) 'Atlantic helps shatter BBC radio leadership', *Irish Times* 25 October.

Foley, Michael (2000) 'Press regulation', *Administration* 48 (1), 40–51.

Gailey, Andrew (1995) *Crying in the Wilderness. Jack Sayers: A Liberal Editor in Ulster, 1939–69*, Belfast: Institute of Irish Studies, Queen University of Belfast.

Gibbons, Luke (1984) 'From kitchen sink to soap', in Martin McLoone and John MacMahon (eds) *Television and Irish Society: 21 Years of Irish Television*, Dublin: RTE/IFI, 21–53.

Gibbons, Luke (1996) *Transformations in Irish Culture*, Cork: Cork University Press.

Gorham, Maurice (1967) *Forty Years of Irish Broadcasting*, Dublin: The Talbot Press for Radio Telefis Eireann.

Gray, Tony (1991) *Mr Smyllie, Sir*, Dublin: Gill and Macmillan.

Hall, Stuart (1973) 'The limitations of broadcasting', Karl Miller (ed.) *A Second Listener Anthology*, London: British Broadcasting Corporation, 18–23.

Hannigan, David (1993) 'The *Kilkenny People* and the censors 1939–45', MA in Journalism dissertation, Dublin City University.

Harvey, Sylvia and Robins, Kevin (eds) (1993) *The Regions, the Nations and the BBC*, London: British Film Institute.

Haughton, J.P. (1950) 'Irish local newspapers: a geographical study', *Irish Geography* 2 (2), 52–7.

Hayley, Barbara and McKay, Enda (eds) (1987) *Three Hundred Years of Irish Periodicals*, Dublin: Association of Irish Learned Journals/Lilliput Press.

Hazelkorn, Ellen (1996) 'New technologies and changing work practices in the media', *Irish Communications Review* 6, 28–39.

Henderson, R.B. (1984) *A Musing on the Lighter Side of Ulster Television and its First 25 years*, Belfast: The Universities Press for UTV.

Hickie, Aileen (1994) 'The history and structure of *An Phoblacht*', unpublished term paper, MA in Journalism, Dublin: Dublin City University.

Holt, Eddie and Sheehan, Helena (1997) 'Television in Ireland', in James Coleman and Brigitte Rollett (eds) *Television in Europe*, Exeter: Intellect Books, 77–86.

Horgan, Jean and Meehan, Niall (1987) *Survey on Attitudes of Dublin Population to Section 31 of the Broadcasting Act*, Dublin: National Institute for Higher Education.

Horgan, John (1984a) 'The press: credibility and accountability', *The Crane Bag* 8 (2) 9–12.

Horgan, John (1984b) 'State policy and the press', *The Crane Bag* 8 (2), 51–61.

Horgan, John (1986) 'The provincial papers of Ireland: ownership and control and the representation of "Community"', in D. Bell (ed.) *Is the Irish Press Independent?* Dublin: Media Association of Ireland.

Horgan, John (1993a) 'Government, propaganda and the Irish News Agency', *Irish Communications Review* 3, 31–43.

Horgan, John (1993b) 'Over the sea from Skye: cross-channel competition and the Irish media market', *Teaglaim* 1, 35–9.

Horgan, John (1995) 'Saving us from ourselves: contraception, censorship and the "evil literature" controversy of 1926', *Irish Communications Review* 5, 61–7.

Horgan, John (1997) *Sean Lemass: The Pragmatic Patriot*, Dublin: Gill and Macmillan.

Horgan, John (1999) 'The media and the enemies of truth', in Dermot Lane (ed.) *New Century, New Society: Christian Perspectives*, Dublin: Columba Press, 93–102.

Horgan, John (2000) 'The media and the state: television and the press 1949–1999', in Ray Ryan (ed.) *Writing in the Irish Republic: Literature, Culture, Politics, 1949–1999*, London: Macmillan, 242-63.

Hourigan, Niamh (1996) 'Audience identification and Raidio na Gaeltachta', *Irish Communications Review* 6, 1–6.

Inglis, Brian (1960) 'Moran of the *Leader* and Ryan of the *Irish Peasant*', in Conor Cruise O'Brien (ed.) *The Shaping of Modern Ireland*, London: Routledge and Kegan Paul.

Inglis, Brian (1962) *West Briton*, London: Faber.

Integra (2000) *Perception is Power: Social Exclusion and the Media*, Dublin: WRC Social and Economic Consultants.

Irish Marketing Surveys (1975) *A Report on the Public Preference for a Second Television Channel*, Dublin: Irish Marketing Surveys Ltd.

Johnston, C.S. (1981) *Irish Political and Radical Newspapers of the Twentieth Century: A Guide*, Jordanstown: Ulster Polytechnic Library.

Joint Committee on State-Sponsored Bodies (JCSSB) *Minutes of Evidence*, Dublin: Stationery Office.

Kelly, Mary (1984) 'Twenty years of current affairs on RTE', in Martin MacLoone and John MacMahon (eds) *Television and Irish Society: 21 Years of Irish Television*, Dublin: RTE/IFI, 89–107.

Kelly, Mary (1992a) 'Television content: *Dallasification* of culture?', in Karen Siune and Wolfgang Truetzschler (eds) *Dynamics of Media Politics: Broadcast and Electronic Media in Western Europe*, London: Sage, 75–101.

Kelly, Mary (1992b) 'The media and national identity in Ireland', in P. Clancy et al. (eds) *Ireland and Poland: Comparative Perspectives*, Dublin: Department of Sociology, University College Dublin, 75–89.

Kelly, Mary and Rolston, Bill (1995) 'Broadcasting in Ireland: issues of national identity and censorship', in P. Clancy et al. (eds) *Irish Society: Sociological Perspectives*, Dublin: Institute of Public Administration, 563–92.

Kennedy, Dennis (1988) *The Widening Gulf: Northern Attitudes to the Independent Irish State 1919–49*, Belfast: Blackstaff Press.

Kenny, Colum (1993) 'Commerce and culture: Irish broadcasting at the cross-roads should take the middle path', *Teaglaim* 1, 44–6.

Kenny, Colum (1994) 'Section 31 and the censorship of programmes', *Irish Law Times & Solicitor's Journal* (n.s.) 12 (3).

Kenny, Colum (1997a) 'Maple and shamrock: seeking a strategy for survival in the audiovisual jungle', *Irish Communications Review* 7.

Kenny, Colum (1997b) 'TV3 and the regulation of competition in broadcasting', in Marie McGonagle (ed.) *Media: The Views of Journalists and Lawyers*, Dublin: Round Hall – Sweet & Maxwell.

Kenny, Colum (1998a) 'Ireland to lead Europe in TV by microwave', *Irish Times* 28 April.

Kenny, Colum (1998b) 'The politicians, the promises and the mystery surrounding Radio Bonanza', *Sunday Independent* 21 June, 4.

Kenny, Colum (1998c) 'Whistling in the dark, or, a job for journalists in the Tower of Babel', in Eamonn Conway (ed.) *The Splintered Heart: Conversations with a Church in Crisis*, Dublin: Veritas.

Kenny, Ivor (1994) *Talking to Ourselves: Conversations with Editors of the Irish News Media*, Galway: Kenny's Bookshop.

Keogh, Dermot (1994) *Twentieth-Century Ireland*, Dublin: Gill and Macmillan.

Keogh, Dermot (1995) 'Ireland and "emergency culture": between Civil War and normalcy 1922–1961', *Ireland: A Journal of History and Society* 1 (1), 21–33.

Kiberd, Damien (ed.) (1997) *Media in Ireland: The Search for Diversity*, Dublin: Open Air.

Kiberd, Damien (ed.) (1999) *Media in Ireland: The Search for Ethical Journalism*, Dublin: Open Air.

Kilfeather, Frank (1997) *Changing Times: A Life in Journalism*, Dublin, Blackwater Press.

Kyle, Keith (1970) 'Ulster and the BBC', *A Listener Anthology, August 1967–June 1970*, London: British Broadcasting Corporation, 47–51.

Lansdowne Market Research (1981) *The Role of Provincial Newspapers with Particular Reference to Advertising*, (mimeo), Dublin: Lansdowne Market Research Ltd.

Lee, Joseph (1997) 'Democracy and public service broadcasting in Ireland', in Declan Kiberd (ed.) *Media in Ireland: The Search for Diversity*, Dublin: Open Air, 10–23.

Lee, Joseph (1989) *Ireland, 1912–1985: Politics and Society*, Cambridge: Cambridge University Press.

Library Association of Northern Ireland (1987) *Northern Ireland Newspapers, 1737–1987: A Checklist with Locations*, Belfast : Library Association (Northern Ireland Branch).

Longford, the Earl of and O'Neill, Thomas (1970) *Eamon de Valera*, London: Hutchinson.

Lucey, Cornelius (1937) 'The freedom of the press', *Irish Ecclesiastical Record*, vol. 8 (July–December), 589–99.

Lyons, F.S.L. (1979) *Culture and Anarchy in Ireland 1890–1939*, Oxford: Clarendon Press.

Madden, Paul (ed.) (1979) *The British Media and Ireland: Truth the First Casualty*, London: Information on Ireland.

McCafferty, Nell (1987) *Goodnight Sisters: Selected Articles*, Cork: Cork University Press.

McCann, Eamonn (1971) *The British Press and Northern Ireland*, Derry: Northern Ireland Socialist Research Centre.

McCluskey, Dara (1994) 'The press of the political parties', unpublished term paper, MA in Journalism, Dublin City University.

Mac Conghail, Muiris (1979) *Television in the Eighties* (mimeo), Review paper presented to RTE Authority Seminar, 14/15 December.

MacDermott, Linda (1995) *The Political Censorship of the Irish Broadcast Media 1960–1994*, MA thesis, Department of Communications and Theatre, Notre Dame University.

MacEntee, Sean, MacEntee papers, Dublin: UCD Archives.

McGurk, Tom (2000) 'Time for Irish TV for the North', *Sunday Business Post* 11 June.

McLoone, Martin (1984) 'Strumpet City: the urban working class on television', in Martin McLoone and John MacMahon (eds) *Television and Irish Society: 21 Years of Irish Television*, Dublin: RTE/IFI, 53–89.

McLoone, Martin (ed.) (1991) *Culture, identity and broadcasting in Ireland: local issues, global perspectives*, Belfast: Institute of Irish Studies.

McLoone, Martin (ed.) (1996a) *Broadcasting in a Divided Community*, Belfast: The Institute of Irish Studies.

McLoone, Martin (1996b) 'The construction of a partitionist mentality: early broadcasting in Ireland', in Martin McLoone (ed.) *Broadcasting in a Divided Community*, Belfast: The Institute of Irish Studies, 20–35.

McLoone, Martin and MacMahon, John (1984) *Television and Irish Society: 21 Years of Irish Television*, Dublin: RTE/IFI.

MacManus, Francis (ed.) (1967) *The Years of the Great Test, 1926–39*, Cork: Mercier Press.

MacRedmond, Louis (ed.) (1976) *Written on the Wind: Personal Memories of Irish Radio 1926–1976*, Dublin: Radio Telefis Eireann.

Maume, Patrick (1997) *D.P. Moran*, Dundalk: Historical Association of Ireland.

Mercier, Vivian (1945a) 'The Times (Irish)', *The Bell* 9 (4), 290–7.

Mercier, Vivian (1945b) 'The Irish Press', *The Bell* 9 (6), 475–85.

M.H. Consultants Ltd (1978) *A Study of the Evolution of Concentration in the Irish Publishing Industry*, Evolution of Concentration and Competition series 14, Brussels: EEC Commission.

Miller, David (1994) *Don't Mention the War: Northern Ireland, Propaganda and the Media*, London: Pluto.

Morris, Michael (1973a) *Broadcasting Research and Studies: A Study of Irish Broadcasting and its Relationship to Irish Culture*, Dublin: Radio Telefis Eireann.

Morris, Michael (1973b) *Towards an Anthropology of the Contemporary Arts: Cultural Implications of the New Media of Communication*, Dublin: Radio Telefis Eireann.

Morris, Michael (1973c) *The Social Effects of Television Violence – The Irish Context*, Dublin: Radio Telefis Eireann.

MRBI (1983) *21st Anniversary Poll: The People of Ireland – A Tribute*, Dublin: Market Research Bureau of Ireland.

Mulryan, Peter (1988) *Radio Radio: The Story of Independent, Local, Community and Pirate Radio in Ireland*, Dublin: Borderline Press.

Murphy, John A. (1979) *Ireland in the Twentieth Century*, Dublin: Gill and Macmillan.

NACB/Veritas (1998) *A Voice for Everyone: All You Need to Know about Community Radio*, Dublin: Veritas.

National Newspapers of Ireland (1997a) *The Safety and Suitability of Shredded Newspaper as a Bedding Material for Dairy Cows*, Dublin: NNI, Teagasc and the Department of Local Government.

National Newspapers of Ireland (1997b) *Code of Practice on Privacy*, Dublin: NNI.

National Newspapers of Ireland (1998) 'Fact Sheet on the Freedom of Information Act 1997', Dublin: NNI.

Nic Pháidín, Caoilfhionn (1987) 'Na hIrisí Gaeilge', in Barbara Hayley and Enda McKay (eds) *Three Hundred Years of Irish Periodicals*, Mullingar: Lilliput Press, 69–85.

Nolan, Dan (1966) *The Provincial Press in a Changing Economy*, Tralee: The Kerryman.

O'Brien, Conor Cruise (1998) *Memoir: My Life and Themes*, Dublin: Poolbeg.

O'Brien, Denis (1992) 'Independent local radio – an Irish success story', *Irish Communications Review* 2, 54–8.

O Broin, Leon (1975) 'Amending Irish broadcasting law I', *European Broadcasting Review* 25 (5), 39–41.

O Broin, Leon (1976) 'Amending Irish broadcasting law II', *European Broadcasting Review* 27 (1), 38–40.

O Broin, Leon (1977) 'Amending Irish broadcasting law III', *European Broadcasting Review* 28 (2), 48–9.

O Broin, Leon (1985) *Just Like Yesterday*, Dublin: Gill and Macmillan.

Ó Cíosáin, Éamon (1993) *An tÉireanneach 1934–37: Nuachtán Soisíalach Gaeltachta*, Baile Atha Cliath: An Clochomhar.

O'Connor, Barbara (1984) 'The presentation of women in Irish television drama', in Martin MacLoone and John MacMahon (eds) *Television and Irish Society: 21 Years of Irish Television*, Dublin: RTE/IFI, 123–33.

O'Donnell, Donat (Conor Cruise O'Brien) (1945a) 'The *Irish Independent*: a business idea', *The Bell* 9 (5), 386–94.

O'Donnell, Donat (Conor Cruise O'Brien) (1945b) 'The Catholic press: a study in theopolitics', *The Bell* 9 (5), 386–95.

Ó Drisceoil, Donal (1996a) *Censorship in Ireland 1939–45*, Cork: Cork University Press.

Ó Drisceoil, Donal (1996b) 'Moral neutrality: censorship in emergency Ireland', *History Ireland* summer.

Ó Glaisne, Risteard (1982) *Radió na Gaeltachta*, Co. na Gaillimhe: Cló Chois Fharraige.

O'Halpin, Eunan (1999) *Defending Ireland: The Irish Free State and its Enemies since 1922*, Oxford: Oxford University Press.

Ó hUanacháin, Micheál (1980) 'The broadcasting dilemma', *Administration* 28 (1), 33–71.

O'Neill, Caithriona (1984) 'Ownership and control in the provincial press', BA (Communications) dissertation, Dublin: National Institute for Higher Education.

Oram, Hugh (1983) *The Newspaper Book: A History of Newspapers in Ireland 1649–1983*, Dublin: MO Books.

Oram, Hugh (n.d. 1989?) *Paper Tigers: Stories of Irish Newspapers by the People who Make Them*, Belfast: Appletree Press.

O'Reilly, Emily (1998) *Veronica Guerin: The Life and Death of a Crime Reporter*, London: Vintage.

O'Sullivan, Timothy (1984) *Fair and Accurate? The Press and the Amendment*, Dublin: Veritas.

O'Toole, Fintan (1990) *A Mass for Jesse James: A Journey Through 1980s Ireland*, Dublin: Raven Arts Press.

O'Toole, Fintan (1996) 'Brand leader', *Granta* 53, 45–75.

O'Toole, James(1998) *Newsplan: Report of the Newsplan Project in Ireland*, London and Dublin: The British Library and the National Library of Ireland.

Phoenix, Eamon (ed.) (1995) *A Century of Northern Life: The Irish News and 100 years of Ulster History 1890s–1990s*, Belfast: Ulster Historical Foundation.

Picard, Robert (1983) 'Government intervention and press subsidies', *Editor and Publisher* 13 June.

Picard, Robert (1989) *Media Economics, Concepts and Issues*, New York: Sage.

Pine, Richard (1985) *Leisure and Broadcasting*, Dublin: Radio Telefís Eireann.

Powell, Frederick W. (1992) *The Politics of Irish Social Policy 1600–1990*, New York, The Edwin Mellen Press.

Preston, Paschal (1995) *Democracy and Communication in the New Europe*, New Jersey: Hampton Press.

Provincial Newspapers of Ireland (1976) *Survival: The Case for the Provincial Press*, Mullingar: The Westmeath Examiner.

Purcell, Elizabeth (1984) 'Provincial press, policy and practice', BA (Communications) dissertation, Dublin: National Institute for Higher Education.

Radio Pobal na Tire (1980) *Nationwide Community Radio: Proposals for the Eighties*, Dublin: RTE.

Radio Telefis Eireann (1971) *A View of Irish Broadcasting*, Dublin: Radio Telefis Eireann Authority.

Radio Telefis Eireann (1989) *Broadcasting Guidelines for RTE Personnel*, Dublin: Radio Telefis Eireann.

Radio Telefis Eireann (1995) *RTE Response to the Government's Green Paper on Broadcasting*, Dublin, Radio Telefis Eireann Authority.

Report of the Television Commission (1959) Dublin: The Stationery Office.

Reynolds, Brian (1976) 'The formation and development of Fianna Fail 1926–32', PhD thesis, Trinity College, Dublin.

Rolston, Bill (ed.) (1996) *War and Words: The Northern Ireland Media Reader*, Belfast: Beyond the Pale Publications.

Rose, Richard (1971) *Governing without Consensus: An Irish Perspective*, London: Faber.

Ryan, Brendan (1995) *Keeping Us in the Dark: Censorship and Freedom of Information in Ireland*, Dublin: Gill and Macmillan.

Sanchez-Taberno, Alfonso (1993) *Media Concentration in Europe: Commercial Enterprise and the Public Interest*, Dortmund: European Institute for the Media.

Savage, Robert (1982) 'The origins of Irish radio', MA thesis (3027): University College, Dublin.

Savage, Robert (1996) *Irish Television: The Political and Social Origins*, Cork: Cork University Press.

Schulz, Thilo (1999) *Das Deutschlandbild der Irish Times 1933–45*, Frankfurt-am-Main: Peter Lang.

Shearman, Hugh (1987) *Newsletter 1737–1987: A History of the Oldest British Daily Newspaper*, Belfast: Newsletter Publications.

Sheehan, Helena (1987) *Irish Television Drama: A Society and its Stories*, Dublin: Radio Telefis Eireann.

Smith, Anthony (1972) 'Television coverage of Northern Ireland', *Index on Censorship* 1 (2), 15–32.

Smith, Raymond (1995) *Urbi et Orbi and All That*, Dublin: Mount Cross Publishers.

Stapleton, John (1974) *Communications Policies in Ireland*, Paris: UNESCO.

Stokes Kennedy Crowley (1984) *Review of Radio Telefis Eireann*, Report to the Minister for Communications, Dublin: Department of Communications.

Taylor, Peter (1978) 'Reporting Northern Ireland', *Index on Censorship* 7 (6), 21–5.

Television Commission (1959) Report, Dublin: Stationery Office.

Tobin, Fergal (1996) *The Best of Decades: Ireland in the 1960s*, Dublin: Gill and Macmillan.

Toibín, Colm (1990) *The Trail of the Generals: Selected Journalism 1980–1990*, Dublin: Raven Arts Press.

Tribunal of Inquiry into the Programme on Illegal Moneylending (1970) *Report*, Dublin: Stationery Office.

Truetzschler, Wolfgang (1991a) 'Foreign investment in the media in Ireland', *Irish Communications Review* 1, 1–4.

Truetzschler, Wolfgang (1991b) 'Broadcasting law and broadcasting policy in Ireland', *Irish Communications Review* 1, 24–37.

UTV (1999) *Annual Report*, Belfast: Ulster Television.

Walsh, C.H. (1992) *Oh Really, O'Reilly*, Dublin: Bentos Publications.

Watson, Iarfhlaith (1997) 'A history of Irish language broadcasting: national ideology, commercial interest and minority rights', in Mary J. Kelly and Barbara O'Connor (eds) *Media Audiences in Ireland: Power and Cultural Identity*, Dublin: University College Dublin Press, 212–30.

Whyte, John (1990) *Interpreting Northern Ireland*, Oxford: The Clarendon Press.

Williams, Raymond (1973) 'The question of Ulster', in Karl Miller (ed.) *A Second Listener Anthology*, London: British Broadcasting Corporation, 15–18.

Winchester, Simon (1974) *In Holy Terror*, London: Faber.

Woodman, Kieran (1985) *Media Control in Ireland, 1923–1983*, Carbondale: Southern Illinois University Press.

Women in Broadcasting Study Group (1980) *Women and RTE: A Question of Balance*, mimeo, Dublin: WIBSG.

Index